"All people dance when they are in conflict, either around each other or in an embrace—similar movements, but worlds apart. This book will help people stop stepping on each other's toes and move them toward looking into each other's eyes and really dancing."

NICOLE JOHNSON
actress and television host, dramatist with Women of Faith

"While leading biotechnologists have successfully cracked the DNA code, searching for hidden scientific mysteries in the human body, Dr. Gary Smalley and his team of experts reveal life-changing paradigms that will revolutionize relationships for decades to come. *The DNA of Relationships* magnifies the essence of all relationships—marital, family, and friend—for a well-rounded dynamic life."

DR. JAMES O. DAVIS
cofounder, president, and CEO of Global Pastors Network

"Once again Gary Smalley is on the cutting edge in helping us develop great relationships with those most dear to us. Gary's earlier books have nourished our fifty years of marriage. We believe *The DNA of Relationships* is his best work to date."

JACK and SHERRY HERSCHEND
cofounders and co-owners of seventeen themed family venues, including Silver Dollar City,
Dollywood, Stone Mountain Park, and Dixie Stampede

"Gary's books have been a special help to us over the years. We didn't think he could do it, but this new book is the best yet—over the top."

CHUCK (actor) and GENA NORRIS

"It's both rare and refreshing to find a new approach to strengthening and enriching relationships. That's just what Gary Smalley and the relationship team have done. After years of research and rigorous clinical development, this group of outstanding professionals has developed a unique approach that can heal broken relationships and strengthen healthy ones. This isn't just another relationship book. It may be the most practical and helpful book you'll ever read."

GARY J. OLIVER, TH.M., PH.D.
executive director of The Center for Marriage and Family Studies, author of *Raising Sons and Loving it!*

"When people find out I'm a director in Hollywood, they inevitably ask who I've liked working with the most—Heston, Selleck, Landon, Cher, Jane Fonda, Kathie Lee, Chuck Norris? I always give the same answer. I've loved working with all of them, but the one person who has made the single greatest impact on my life is Gary Smalley. The communication and relationship skills that he taught me not only made my marriage the most fulfilling part of my life but also helped me achieve extraordinary success in my business as well. Gary's communication techniques alone provided the critical foundation on which my partners and I have built businesses that have achieved billions of dollars in sales."

STEVE SCOTT
cofounder of American Telecast

"How can a man's passion grow stronger and stronger with each passing year? How can a man's wisdom grow more effective with each book he writes? How can a man literally revolutionize millions of marriages around the world? It must be the hand of the Lord on that man's life! My friend, encourager, and mentor Dr. Gary Smalley has done it again. Peer into Gary's heart, and draw on his wisdom, which will set your life ablaze!"

JOE WHITE
founder and president of Kanakuk Kamps

"The DNA of relationships and the secrets of rebuilding relationships are revealed in this book. Gary Smalley shares the discoveries from marriage intensives created by Greg Smalley, Robert Paul, and colleagues. These secrets will enable people to learn to deal with their 'hot buttons' and be able to create a 'safe zone' for creating greater intimacy."

DAVID H. OLSON
Ph.D., author of *Empowering Couples*, president of Life Innovations

"Gary Smalley's teaching has had a lasting effect on the relationships in our family. Since I spend a majority of my time speaking to students, I'm aware of the desperate need this generation has for solid, healthy relationships. I look forward to the impact *The DNA of Relationships* will have on all generations!"

MIKE MCCOY
vice president of Bill Glass Champions for Life and NFL defensive lineman
for Packers, Raiders, and Giants

"We have both benefited greatly from the message presented in the book you're holding. Never before have we been so blessed and had our eyes opened to such new and powerful ways of living a more joyful life. I hope teenagers and other adults can each gain even half of what we have gleaned."

KATHY LENNON
(singer with the Lennon Sisters)
and husband, JIM DARIS

"You will love the unique approach Gary takes to explain how God designed us for relationships. Everyone who reads this new book and learns the new dance steps will improve every relationship."

DR. KEVIN LEMAN
author of *Sheet Music*

"I've known Gary Smalley for over thirty years, and I've watched him improve his insights for helping couples and families. But this new book, *The DNA of Relationships,* is by far his best work. Together with his highly trained research team, he has put together a book that can strengthen or repair any relationship. A must-read."

JIM SHAUGHNESSY
international relationships/manufacturing partner with BYL National Collection Agency and
partner with AT Corporation

"Not only has our marriage benefited from Gary's teachings, but we also believe that the life-changing insights in this book will start a worldwide relationship revolution. Learn the dance steps in this book, and all of your relationships will be greatly enriched."

RICK and CHERYL BARSNESS
founders of the Incredible Pizza Company

"Bravo! Gary Smalley has given us an answer for the current relationship crisis facing this generation. Grasp what he is saying about relationship DNA, and you will have the key to make every relationship a loving, lasting one."

KAREN KINGSBURY
coauthor of the best-selling Redemption series and author of *Let Me Hold You Longer*

"We all want our relationships with our spouses, family, and friends to be strong and healthy. But too often we experience pain and brokenness. We know the frustration of wanting to communicate our feelings without hurting others. Gary reveals the core problem of relationship struggles and provides solutions that work."

DENNIS RAINEY
president of FamilyLife, author of *Rekindling the Romance*

"With the institution of marriage at great risk around the world, the Smalleys have come up with a plan to help at-risk couples find peace and renewed love in their relationship. At the top of every pastor's list of challenges is the question: What can I do to strengthen and stabilize the marriages and other relationships in my congregation? Now they have it—*The DNA of Relationships!*"

H. B. LONDON JR.
vice president of church, clergy, and medical outreach with Focus on the Family,
author of *For Kids' Sake: Winning the Tug-of-War for Future Generations*

The Smalley Relationship Center

in partnership with

National Institute of Marriage

present the

RELATIONSHIP REVOLUTION TEAM

PHOTOGRAPH BY SHANN SWIFT

Left to right: Michael Smalley, M.A., and Dr. Gary Smalley of the Smalley Relationship Center; Dr. Robert S. Paul of the National Institute of Marriage, and Dr. Gregory Smalley, Dir., Church Relationship Ministries, John Brown University.

THE SMALLEY
RELATIONSHIP CENTER
1482 Lakeshore Drive
Branson, MO 65616
+ + +
Phone: (417) 335-4321
Phone: (800) 848-6329
Fax: (417) 336-3515
+ + +
www.smalleyonline.com

NATIONAL INSTITUTE
OF MARRIAGE
1483 Lakeshore Drive
Branson, MO 65616
+ + +
Phone: (417) 335-5882
Phone: (866) 875-2915
Fax: (417) 339-1962
+ + +
www.nationalmarriage.com

THE DNA OF RELATIONSHIPS

Dr. Gary Smalley

Dr. Greg Smalley + *Michael Smalley* + *Dr. Robert S. Paul*

TYNDALE HOUSE PUBLISHERS, INC., WHEATON, ILLINOIS

Visit Tyndale's exciting Web site at www.tyndale.com

The DNA of Relationships

Copyright © 2004 by Smalley Publishing Group LLC. All rights reserved.

Cover photograph of Dr. Gary Smalley © 2004 by Jim Lersch. All rights reserved.

Cover photograph of DNA link © by Alamy. All rights reserved.

Author photo copyright © 2004 by Jim Lersch. All rights reserved.

Published in association with the literary agency of Alive Communications, Inc., 7680 Goddard Street, Suite 200, Colorado Springs, CO 80920.

Some of the names and details in the illustrations used in this book have been changed to protect the privacy of the people who shared their stories with us.

Designed by Dean H. Renninger

Edited by Lynn Vanderzalm

Unless otherwise indicated, all Scripture quotations are taken from the *Holy Bible*, New Living Translation, copyright © 1996. Used by permission of Tyndale House Publishers, Inc., Wheaton, Illinois 60189. All rights reserved.

Scripture quotations marked NIV are taken from the *Holy Bible*, New International Version®. NIV®. Copyright © 1973, 1978, 1984 by International Bible Society. Used by permission of Zondervan Publishing House. All rights reserved.

Library of Congress Cataloging-in-Publication Data

The DNA of relationships / Gary Smalley . . . [et al.].
  p. cm.
  Includes bibliographical references (p.)
  ISBN 0-8423-5530-8 (hc) ISBN 0-8423-5532-4 (sc)
  1. Interpersonal relations–Religious aspects–Christianity. I. Smalley, Gary. II. Title: D.N.A. of relationships.
BV4597 .52.D62 2004
248.4–dc22   2004010263

Printed in the United States of America

10 09 08 07 06 05
8   7   6   5

This book is dedicated
to the three other men on the
Relationship Revolution Team:

DR. GREG SMALLEY,

*who not only assembled the team of experts at Today's Family, the Smalley
Relationship Center, and the National Institute of Marriage to help develop
many of the ideas in this book but also put his fingerprints all over the final
versions; without his mentoring me during the past two years in the concepts
found in this book, you would not be holding the book in your hand;*

DR. BOB PAUL,

*who developed much of the original concepts contained
in this book through his marriage intensives;*

and

MICHAEL SMALLEY,

*who has recently given me three very important things:
help with this book; new life, literally, by donating one of his kidneys
to me; and finally, the outstanding companies
of Alive Communications, Tyndale House Publishers,
and Allegiant to carry out my dreams
for the next twenty years.*

CONTENTS

ACKNOWLEDGMENTS

Thank you to my colleagues in writing this book: Greg Smalley, Michael Smalley, and Bob Paul. Even though I dedicated this book to these men, I can say so many more things about them. As a father and friend of these men, I have been thrilled to have each of them mentor me over the past few years. I continually learn how much I don't know about helping people. These men have lovingly and carefully taught me such vital information, and it always overwhelms me that two of them are my own children. I taught them, and now they are teaching me. What a wonderful life cycle. Michael brought us to Alive Communications, Tyndale, and Allegiant. All of these wonderful companies are making this massive relationship revolution possible. Greg and Bob have contributed to the content. Greg's excellent leadership throughout the development of this book and Bob's ability to uncover his insights have made the whole project possible. And now I'm ready to deliver this message for the rest of my life.

Thank you to Rick Christian and Lee Hough of Alive Communications and to Greg Johnson for their outstanding help in bringing this project to reality. Thank you to Tyndale House Publishers—Ron Beers, Ken Petersen, Lynn Vanderzalm, Jon Farrar, Mary Keeley, and Kathy Simpson—for believing in us. I have never had a more committed and involved publisher. They have stuck with us through hours of meetings and creative thinking in order to bring you this newest and most exciting book I have ever worked on.

Thank you to Dave Bellis for his inspiration and motivation to complete this giant dream. Dave, you will never know this side of heaven how much I appreciate you for giving me the dream of starting a relationship revolution. Thank you to Kevin Johnson and Steve Halliday for all you have done to make this dream come true. Without your wordsmanship, this book would have remained just a dream.

Thank you to Ted Cunningham, Kathy Lennon Daris, James Daris, Dan Lennon, Amy Smalley, Jeanie Williams, and Chuck Zehnder for their help in reviewing the manuscript and giving invaluable insight.

Thank you to the other staff at the Smalley Relationship Center—

Norma Smalley, Jeff Smethers, Sheila Smethers, Roger Gibson, Gene Vanderboom, John Nettleton, Jim Brawner, Terry Brown, Thecia Dixon, Rose Shook, Jimmy Funderburk, Kelly Silvy, Charity Kaempher, Josh Strom, Sue Parks, John Webster, and Marian Webster—for your amazing dedication to helping everyone in their most important relationships. I never stop thanking God for your faithfulness and creativity.

Most important, thank you for the years of hard work, insights, and contributions of the team of professionals who during their tenure at To-day's Family, the Smalley Relationship Center, and the National Institute of Marriage helped in the initial research and development of some of the ideas discussed in this book—Robert Paul, Dr. Scott Sticksel, Dr. Peter Larson, Dr. Greg Smalley, Dr. Robert Burbee, Dr. Shawn Stoever, Tricia Cunningham, Dr. Brett Sparks, Beth Warzanyiak, Tamara Hanna, Dr. Kelly Vick, Pat McClean, Cindy Irwin, Chris Arnzen, Dr. David Swift, and Sheryl Haile.

Thank you to the other staff of the National Institute of Marriage—Mark Pyatt, Vicki Wrosch, Sue Head, Tamara Hanna, and Sheila Brawley—for your dedication to see a marriage awakening come to America.

And finally, thank you to my current small group—Dan and Shelly Bergland, Chris and Carole Essick, Mike and Becky McKnight, Mitch and Susie McVicker, and Elton and Carrie Youngblood—for your love for and commitment to each other and for your concern that America's relationships grow to what God intended them to be.

Gary Smalley

PART ONE
THE FIRST STEP

1

A RELATIONSHIP REVOLUTION

LIFE IS RELATIONSHIPS;
THE REST IS JUST DETAILS.

THIS IS THE GREATEST TRUTH.

EVERYTHING IN LIFE THAT TRULY
MATTERS CAN BE BOILED DOWN
TO RELATIONSHIPS.

Almost everything we do touches a relationship in some way. Just think about your day. Whether you're at home or at work, driving your car, playing, exercising, shopping, vacationing, worshipping at church, or doing any one of the many activities you and I do every-day, we are constantly involved with people. We even interact with people in our sleep. There is no escaping relationships.

That is why for the past thirty-five years, I have felt passionate about helping couples, families, and individuals to strengthen, deepen, and enrich their most important relationships. That is what God has called me to do.

In this quest to improve relationships, I am always searching for what works and identifying what doesn't work. I love to take relationship theories, apply them to my own relationships, and see if they work for me personally. It makes no difference to me if I make the discovery on my own or if the new relationship idea comes from someone else. I'm always hunting.

So for three and a half decades I have traveled all over the world, delivering my message about how to improve relationships. Everywhere I go, I meet people who tell me that one of my conferences or one of my videos or books has helped save their marriage or improve their friendships or reconnect with family members. I feel deeply humbled and grateful for each of these encouraging reports.

Yet I also frequently hear something not quite so thrilling. Many people take me aside to say, "I watched your videos—but I lost my marriage." Or, "I read your book—but my wife still left me." Or, "I tried your material—but things just didn't work out." Whenever I hear stories like these, a deep sadness fills my heart. I know my message has helped a lot of people, but I also know it hasn't helped everyone. That's why I'm constantly on the lookout for anything that really *works* for the vast majority of people I meet.

A Revolutionary Discovery

Two years ago, while searching for information to improve relationships, I made what I now believe is the greatest discovery of my lifetime. Interestingly, it happened right under my nose, in my own backyard. It came from my son Greg's marriage counseling and research center, now called the National Institute of Marriage.

Soon after Greg earned his doctorate in psychology, he began assembling a team of professional counselors, including Bob Paul, Dr. Scott Sticksel, Dr. Peter Larson, Dr. Robert Burbee, Dr. Shawn Stoever, and Dr. Brett Sparks. Almost immediately they started hearing reports, both encouraging and challenging, about my ministry. People told them that they loved the books and videos and conferences I had done—but many said they needed *more*. They needed someone to come alongside them, to get "life-on-life" with them, and to help them put our material into practice.

Greg, Bob, and their highly trained relationship experts began doing what they call "marriage intensives," where couples on the brink of divorce come for two or four days of intensive work on their relationships. While I wholeheartedly endorsed the efforts of Greg, Bob and the team, at that point I didn't get deeply involved. I left them alone to do their good work.

But when their research team recently finished its first five-year study of the couples who came for the intensives, the results were staggering. The team found that 93 percent of the couples are still together—and thriving in solid, healthy relationships! Take a moment to digest that amazing number: *That's a success rate of better than nine in ten!* When highly distressed couples learned and applied the material you're about to read, 93 percent of them not only managed to keep their marriages intact but also have reported much higher satisfaction with their relationships!

After hearing such glowing accounts, I finally decided that I had to find out for myself what was going on. The team penciled me in to take part in both a four-day intensive and a two-day intensive. What I saw was amazing. I haven't been the same since.

As the intensives began, I observed angry couples who couldn't even stand to look at each other. They refused to hold hands. Many clearly didn't even want to be there. Tears flowed freely from both the men and the women. I heard wrenching details of illicit affairs and habitual cheating, of serious financial problems, of fierce arguments and violent shouting matches.

Let me share the story of one couple to illustrate what I mean. Jim and Mary had already decided to give up on their marriage. After fifteen years together and three children, the couple came to the marriage intensive as a final attempt to salvage their marriage. I heard Jim say that if the marriage intensive didn't change things, he was going to file for divorce the following week. He thought that this week would be a total waste of his time.

To me their situation seemed impossible. I wondered if they had any chance at all. They sat glaring at each other, hostility and tension written all over them.

The first years of their marriage had been reasonably good,

but as Jim became increasingly involved in work and Mary became focused on the kids, their relationship began to spiral into worsening emotional distance, combined with periodic angry outbursts toward one another. Mary felt Jim abandoned her, and she did everything she could to get him to talk about their problems and to work with her to make their marriage and family better. In response to Mary's pursuit, Jim grew cold, and at the time they entered the intensive, he admitted that he had lost all feelings of love toward Mary. He talked about being so tired of her trying to control his every movement and to manipulate him to do the marriage her way. Over the years they had sought help from several marriage counselors and a pastor, but nothing seemed to make any lasting difference.

The final straw was when Mary discovered that Jim was having an affair with a coworker. Mary felt completely devastated and deeply betrayed. The pain of losing her husband to another woman felt like the death of a loved one. She felt totally alone. But most of all, she felt helpless to keep Jim from this other woman. Mary had seriously considered ending the marriage, but her faith in God and her concern for her children caused her to look for an alternative. She was unsure if she could ever forgive Jim and wondered if she could ever trust him again.

Jim felt just as confused and distraught. His love for his wife was such a distant memory that he seriously doubted whether he could ever love her again. Worst of all, he questioned whether he even wanted to try. The only reason he came to the intensive was concern for his children and a desire to be able to say that he had tried "everything" to save the marriage. Neither Jim nor Mary was overly motivated to make things work.

Before they left for the intensive, their thirteen-year-old daughter, Sandra, had left a note for them:

Dear Mom and Dad,
I don't know how God will solve this, but I just can't imagine my parents divorcing and our family breaking apart. Thank you for trying. Yet, I feel like a young puppy left outside in the cold with no shelter. It feels like it's getting colder and colder each night, and winter will soon be here. The other dogs tell me that I won't believe how cold it will get. I know the snow is coming,

and I feel so helpless to find a way to keep warm. I'm so scared that I'll freeze to death before it's over. It's such a terrible feeling to be alone and to feel like no one understands what I'm going through. My friends have explained the pain I'll feel once you divorce, and it scares me. I feel so helpless, like I'm just sitting in my room waiting for the ice storm to hit. Each day is longer and longer, and it feels darker and darker. I'm sick inside all of the time. Please keep trying!

Sandra

Before the intensive begins, the team asks each couple, "Do you believe that God could do a miracle in your marriage and provide a way for you not only to stay together but actually to fall back in love the way you once were?" During the four-day intensive, both Jim and Mary had a series of miraculous encounters that totally surprised them. They began to understand the powerful truths I will unpack for you throughout this book. As they worked through the various steps I'll share with you, they felt a deep sense of compassion and care for the other. They hadn't felt this way toward one another for a long time. They also became aware of several significant beliefs that had led to frustration and failure. At one point Jim said, "No wonder our marriage has felt impossible for so long." And Mary asked with exasperation, "Why hasn't anyone ever told us about this before?"

By the end of the four days, they both recognized they had a challenging road ahead, but they each felt tremendous hope for the future of their marriage and their family. Jim's heart began opening to his wife, and he was overwhelmed with gratitude toward God. Mary was thrilled with a new understanding of herself, and of Jim and their marriage. She felt the new knowledge and key skills were exactly what they needed to create a satisfying and safe marriage that both could be thrilled with. Like most couples who attend one of these intensives, after the third day, Jim and Mary were seen holding hands on the way to dinner.

When Jim and Mary arrived home, they sat down with their children. Jim began, "Kids, we have good news and some bad news. The bad news is that your mom and I will need more prayer and help with our relationship. The good news is that we are staying together. We believe with God's help and the things we learned in the intensive that we can make it. We want this for us and for you. We love you and want to stay together as a family."

Instantly, Sandra jumped into their arms. With tears running down her checks, her words were powerful, "Thanks for getting me out of the cold and letting me back into the warm house. Thank you. Thank you. Thank you!"

The astounding turnaround just floored me. I'm in my early sixties, and this new discovery not only has changed me but also has taken me to a whole new level of understanding how to enjoy my important relationships. What Greg's team has taught me these past few years has empowered me to determine how happy I am with each relationship, no matter what others are doing. I get to choose how fulfilled I am and that other people can't rob me of my being full. When you finish this book, you'll understand why I'm so excited about this new way of living.

Can you imagine my joy as I saw dozens of couples stabilize their relationships? And it made me wonder: *What is the secret to these miraculous turnarounds?*

A Definable Pattern

As Greg, Bob, and the team began to chronicle and analyze their experience with the intensives, an unexpected fact surprised everyone: The negative behavior that hurt the relationship of *every* couple resulted from an easy-to-identify, recurring pattern. None of these men and women realized that their spouses had been doing and saying things that prompted this vicious cycle to kick in, but whenever it happened, they stepped right into their own place in the pattern, injuring the relationship. Every time this hurtful pattern of behavior went into motion, it did so in consistent, predictable ways—ways that could be graphically charted out on a whiteboard.

It seemed almost as if these men and women were saying, "My spouse is making me feel disrespected or belittled. I feel like I'm a failure, or I feel abnormal. Since I don't like these feelings, I have to do something to get my partner to stop." So what did they do? They immediately fell into the well-worn ruts of their hurtful pattern, triggering round after round of the same sad cycle. Without even realizing what was happening, these sparring partners would begin a destructive dance.

Learning New Dance Steps

After the team helped these distressed couples understand how their destructive dance was destroying their marriages, they helped them to break the rhythm of that dance and learn new dance steps that would restore their relationships and renew their love for one another. Sounds like a tall order, doesn't it? Yet the team consistently filled that order.

How? What on earth did they do to manage such a tremendous feat? They taught these men and women three things:

- the DNA of relationships
- the pattern of their unique relationship dance
- five effective dance steps for building healthy relationships

By committing themselves to learning and practicing these principles and steps, these couples not only rediscovered their passion for one another but also learned how to build a fulfilling relationship, which had seemed frustratingly out of reach before.

Now, let's get real honest. Does it sound doubtful to you that couples *even on the brink of divorce* could, in a matter of days, do a 180-degree turnaround and start enjoying the marriage they always wanted? Does it seem far-fetched that by understanding and applying a few key concepts, sour relationships can turn sweet and anger can give way to joy? I used to think so. But then I saw with my own eyes what can happen when God steps in and lends his infinite power to the remarkable plan for relationship success that we want to share with you. Let me share another "impossible" story that proves miracles really can—and do—happen!

Bob Paul, one of the main creators of this new material, is married to Jenni. Both of them would tell you that the first several years of their marriage were anything but satisfying. Bob's constant demands and insensitive instructions about how she ought to meet his needs led to almost daily fights. She grew to hate him. In total disgust she shut him out of her emotional, spiritual, and physical life and once even told him, "The thought of ever making love to you again makes me feel like I'm going to vomit." If any relationship seemed impossible to save, this was it. However, many of the insights described in this book are a result of Bob's long journey as he allowed God to change him and completely transform his marriage. The process has dramatically influenced the way he works with people. Bob and Jenni have now passed their twenty-third anniversary, and they've reached that milestone as a happy, contented couple, delighted to be together and thrilled with their marriage.

Sound impossible? It's really not. We're going to show you how to become part of this relationship revolution. This book will open the door to miracles in your own relationships. It fascinated me to hear Bob say to the couples that visited our counseling center, "I don't know how God is going to do this, but I've experienced a miracle in my own marriage and get to witness miracles occurring in other marriages almost every week of my life. A miracle really can take place in your relationship."

We're going to show you in this book how to experience that kind of miracle. In fact, let me offer you a guarantee: The powerful principles and techniques that you're about to learn can help to revolutionize *your* relationships and turn them into something deeply satisfying and even thrilling.

And you know what? It's easier than you think.

A Pattern for *All* Relationships

The exciting concepts and methods hammered out in our marriage intensives apply to *all relationships*, not merely to marriage. I made this discovery for myself as I saw major improvements taking place in my own home and with friends.

After seeing the results of the patterns that Greg and Bob's team had discovered, I started thinking, *Wait a minute! If this material has so effectively helped me to handle my conflicts with Norma, maybe it can also help to explain why I lost some key friendships back in the seventies and eighties.* I was closer than a brother to several men, and yet we fell out of fellowship and into terrible disharmony.

Dreadful memories flooded my mind, painful memories full of sadness and regret and grief. I thought of two men in particular, once dear and close friends, but from whom I had so totally disconnected that we no longer even spoke with one another. Here I was, a respected marriage and family "expert," and yet I couldn't even get along with men whom I once counted as my closest friends! The thought deeply embarrassed and troubled me.

As I replayed old mental tapes and pondered what might have

happened between us, eventually it dawned on me. I began to see how these men and I had been involved in a destructive dance. As a result we simply went our separate ways—angry, hurt, and confused. And so we lost a treasured friendship.

But maybe it didn't have to be that way! Maybe I could employ the same principles that worked so well with Norma to strengthen my current friendships and rebuild damaged ones!

I've been learning ever since! And what I've been learning and applying in my own life, I want to teach you.

The Joy Can Be Yours

We all want warm, fulfilling relationships—in our marriages, in our families, in our friendships, and in the workplace. I long for you to experience and enjoy the same newfound life and vitality in relationships that I've come to experience in the past few years as a result of applying the concepts in this book.

What a difference it can make when you understand the DNA of relationships, the relationship dances, and the five dance steps. As you join me in this delightful adventure of discovery, you'll experience God's love and power in fresh and exciting ways:

*You'll learn about the amazing **Power of One**.* You'll see how to take personal responsibility for your part in all relationships. You'll see how to become completely empowered to choose how you feel within all of your relationships. This message has completely changed our family, our staff, and our lives. We just have to send it out to the world, to churches and families and couples and singles, so that others can enjoy the same freedom and enthusiasm that we're enjoying! Can you just imagine teenagers—or anyone else for that matter—not blaming others for being unhappy? They could learn how to be responsible for their own emotions. That would be a great day.

*You'll learn about **Safety**,* about creating an environment that feels safe, where true intimacy can take root and bloom. You'll learn how personal differences can enhance your relationship instead of causing problems and how you can adopt an attitude of curiosity instead of judging others. And you'll discover how to effec-

11

tively and positively deal with "walls" that your partner or friends may put up. Just imagine friends, couples, and kids feeling completely safe to open up and share their deepest thoughts with others who love them.

*You'll learn about **Self-Care,*** how God wants you to take care of yourself so that you can become a channel of his love to others. We'll show you how to make sure that your internal battery is charged, ready to connect for satisfying and fulfilling relationships. Imagine a host of people learning how to take care of themselves in ways that enable them to care for others. Can you see workplaces and churches filled with people who are not expecting others to fill them up but rather are taking care of themselves during the week and coming to work or church to enrich each other?

*You'll learn about **Emotional Communication,*** a powerful communication method with the strength to eliminate the main causes of divorce and the primary causes of separation between friends. You'll learn how to connect deeply with the heart of another person. We'll show you how to find the emotional "nugget" that leads to effective and fulfilling communication, enabling you to feel confident that you will be understood. And we're going to show you how to make communication easier and more efficient than you've ever experienced! Imagine feeling that others deeply understand you.

*You'll learn about **Teamwork,*** about adopting a no-losers policy that will help you walk in harmony and complete unity with your spouse, family members, and friends so that you never again have to worry about losing an argument. We'll show you how to identify the obstacles that make your relationships difficult, as well as how to remove those hurdles. Imagine families and neighbors and colleagues working through conflict in ways that don't damage relationships.

Does any of this sound appealing to you? Does it sound like something you would like in your own life?

Well, how could it *not*?

We Have a Relationship Crisis Today

What you will learn and experience in this book will have an impact far beyond your personal relationships because we are surrounded by millions of people in relationship crises. The following could be read as the headlines of a culture losing the battle for relationships:

- Lifelong friendship goes sour
- Teenager runs away from home
- Coworkers quarrel, one leaves the company
- Girlfriend and boyfriend split up
- Newlyweds have first fight
- Adult siblings stop talking to each other—for years
- Soldier returns home from defending country and abuses his wife
- Marriage of fifteen years shatters in divorce
- Lonely teenager commits suicide
- Pastor's marital infidelity splits church
- Two students, estranged from friends and society, assassinate a dozen schoolmates and then end their own lives
- Nineteen terrorists wreak havoc on a country, killing thousands of innocent people

Something has gone very wrong. We all know it. At least one of these scenarios has touched nearly every person on earth. The effects of broken relationships cut across the generations, from school children to married couples to senior citizens. And the consequences are staggering. Worse yet, the tragic stories of disrupted friendships, marriages, families, communities, and nations grow increasingly frequent.

We see that practically all the world's crises, little or large, can be reduced to one thing: *the breakdown of relationships.*

We believe that the message of this book can have a profound impact on our culture. Our ultimate goal is not merely to help you build great relationships but also to encourage you to take what you learn and multiply it in the lives of others around you.

Later we'll describe in more detail how we're working to recruit an army of a million relationship champions who will gather weekly with a small group of other champions to help one another learn and apply the DNA of relationships principles. It excites us beyond words to think of the potential of partnering with you and a million or more other people around the world!

We're also actively praying for 100,000 churches to join us as we work to ignite the relationship revolution that will transform our country and our world. Could you be one of the leaders in your own church for whom we're searching? If so, we promise to equip you through our Web site, through a series of resources currently under development, a radio program, and several other resources. You can read all about these connections in chapter 10 and the resources pages of this book. In short, we'll be here for you until you understand this new message and can apply it easily in your life and relationships. We believe that we've found a relational gold mine, and we want you to profit from all its awesome riches.

More Excited Than Ever

In all my thirty-five years of ministry, the material in this book has taken me to a whole new level of understanding about how to help people in all of their most important relationships. If in the past you have found any help in what I've presented, then I promise that you're going to find vastly more help in what you're about to read.

As I said, God has called me to hunt for and discover what actually *works* in strengthening the relationships of couples, families, and singles. I don't know how to say it any more strongly: the material in *The DNA of Relationships* works not just theoretically but practically. I've seen its effectiveness in the lives of hurting couples as well as in my *own* life, in my *own* marriage, in my *own* relationships with family, and in my *own* friendships.

Believe me, this new stuff *works!*

But it gets even better! Not only does it work, but it also makes relationships far *easier* than I've ever known them to be. Just think about that: better *and* easier! What we're presenting here will not complicate your life. Much to the contrary, it will make it far simpler.

And how can you beat *that?*

JOIN THE ADVENTURE
Life is relationships; the rest is just details.[1]

We would never write a book like this if we didn't think God has shown us a better and easier way to build strong, satisfying relationships, able to bring joy for a lifetime. We've both seen and experienced how God can turn around disastrous relationships and bring them to a place of health, satisfaction, and joy.

Would you like to see and experience the same thing? Then join us. Hop aboard for what could be the most thrilling ride of your life. And let's begin where all good rides start: at the beginning, at how God designed us. For without starting there, we'll miss out on the full relationship experience God means us to have.

LIFE IS RELATIONSHIPS;
THE REST IS JUST DETAILS.

THE DNA OF
RELATIONSHIPS

"A miracle!" That's what people who've been through one of our intensives say after their experience, and it's what we believe is going to create a relationship revolution in America today.

When you and I look around, we see countless relationships that need a miracle. Every day we see shattered relationships—husband and wives, parents and children, sisters and brothers, neighbors and coworkers who aren't talking to each other, who intentionally or unintentionally hurt each other. You know what I'm talking about. We see people at home, at work, or at church, and even though they are smiling, we find that when we get really close to many of them, they are hurting and lonely. They are settling for mediocre relationships.

Relationship pain keeps growing in our country. Did you know that a very heartbreaking experience greets thousands of kids every day in America? Kids just like Jeremy.

"Daddy? Where are we going?" Jeremy asks excitedly about their afternoon date. He even checked out of school for this special occasion.

"We're going to your favorite place, Son. McDonald's, the one with that cool inside play place," his dad replies. Daryl tries to inject some excitement into his voice to compensate for his heavy heart. Today is the day he needs to tell his son the bad news. He hopes taking

Jeremy to one of his favorite hangouts will ease the pain of what his son will soon learn.

"Jeremy," Daryl begins, taking in a deep breath. "I don't know how to tell you this, but Mommy won't be coming home tonight. She's never coming home again."

"Mommy not come home? Why not?" Jeremy whispers.

Daryl can't bring himself to look into his son's eyes. "You know that Mommy and Daddy aren't getting along that well, so we've decided to get a divorce."

"A divorce?" the seven-year-old asks, confused. "I don't get to see Mommy anymore?"

"No son, it's not like that. It's just that you'll have to visit Mommy at her new house from now on. She won't be living with us anymore. She will be living at a different place with a different family now."

"But, Daddy, what about our family? Why would Mommy leave me?" Jeremy sobs, pain seared on his face. "I don't want Mommy to have a new family! What's wrong with me? Why didn't you ask me what I wanted?"

People like Daryl and Jeremy and the mother who left him are the main reason why I want to be a part of a national relationship revolution. There's too much relational emptiness and pain just in our country alone. More than two thousand children every day hear what Jeremy heard. In ten years, that can translate into negatively affecting more than 7 million relationships. This has to stop!

I believe the best way to address this crisis is to understand how God designed us to live, to understand our relational DNA. Just as understanding our physical DNA reveals the mysteries of how our bodies work, understanding our relational DNA unlocks the miracles and mysteries of how our relationships work. After five years of watching the amazing miracles happen in our marriage intensives, we have concluded that people change as soon as they understand and apply themselves to what we are calling the basic DNA of all relationships. We discovered the DNA, first, by watching these miracles and, second, by seeing the same pattern in the story of the first humans. Later in this chapter, we'll give you the third reason why we came up with the DNA of relationships.

We never see anyone who doesn't want to be connected with others, to love and be loved, to share dreams and hopes, to be valued.

Everyone longs for emotional, physical, and spiritual closeness and intimacy with others. Where does that longing come from? We believe it's part of our relational DNA.

What is the DNA of relationships? It is simply the genetic relationship code with which we were created. It's our relational hardwiring. It's the unalterable, immutable relationship truth that is true for all people, for all times. We've never seen the exception.

To help you understand how we came up with the DNA of relationships, we want to take you back to the beginning, to the oldest story of mankind, Adam and Eve, which is really the story of us.

The Story of Us

Adam was the first person created. He must have felt a harmonious connectedness to his environment and an intimate connectedness to God. The Garden of Eden was a true paradise, a safe place to exist. There was no war, famine, natural catastrophes, or sin. But Adam felt not only safe and at peace with God but also at peace with himself. Adam was confident of his place in the universe. God gave Adam everything he needed: work to do, a close relationship with his Creator, everything he needed to take care of himself.

While we have no record that Adam complained about his condition in the pristine Garden, something was, in fact, missing. Even though Adam's relationship to God was very fulfilling, God wanted to give Adam something even more—a human companion, a human connectedness. God said, "It is not good for the man to be alone."[1]

We can only imagine how Adam might have responded when he first saw Eve. I suspect he felt an irresistible longing for her, for a deeper intimacy than their physical senses could experience. For God had planted deep within them a desire for an emotional and physical connection, a bonding of the inner spirit, an intimate attachment of the soul called *human relationship*.

The rest of the story is familiar to everyone. God gave Adam and Eve responsibility over everything else he had made and allowed them unlimited access to the fruit of the tree of life in the center of the Garden. Life was very good for Adam and Eve. They were safe and deeply satisfied in their relationships with God and each other.

There was only one catch. God told them not to eat any fruit from the tree of the knowledge of good and evil. But the deceiver convinced them otherwise. He told them that if they ate the fruit from the tree, they would be like God. Wanting the same wisdom and power as God, Adam and Eve chose to disregard God's instructions, and they chose what they thought was the better deal.

The next time God came walking in the Garden to spend time with them, Adam and Eve hid from him because they were ashamed and afraid of the consequences of their actions.[2] When God questioned them, Adam pointed the finger at Eve, and Eve blamed the serpent. Neither was willing to take responsibility.

Adam and Eve's choice changed everything. Gone was the harmonious relationship they had enjoyed with God. Gone was the satisfying relationship with each other. Their relationships were shattered. And as a result we have been struggling with shattered relationships ever since.

The DNA Code

Everything we need to know about the DNA of relationships is encoded in this story. The relationship DNA code is made up of three simple yet profound strands:

1. *You are made for relationships.*
2. *You are made with the capacity to choose.*
3. *You are made to take responsibility for yourself.*

While these sound simple—and they are—understanding them could revolutionize your life and your relationships. That's what this book is about—applying these three profound concepts to the relationship problems you're facing right now.

We still see people who show up at our marriage intensives with the attitudes Adam and Eve had. When people exclude God and try to navigate their own way through the relationship maze, we see much more fear prevalent in their lives. But we have also found that relationships change the fastest and easiest when people understand the relational DNA and apply the principles to their relationships.

1. YOU ARE MADE FOR RELATIONSHIPS

The other day, I received a letter from a young man who had gotten back together with his girlfriend after a difficult conflict and a terrible fight. Eric had been working through some things at our counseling centers, and it apparently had helped him and his girlfriend, and they got back together. Eric's closing sentence was, "Sometimes I feel that I can't live with her, and yet I know I can't live without her."

DNA OF RELATIONSHIPS

1. You are made for relationships.

2. You are made with the capacity to choose.

3. You are made to take responsibility for yourself.

How often do we hear that said? Well, there's a reason for that. It's the DNA: You are made to need relationships. Even when they are hard, difficult, or just plain frustrating, you need relationships. It's the way you are wired. You have a longing to belong to someone, to be wanted and cherished for the valued person you are.

Relationships are not an option. From the moment you're born, you're in relationship with parents. Soon you're in relationship with other children. Later you have relationships in the workplace, and you develop relationships with close friends. And eventually most people develop a relationship with someone they deeply love.

When a relationship becomes difficult or painful, we tend to dismiss the relationship and may for a while try to abandon all relationships. But eventually we come back and seek connection once again.

While we can choose *how* we will participate in relationships, we have no choice about *whether* we will participate in them. This is a critical point. Your only real choice is whether you will work to make your relationships healthy, whether you will do things that hinder or enhance them.

Let's look more closely at the components of the first strand

21

of the DNA of relationships. Encoded in the Adam and Eve story is this relationship truth: *You are made for three kinds of relationships—with others, with yourself, and with God.* This design feature is true for all of us—whether or not we recognize it and whether or not we act in line with it. It just *is.* When you map this out, it looks like this:

Most people understand how they're in relationship to others. Many people don't really understand how they're in relationship to themselves (which is a key problem in making sense of all relationships). And some people don't want to admit they're in relationship to God. But they are.

→ YOU ARE MADE FOR THREE KINDS OF RELATIONSHIPS: WITH OTHERS, WITH YOURSELF, AND WITH GOD.

As we will see, each of these relationships is not only important, but each is intricately interrelated. If one relationship is out of balance, the others will be affected.

What's exciting is that we can unravel the secrets of this DNA code and by doing so discover the answers to our relationship problems.

You Have a Relationship with Others

You are created for relationships with others. That seems like a no-brainer. We all have relationships—with family, friends, neighbors, coworkers, teammates, and others. What are your relationships like? Are they strong, satisfying, nurturing, respectful, and exciting? Or are they disappointing, strained, distant, painful, and frustrating? You probably have some of both. If you accept the DNA truth that you are made for relationships with others, every chapter in this book will help you build more loving and healthy relationships. It requires a lifetime of necessary but satisfying work.

Not long ago I was on a plane to San Francisco for a relationship conference. A woman recognized me, introduced herself, and mentioned that she had used some of the videotapes I did some years back. Sarah thanked me for helping her through a difficult time. Expecting to hear a success story, I asked her how the relationship was going now.

Sarah hesitated, then simply said, "Well, that relationship ended awhile ago."

"Sorry to hear that," I said. "What was the problem?"

This time she didn't hesitate: "The problem was *him*. He didn't really respect me."

"I see," I responded.

"I'm in another relationship now. This one's better." Sarah laughed. "He's got problems too, but this one's better."

Sarah's story is really not that remarkable. And that's the point. Her situation is a common one, repeated in many lives over and over: "The problem was *him*." Sadly, if Sarah doesn't learn, she'll soon start blaming the new man in her life for her unhappiness.

Does this sound at all familiar? Things haven't changed much through the millennia. It's the same blame game that Adam and Eve played, pointing to the other person as the source of the problem.

What about your troubled relationships? Do you hear yourself making similar statements about the other people? Do you see the problems as their fault?

Most psychologists and counselors recognize this basic relationship truth: *It's never just about the other person.* If the problem were always the other person, then we wouldn't have counselors and therapists. We'd hire a "relationship repairperson" and send him or her over to the other person's house!

IT'S NEVER JUST ABOUT ← THE OTHER PERSON.

I want you to think about this: The problem you have with another person is often a problem you have with yourself. Now, you may be talking back at me, saying, "No, Gary, I have to tell you, this other person really is bad and did me wrong."

Maybe so. But I'm guessing that there's more to it than that. Because usually there is.

Usually the pain that another person causes you is coming out of a fear or insecurity you have about yourself. Think about it: If someone says something about you that you know isn't true, then it's not really a problem. You are hurt by what people say or do only when something rings true.

Let me use a simple and obvious example. Let's say you're six-feet-two-inches tall. By most standards, you're considered a tall person. Let's say that at a party a friend calls you "Shorty." Now, there's no reason for you to take offense, and you probably wouldn't. In fact, other people would look at your friend oddly because she was saying something that was obviously not true about you. You aren't particularly offended because you are confident inside yourself that what was said wasn't true.

But let's say that at the same party, your friend calls you "Skyscraper." Now this bothers you. Why? Perhaps because you're insecure about being too tall. What she said pushes a button inside you. You're thinking, *It might be true. I'm too tall. I'm faulty as a person.*

At that point, you assume your friend was doing you wrong, was making fun of you. Yet, for all you know, maybe she was saying it as friendly teasing, or even perhaps she (being on the short side) admired you for being taller. And yes, it's possible she was being mean. But even then, the real problem isn't really what she said. The problem is *how you see yourself.* You reacted to what she said based on some inner fear of not being normal or feeling somehow defective. How many times in relationships are you blinded by what others say? You're offended by someone else, and that, then, becomes a relationship problem. Instead, you need to take a look at yourself, clearly and objectively. You need to point the camera at yourself through the right lens.

Note that I'm not saying that the problem here is that you *are* too tall. You may not be. Many times the statement that offends us isn't true at all. The problem is how we *react* to what others do or say. Any accurate snapshot of a relationship problem never focuses just on the other person—the picture must also include you.

You can probably see the third DNA strand—you are made to take responsibility for yourself—weaving itself through this discussion. When you violate that DNA and blame other people, you are placing the responsibility for the relationship problems on them. Only when you recognize your own responsibility will you begin to find a way out of the problem. I call this the Power of One, and because it is so important, I'll discuss it fully in chapter 4.

You Have a Relationship with Yourself

Does it surprise you to think about having a relationship with yourself? Somehow this simple relationship truth escapes so many of us so much of the time. But this understanding is *critical* to successful relationships.

Part of your resistance to paying attention to your relationship to yourself may be that it sounds, well, self-centered. And it is to some extent. But as with all relationships, it's all about balance. It is unhealthy to be too focused on your relationship to yourself; it can lead to what psychologists call narcissism. However, it is just as unhealthy to belittle, dismiss, or ignore yourself.

Do you have a healthy, dynamic relationship with yourself? Are you on good terms? Do you think of yourself as important? Do you like yourself? Do you accept yourself? Do you forgive yourself? Do you take care of yourself?

One of the things I see so clearly in the people who come for counseling is the difference between people who don't have a healthy relationship with themselves and those who do.

One of the women is Mary, who is dealing with alcoholism. It's quite a struggle. Besides the problem of her dependency on alcohol, her addiction affects all the relationships in her life. She has become distant from her husband and neglectful of her children. She has good days when she is more communicative, but other days she drops out of sight for hours on end. She barely speaks to her husband, Tom, and she forgets to pick up her kids from school.

Mary is unaware of what she does to the people in her life, unaware of how her behaviors affect relationships. When asked why she does what she does, she mutters, "I dunno" and has a blank look on her face. She looks and sounds helpless about herself. She consistently seems unable to see her own behaviors, to understand anything about how they affect others, or ultimately to have any perspective about herself in the world.

Now, addictions are very hard to overcome, no question. I don't minimize the difficulties that Mary faces on a daily basis. But she'll never climb out of her situation until she sees herself honestly and objectively, which is the starting place for her developing a healthy relationship with herself. She needs a model, someone like Susan.

Susan also struggles with alcoholism. She was much like Mary, helpless in the face of her addiction and unaware of herself. But then she gave birth to a baby girl. The baby changed Susan's perspective of herself. She suddenly *saw herself through her baby's eyes,* and she saw how her addiction could hurt her child in a major way.

She was able to step apart from herself and see herself objectively as if she were another person. It was as if she saw herself through a camera lens. She didn't like everything she saw—an addicted woman who thought she had no choices—but facing that reality helped her begin the process of change. Once she saw her own actions and how they affected others, she could take personal responsibility for those actions. Susan was finally motivated to change.

Soon Susan started making changes in her lifestyle and fighting the addiction that had controlled her. (Do you see the third strand here again? You are made to take responsibility for yourself.) She started taking care of herself. She got into AA, which has been immensely helpful.

All of this started when Susan saw herself through the camera lens and developed a healthy relationship with herself.

People who *do* have a healthy relationship with themselves—who take responsibility and take care of themselves—are better positioned to deal with relationship problems because they can see themselves objectively.

The relationship truth is this: *Put yourself in the picture.* When you master this skill—seeing a picture image of both the other person and yourself in the same frame—you suddenly have a perspective on yourself with others. You can see the consequence of your own actions and the effect they have on the feelings of your friends and family. And you can adjust your thoughts, words, and behaviors accordingly.

One of the things you immediately notice about people who

have a healthy relationship with themselves is that they take care of themselves—their bodies, their minds, their emotions, and their spirits. This relates to the importance of self-care, which I'll discuss fully in chapter 6. When we teach this concept of a relationship with self, people just come alive. When they accept this truth and start thinking about the future of taking better care of themselves, they get very excited and hopeful.

But be prepared for something else.

I have to admit, sometimes when I see snapshots of myself, I don't always like what I see. I look across a row of beautiful smiling faces—my children and grandchildren, my wife, and then I see my smiling self—and I think, *Is that really me?*

If you look at yourself through the camera lens, you may not like what you see. Some of what you see—in your behaviors, in the responses of other people, in the attitudes that you cast out among others—just won't be pretty.

PUT YOURSELF IN THE PICTURE. ←

The danger is that you'll run from the ugly stuff and put away the camera. In fact, that's why people avoid developing an honest, objective relationship with themselves in the first place—because they're afraid of what they'll see. But some people dare to look at themselves, and when they do, it yields great results in their relationships.

Although it's good for us to look at ourselves through a camera lens, many of us use the wrong lens. Sometimes we use the lens that Hollywood uses when filming aging actors and actresses—the soft-focus lens that blurs out the wrinkles. Other times we use a distorted lens, like carnival fun-house mirrors, which makes us look uglier than we are.

I believe that the most objective and true camera lens is God's. And that brings us to the third key relationship in our DNA.

You Have a Relationship with God

Your most important relationship is with God, the source of all life. Some people may not want to admit that they have a relationship with God. They may say, "I abandoned God a long time ago. I have no relationship with him."

I maintain that we *all* have a relationship with God, whether or not we like it. Even people who don't believe he exists nevertheless have a relationship with him—a distant or dysfunctional one, but a relationship nonetheless. Think of the physical world. You have a father, whether or not you like it. He may be living or dead, a man of integrity or a criminal. But you have a father. Your relationship with him may be wonderfully nurturing or deeply hurtful. It may be intimate or cold as ice. But you have a relationship with him.

The reality is that you have a relationship with God, and he created you to need a relationship with him. The French philosopher Pascal once said that each person is created with a lifelong, deep desire for something more, and that longing is filled only by knowing God. In fact, recent scientific findings have led researchers to believe that the human brain itself is "hardwired" for God. A *Newsweek* cover story carried the intriguing headline, "God and the Brain: How We're Wired for Spirituality."[3]

God is serious about his relationship to you. In fact, the Bible says that "He is a God who is passionate about his relationship with you."[4] If you ignore this relationship, if it becomes out of balance, then all of your other relationships will also be out of kilter.

Adam and Eve learned this the hard way. God offered them everything they needed: first, a relationship with him; second, a relationship with each other. God was utterly dependable. He asked Adam and Eve to trust him to meet their needs. But they trusted the serpent instead. When they walked away from God, they walked away from the lasting source of love, joy, peace, and an overflowing life.

The key to the DNA of relationships is to understand that we are wired to have a direct connection with God. Let me go back to the image of the camera.

As I have said, what we tend to do in relationships is to see only the other person, and we point the lens only at him or her. It looks like this:

This is where many people are. You can see how flat and simplistic this view of a relationship is. This is why so many of us experience the kind of relationship problems we have.

The DNA of relationships says that you are made for relationships with others, yourself, and God. It looks like this:

We've said that relationship problems aren't just about the other person and that we need to put ourselves in the picture too. That looks like this:

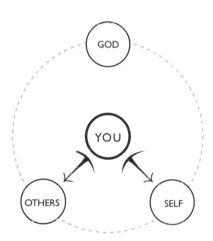

But God also made you for a relationship with himself. He offers you love, acceptance, forgiveness, value, growth, satisfaction, and honor. He equips you with everything you need for a meaningful life and satisfying relationships. He offers you life to the fullest.[5] We have found that the people in our intensives came alive as soon as they included God in the camera viewfinder.

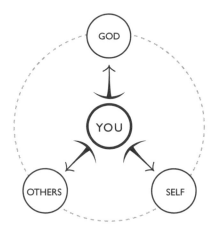

Again, as soon as the people in our marriage intensives realize that they need a relationship with God, they begin to gain the perspective and power to change. Also, when they look to God for their fulfillment, it takes the pressure off of their spouses, children, and friends to fulfill them.

As I mentioned, sometimes when you look at yourself through the camera lens, what you see isn't pretty. Or other times it's too rosy. How do you make sure that in seeing yourself and others through the camera lens, you are getting an accurate picture?

Well, that's another relationship truth: *Get God's lens if you want a healthy view of your relationships.*

→ GET GOD'S LENS FOR A HEALTHY VIEW OF YOUR RELATIONSHIPS.

In other words, you have to get your lens from God. His lens is the most accurate, never portraying you better than you should appear but always showing the true beauty inside you. And God sees you as you really are.

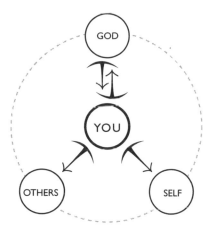

In the bestseller *The Purpose-Driven Life*, Rick Warren describes how God sees you:

> You are not an accident. Your birth was no mistake or mishap, and your life is no fluke of nature. . . . Long before you were conceived by your parents, you were conceived in the mind of God. He thought of you first. . . . He custom-made your body just the way he wanted it. He also determined the natural talents you would possess and the uniqueness of your personality. . . . Most amazing, God decided *how* you would be born. Regardless of the circumstances of your birth or who your parents are, God had a plan in creating you. It doesn't matter whether your parents were good, bad, or indifferent. God knew that those two individuals possessed *exactly* the right genetic makeup to create the custom "you" he had in mind. They had the DNA God wanted to make you. . . . God never does anything accidentally, and he never makes mistakes. He has a reason for everything he creates. . . . God was thinking of you even *before* he made the world. . . . This is how much God loves and values you![6]

Do you believe that description? Do you believe that God loves you and values you? Do you know that you are precious to him?[7] Do you believe that he accepts you and forgives you? Are you convinced that you are of great worth to him?[8] If you want to strengthen your relationship to God, see appendix A: How to Have a Relationship with God.

It's no accident that AA and other addiction programs talk about a higher power. It is not surprising that faith-based programs across the country work in changing the lives and relationships of people in prisons. These are based on the reality that God loves us and provides us with the empowerment to live life to the fullest. They are based on this same relationship truth of getting people to look at life, themselves, and all their relationships through the honest and loving lens of God.

When you have a healthy relationship with God, you are in the best position to see yourself as he sees you, which will result in a healthier relationship with yourself. When your relationship with God is out of balance, you can't see yourself properly and you lack the power to change or enjoy life as he intended. And it's more complicated when the other person also has an unhealthy relationship with God. Then neither of you is seeing yourself clearly. What happens then is that you begin to react to each other for the wrong reasons— sometimes with an inflated sense of who you are, and other times with a deflated sense of who you are. If neither of you can see yourself accurately, how do you expect the relationship to work?

All three DNA relationships are interrelated. When one is out of balance, the other two suffer. When you do something to strengthen one, the other two become stronger too.

→ ALL THREE RELATIONSHIPS MUST BE IN BALANCE.

Let me give you the third reason why we came up with this DNA concept. We recognized that the God-yourself-others relationships are also part of the Great Commandment: "'You must love the Lord your God with all your heart, all your soul, and all your mind.' This is the first and greatest commandment. A second is equally important: 'Love your neighbor as yourself.' "[9] This New Testament teaching underscores what we see in the DNA: Our relationship with God is the first and greatest relationship, and our ability to love others is related to our ability to love ourselves. These three relationships seemed to be a part of our genetic makeup.

2. YOU ARE MADE WITH THE CAPACITY TO CHOOSE

Already you can see how the DNA strands weave themselves into your relationships. You have seen how you are hardwired for relationships—with others, with yourself, and with God.

DNA OF RELATIONSHIPS

1. You are made for relationships.
2. You are made with the capacity to choose.
3. You are made to take responsibility for yourself.

The DNA also reminds you that God created you with the capacity to choose. You can't always choose your relationships—you didn't choose your parents or your siblings or your children—but you *can* choose how you will act in those relationships.

One of the statements we often hear from people who are in troubled relationships is, "I have no choice!"

- Two sisters have heated arguments, and the older one vows she will not speak to the younger sister until she apologizes. She fumes, "I have no choice!"
- A husband is unfaithful, and the wife files for divorce, all the while crying, "I have no choice!"
- A man feels betrayed by his colleague, and he shuts down the relationship, claiming, "I have no choice!"
- A person on a church committee repeatedly is offended by another committee member's opinions. He gets so frustrated that he resigns from the committee, saying, "I have no choice!"

God gave you the power to choose. So when it comes to how you will respond in a relationship that has hit some rough waters, never tell yourself "I have no choice!" That's a lie. The truth is, you *do* have a choice. Lots of choices.

- Will you choose to stay stuck in a relationship—or will you determine to work through the problem areas?
- Will you choose to hold on to your resentment—or will you choose to face that resentment and find freedom from it?
- Will you choose to hurt the other person when he or she hurts you—or will you choose to look beyond the hurt to the deeper problem—possibly one in yourself?
- Will you choose to run when a relationship gets sticky—or will you choose to honor the relationship by facing the problem?
- Will you choose to look at yourself through a distorted lens—or will you choose to see yourself as God sees you?

In counseling people from across the country, I am constantly amazed at how powerful it is when a person makes a choice. I guess I am amazed because I am aware of how hard it is for people to change.

This is another profound truth: *Choice equals change.* Making a choice is often difficult because it requires change. And that change can be threatening.

→ CHOICE EQUALS CHANGE.

Samantha and John had been dating for two years. Samantha wanted to get married, but John was dragging his feet. She became frustrated after a time and threatened to break it off. John didn't want to lose her, but he didn't want to marry, as he put it, "just yet." He sought advice, and after a while, Samantha joined him in a counseling session.

As the couple talked with the counselors, Samantha revealed that she felt John didn't really love her. John revealed that when she kept bringing up marriage in conversation, he felt trapped—precisely the thing that worried him about marriage. It turned out that John's parents had been married all their lives but hadn't really loved each other. John didn't want a marriage like that for himself. Truth was, he really did love Samantha—deeply. But he didn't want a loveless marriage.

In the course of pointing the camera lens at himself and seeking to know more about God's lens and view of himself, John learned more about what was going on inside him. Samantha did the same, realizing more of John's inner struggle and seeing how her own urgency toward marriage was hurting the situation.

What it came down to was that John had to make a choice.

Sometimes it just comes down to that. You have to take control of your life, stop being a victim of your past, and start moving on to something new. You have to make a choice. You have to change. Even when the change is scary.

Fortunately John did. He chose, despite his inner fears, to ask Samantha to marry him. He chose to change. His choice was a sign of growth and maturity. It made possible a step in a whole new life direction. John and Samantha were married within the year.

One of the things John said later is so profound. "I realized," he said, "that if I didn't choose to marry Samantha, that was the same thing as making a choice. By 'not choosing,' I was choosing against her, choosing that I wasn't going to have her in my life. I couldn't bear that."

NOT CHOOSING IS ← ITSELF A CHOICE.

The mistake so many of us make in our relationships is to think that if we just let things stay as they are, if we can postpone making a choice, making a change, then we can get through a difficult experience. We fail to understand that by not making critical choices we *are* choosing. By not doing anything, we force change to be done to us.

What will you choose? You will hear that question throughout this book as a reminder of the second strand in the DNA of relationships. The big question remains in the spotlight: Will you choose to act in ways that hinder or enhance your relationships? The choice you make will affect everything about your life.

I think that the most exciting part of knowing I am made with the capacity to choose is that all of my *thoughts* determine all of my *actions* and *emotions*. It doesn't matter what others do to me or what circumstances I face everyday, I determine all of my feelings, sad or happy, by what I *choose* to think and how I *choose* to react to what happens to me. I love that freedom. When you get to chapter 4, you'll see that your daily thoughts determine everything about you.

3. YOU ARE MADE TO TAKE RESPONSIBILITY
   FOR YOURSELF

We said at the beginning of this chapter that the story of Adam and Eve is the story of us. They were made to take responsibility for themselves. But after they chose to disregard God's instructions, they also violated their DNA. When faced with the consequences of their choices, neither Adam nor Eve was willing to take responsibility. Each pointed the finger and blamed someone else. We're like that. When we find ourselves in a relationship difficulty, we point the finger at the other person. It's *him*. It's *her*.

One of the key messages throughout this book is our need to take personal responsibility for our actions and choices. Unfortunately, it's a message that is new for many people. It's far too easy for us to slip into the pattern set way back in the Garden of Eden: blame the other person.

It's the pattern Carlos and Andrea know too well. During the five years of their marriage, Andrea has managed the household budget and finances. Carlos works in construction, and she teaches third grade in the public school. Together they make a decent living, but they don't have much extra at the end of the month. Carlos spends money on movies, DVDs, and computer games, and Andrea struggles to make ends meet.

Carlos and Andrea fight about money. Carlos spends, Andrea cuts the budget. Every time Andrea restricts spending more, Carlos spends more, which makes Andrea cut the budget more. And on and on. Money is a constant source of conflict. And when the fighting gets too bad, they get some help.

In the counseling office, Carlos points at Andrea and says, "She doesn't let me spend any money."

Andrea points at Carlos and says, "He's irresponsible and spends too much money on entertainment. If he keeps that up, we won't have money for rent and groceries. I have to set limits."

Carlos responds, "She makes me feel like a little kid who needs to ask his mommy for permission to buy anything."

When Carlos and Andrea visited our Marriage Institute, it wasn't long before they both realized they were blaming each other instead of looking at their own actions and words. We stop a couple from even thinking about focusing on the other person. Then we challenged Carlos to see himself as part of the problem and concentrate only on his own part. When he was willing to do that, he was able to take responsibility for his spending habits and work with Andrea to keep a balanced budget. We also challenged Andrea to see herself as part of the problem and to take responsibility to work on her controlling and belittling words. She heard how Carlos felt when she was on his back about his spending. The better they both understood the other and felt what they were going through, the easier it was to start working on themselves.

Later in this book we will talk more about personal responsibility, about communication in relationships, and about creating a win-win situation. But it starts with understanding your DNA relationship code:

1. You are made for relationships.
2. You are made with the capacity to choose.
3. You are made to take responsibility for yourself.

Life is relationships; the rest is just details. God made you for relationships. You can't change that. You can work either with or against this DNA, but you can't choose whether it exists. The only choice you have is whether you will work to make those relationships great or allow them to cause you—and others—great pain.

So choose wisely. Choose life. And be prepared to take personal responsibility to make the decisions—even the hard ones—that can keep joy, peace, and satisfaction flowing into your relationships.

In the next chapter we'll show you the definable pattern that appears almost every time you have a conflict with others. It's a unique relationship dance we all do, and when you recognize it and avoid it, you'll see less and less conflict in all of your relationships. I guarantee that understanding your relationship dance will change your life.

LIFE IS RELATIONSHIPS;
THE REST IS JUST DETAILS.

ONE-MINUTE REVIEW
THE DNA OF RELATIONSHIPS

1. **The DNA of Relationships:**

    - *You are made for relationships.* Relationships are part of the creation design. You are created to need relationships.
    - *You are made with the capacity to choose.* You can't always choose your relationships, but you *can* choose how you will act in those relationships.
    - *You are made to take responsibility for yourself.* You are responsible for your choices and actions. You cannot change the other person, but you can take responsibility for your own behavior.

2. **You have a relationship with others, with yourself, and with God.** Each of those relationships is not only important, but each is intricately related to the others.

3. **It's never just about the other person.** The problem you have with another person is often a problem you have with yourself.

4. **Put yourself in the picture.** When you see yourself in the same "frame" as the other person, you begin to see yourself as part of the problem as well as part of the solution.

5. **Get God's lens for a healthy view of your relationships.** Only when you see your relationships through an accurate lens—God's lens—can you see others as he sees them and see yourself as he sees you. That lens is the basis for healthy relationships.

6. **All three relationships must be in balance.** Each of the three relationships is so tied to the others that if one is out of balance, the other two will be out of balance too.

7. **Choice equals change.** All relationships involve choice. When you choose to work toward healthy relationships, you often find things need to change. You must choose to change, even when the change is scary.

8. **Not choosing is itself a choice.** If you postpone making a choice, making a change, then you *are* choosing. By not doing anything, you force change to be done to you.

3

THE DANCE THAT
DESTROYS RELATIONSHIPS

Between sessions at a marriage seminar in the Midwest, a clearly distressed couple, Dan and Celeste, approached my son Michael.[1] He had just finished a segment on how couples should always try to find a win-win solution to their conflicts so that neither partner feels like a loser (see more about this in chapter 8).

"We just don't see how we can possibly find a win-win to our problem," the exasperated woman said.

"Really?" Michael answered.

"It's impossible," Celeste insisted. "My husband has been out of work for six months, and our conflict is about where we should live."

Dan cut in and quickly explained that he had been applying for work everywhere but had found nothing. Recently an employer about three states away had offered him a job. "But my wife is not agreeing to the move," he said, irritation in his voice. "She won't let us go. She just won't do it." Both partners seemed very tired, a little angry, and extremely frustrated.

"So what do you think your problem is?" Michael asked.

"The problem is that my wife wants to stay here, in the town where we've lived for the last ten years, and I want to move so I can work and provide again for my family."

"Okay," Michael said, "so the conflict is about whether you stay or go?"

"Yes, basically," Dan agreed.

Michael shook his head. And then, to the great surprise of both husband and wife, he declared, "That's not actually your problem." And with that, he started teaching them about the dance that was destroying their relationship.

What's the Problem?

What Michael was saying to Dan and Celeste is that their "surface" problem is not the real problem. He was touching on a DNA truth: The external problem is rarely the real problem. In other words, what appears to be the problem is often not the problem.

→ THE EXTERNAL PROBLEM IS RARELY THE REAL PROBLEM.

As we move into this chapter, think about the trouble spots in your own relationships. What do you think the problem is in each of them? Try to name it. Now keep an open mind as you think about the DNA truth—that the conflict you've named may not be the core problem.

So what was Dan and Celeste's problem? In order to help them find out what it was, Michael kept asking them one basic question: So what? This was not a flippant question that dismissed their problem as if it were nothing important. It was a serious question: Why, in your mind, is that a problem?

He started by asking Celeste, "So what if you move to this new state? Why is that a problem?"

"Well, I wouldn't be around my family and my friends," she answered.

"So?" Michael responded, trying to help the woman understand the deeper issue. "Why is that a problem for you?"

"Because they're an important support group for me," she said.

"Okay," Michael replied, "but you have a husband who will support you. And you'll find other people. Why is it a problem that you would have to leave this particular support group?"

After a few minutes of gentle probing, this visibly distressed woman finally came out with it: "I just don't feel like I'm No. 1 in my husband's life."

"Ah," Michael declared. "I think we're finding out what the real problem is."

At last she found the words to articulate the real problem, and it wasn't the move. "I feel unimportant, as if I'm not a priority," she said to Michael, "so it scares me to move. I'm afraid I'll end up alone." Then she started crying.

As the husband silently took in all of this, Michael stopped and turned to him. For the next few minutes, the two men went down a similar line of questioning. At the end, the man also started crying. "Honey," he said to his wife, "I don't feel like a man. I'm afraid that if we stay in your hometown, I will continue to feel powerless. I feel that your family controls everything about our lives."

Do you see it? The problem was not the move. The problem was that Celeste felt unimportant and that Dan did not feel as if he had control over his life.

And notice something else very important about their problem. At the heart of the matter, they both felt afraid.

What about you? Ask yourself the "So what?" question. Ask it several times. Where does it lead you? Where it leads you may be at the heart of your relationship problems.

The Core Problem

Remember the pattern that Greg and Bob's team discovered when they analyzed the effectiveness and success of the process used in the marriage intensives I mentioned in chapter 1? The team came to this startling conclusion: The destructive dance that *every* couple was involved in stemmed from fear. Every husband and wife was acting out of a core fear.

Let me be so bold as to say that every person on the planet wrestles with some core fear. And that includes you. You may not like to hear that. You may be contradicting me already, "But, Gary, I'm not afraid of anything. I feel perfectly safe in my home. I'm not afraid of other people." That's good, but that isn't the kind of fear I'm talking about. I mean things like fear of failure or fear of not being loved or fear of being alone.

If you think about it, this shouldn't be so surprising. Fear is as

→ YOU WRESTLE WITH A CORE FEAR.

old as the Garden of Eden. In the beginning, Adam and Eve enjoyed a perfect and satisfying relationship with God and with one another. But the moment they disregarded God's instructions and chose instead to follow the serpent's advice, fear took over. It spoiled their relationship to God and to each other. And we have been feeling its destructive effects ever since.

So what are those fears? We have found that most women have a core fear related to disconnection—they fear not being heard, not being valued, somehow losing the love of another. Most men, on the other hand, have a core fear of helplessness or feeling controlled—they fear failure or getting stepped on. Some version of these two core fears seems to exist in everyone, to some degree. In her book *You Just Don't Understand,* author Deborah Tannen calls attention to these two core fears in order to help male and female friends better understand one another.

Of course you might not use those exact words to describe how you feel. You may be more aware of feeling rejected or abandoned than feeling disconnected, for example, or of feeling embarrassed or disrespected more than feeling helpless. Here's the key: *Without identifying your own core fear and understanding how you tend to react when your fear button gets pushed, your relationships will suffer.* Every time!

What is your core fear? Do you already know what it is? Most people don't. Most people are not aware of the fear that lurks behind many of their troubled relationships. If you don't know or feel unsure about what your fear is, identify your core fear by using the following list, which the National Institute of Marriage isolated as the most common fears among men and women. We noticed that the common core fears are all related to two main primary fears: the fear of being controlled (losing power) and the fear of being disconnected (separation from people and being alone). (I recommend that you finish this chapter and then take the Fear Dance quiz in appendix B.)

MY CORE FEAR IS THAT I FEEL . . .

1. Helpless, powerless, impotent, or controlled
2. Rejected, as if people are closing me out of their lives
3. Abandoned or left behind, as in divorce
4. Disconnected from others or alone
5. Like a failure
6. Unloved, as if no one could love me
7. Defective, as if something is wrong with me, as if I'm the problem
8. Inadequate, as if I just don't measure up to others like I should
9. Pained both emotionally and physically
10. Hypocritical or like a phony
11. Inferior, as if I'm being placed below everyone else in value (belittled)
12. Cheated or ripped off or taken advantage of
13. Invalidated, as if my words and actions are being ignored or devalued
14. Unfulfilled, as if what is happening to me will lead to a dissatisfied life
15. Humiliated, as if I have no dignity or self-respect
16. Manipulated, as if others are deceiving me
17. Isolated, as if others are planning to ignore me

I encourage you to "nail" your fear in a way that really clicks for you. The steps for building solid relationships that I'm about to lay out in the rest of this book will work much better for you when you clearly identify your core fear. Then, all of a sudden the whole world opens up. I've seen it happen time after time.

The Fear Dance

Identifying your core fear is important because fear is the music that starts the relationship dance Greg and Bob's team identified in the couples who came to the marriage intensives. The team called that dance the Fear Dance. You would think that the Fear Dance is not a dance anyone would *choose* to do. You would think most people would rather do a Love Dance or a Joy Dance, something positive. But unless we understand the Fear Dance and how we can *choose* not to do it, it seems to be the default dance in most relationships.

So how does the Fear Dance work? Let's look at an event from the lives of my son Greg and his wife, Erin. Read the following story, understanding their core fears: Greg's core fear is a fear of *failure*; Erin's core fear is a fear of *invalidation*, of not being valued for what she says and does.

One night while Erin was working the evening shift at the hospital, Greg was bored, and since he loves to decorate the house, he decided to change the arrangement of the master bedroom furniture. Erin usually loves what he does. He moved the bed, repositioned the knickknacks and their shelves, relocated the dresser, and generally gave the room a new look. Then he went to bed and turned out the lights.

When Erin got home hours later, she didn't switch on the lights because she didn't want to wake Greg. She tiptoed into the bedroom and immediately smashed her shin on a table that hadn't been there when she left for work. She tripped and crashed into a pair of antique skis that were placed against the wall. The skis in turn tumbled onto a shelf containing all her beloved Precious Moments figurines, shattering most of her treasures, which continued to fall until they smacked onto Greg's head.

The combination of breaking glass, falling objects, and screams awakened Greg. He bolted from bed, forgot that he had moved everything, and ran straight into the wall, bloodying his nose. Not one of your typical nights.

When the lights came on, they began shouting at each other. Erin criticized Greg for moving the furniture without first talking with her about it; her angry words made Greg feel like a failure. Greg minimized Erin's concerns and defended his decision to redecorate the bedroom; his words made her feel as if her opinions didn't matter. The shouting and defending and sarcasm continued—and the Fear Dance was in full swing.

Do you see it? They pushed each other's fear buttons. Erin pushed Greg's "fear of failure" button. Greg pushed Erin's "fear of invalidation" button. It's all they needed for a wild night of dancing. It's amazing how we all try to get the other person to *stop* making us feel "failed" or "invalidated" or whatever core fear we have. In reality, others are simply revealing our core fear and giving us an opportunity to choose a better course of action that allows us to deal with our core fear in a healthy way.

The sad thing is, Greg and Erin did the same destructive dance for years. They look back and see the same pattern playing itself out in every major argument of their marriage. They recognized the pattern early on, but they had no clue how to break it. Either Erin or Greg withdrew, and even though things eventually calmed down, they always seemed to return to the same hurtful dance.

Their habits didn't change until they finally understood the steps in the Fear Dance and the *choices* they had to break the rhythm of dance and learn some important new dance steps.

Does any of this sound the least bit familiar? Can you see yourself in the actions of Greg and Erin? The truth is, we face these dynamics not only in marriage but also in every other relationship. The Fear Dance, unfortunately, is a universal dance. Do you see a Fear Dance in your troubled relationships? Do people push your fear buttons? How do you react?

The Steps in the Fear Dance

So, what are the steps in the Fear Dance? The diagram traces the steps of the dance, what goes on inside us, and how our actions cause the same or similar patterns in others.

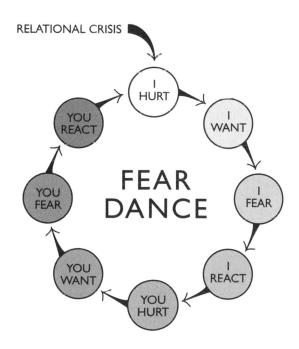

Let's look again at Greg and Erin's story to see if we can see the four Fear Dance steps: hurt, want, fear, and react.

Let's start with Erin. The situation began when Greg redecorated the room without talking it over with her.

1. Erin *hurts.* Remember the DNA truth here: The problem is rarely the problem. The problem isn't that Greg redecorated the room; some wives would love that! The problem is that he doesn't think Erin's opinions were valuable enough to talk with her before he did it. Erin feels hurt by that.

2. Erin *wants.* She wants to be validated, to have Greg value her feelings, ideas, and pain. She wants him to value the fact that she felt left out of a decision that ultimately caused her physical pain and broke her collection of figurines. She wants her husband to meet her needs. She sees him not only as the cause of their problem but also as the solution to all her wants. She wants Greg to change his behavior so that she doesn't feel invalidated anymore.

3. Erin *fears.* When Erin senses Greg's unwillingness and inability to fulfill those wants, she fears that she will be invalidated. Ultimately, she fears loss of connection from Greg. She thinks, *If he doesn't value who I am, what I do, or how I feel, then maybe he won't want to be around me.*

4. Erin *reacts.* Out of her fear, Erin reacts and starts shouting at Greg. She demands, "Why did you move our bedroom around without asking me first?" She continues to shout at him, belittling him, and criticizing him. She chooses all of her words simply to get him to change his behavior because she is convinced that he is her problem.

Now let's take a look at what happens in Greg as Erin is reacting to her hurt, wants, and fear.

1. Greg *hurts.* When Erin starts to bombard Greg with questions and criticism, he feels hurt. He can't understand why she can't see that the whole thing was an accident. Something he intended to be good is suddenly turning into a disaster. He feels hurt.

2. Greg *wants.* He wants to feel successful as a husband. He wants his wife to fulfill his wants, to help him feel successful. He sees her not only as the cause of their problem but also as the solution to all his wants.

3. Greg *fears.* When Greg senses that Erin is unwilling to help

him feel successful, he *fears* that he is a failure. He thinks, *I'm a lousy husband. I hurt my wife; I can't do anything right.*

4. Greg *reacts*. Out of his fear, Greg reacts by shouting back because he feels like a failure. He wants Erin to change her behavior so that he doesn't keep feeling like a failure. She is his problem. "Erin, I didn't know that you want me to ask your permission before I move furniture. If you want me to check things out with you before, you need to let me know these things. I'm not a mind reader. Why are you making such a big deal out of this? What happened, happened. It was just an accident. You're not perfect, either." All of his words further invalidate her. And the dance goes on and on.

Your Fear Dance

To make sure you understand the dance, let's take a look at what the Fear Dance might look like for you.

1. You *hurt*. What does your hurt look like? Think of the range of emotions you feel when you are wounded: bewilderment, sadness, disconnection, anger, confusion, worry, rage, frustration, horror, embarrassment. Those are just a handful of the words that could describe your real-life hurts.

2. You *want*. When you hurt, you want a solution. You want things that will make you feel better. Sometimes you might think that eating will make you feel better, shopping will replace the hurt, focusing on the children or other things will make you forget your troubles, drinking will dull the pain. You spin lists of things that you believe would satisfy your wants. Or you reduce the conflict to that one, solitary thing that you believe you need to feel satisfied: if only the other person would change so that you could feel better.

Without realizing it, you often expect that the other person will change to satisfy you and give you what you want. You see that person both as your problem and as your solution: You think, *If only my spouse would change.* Or, *If only I had a different boss, I would get the promotion at work.* Or, *If only she would just . . .* Or, *If only my friends would . . .* The end of that sentence is always: *then I could be happy.*

DON'T EXPECT THE OTHER ←
PERSON TO BE YOUR SOLUTION.

Do you see the common thread in all this thinking? Two words: *misplaced expectations*. When you expect people, places, and things to fulfill your wants, you will be disappointed. And anytime you put your expectations for help in the wrong place, the result is fear.

OUR WANTS
- ACCEPTANCE—I want to be warmly received without condition.
- GRACE—I want something good (e.g., forgiveness) that I don't deserve.
- CONNECTION—I want to be united to others.
- COMPANIONSHIP—I want deep, intimate relationships.
- SUCCESS—I want to achieve or accomplish something.
- SELF-DETERMINATION—I want to have independence and free will.
- UNDERSTANDING—I want to be known.
- LOVE—I want to feel attractive to others.
- VALIDATION—I want to be valued for who I am.
- COMPETENCE—I want to have skills and ability that bring success.
- RESPECT—I want to be admired and esteemed.
- WORTH—I want to feel important.
- HONOR—I want to feel like a priceless treasure.
- COMMITMENT—I want to have unconditional security in relationships.
- SIGNIFICANCE—I want to have meaning and purpose.
- ATTENTION—I want to be noticed.
- COMFORT—I want to feel a sense of well-being.
- SUPPORT—I want to be cared for.
- APPROVAL—I want to be liked and accepted.
- WANTED—I want to be sought after.
- SAFETY—I want to feel protected and secure.
- AFFECTION—I want to feel fondness and warmth.
- TRUST—I want to have faith in others.
- HOPE—I want confidence that I will get what I love and desire.
- JOY—I want to feel satisfied and happy.

3. You *fear*. Through thousands of marriage intensives, both at our counseling centers and with people around the world, we have come to realize that when a conflict stirs powerful emotions of hurt

and want, it also touches specific fears. Think about your own troubled relationships. You want to connect, but you fear you're not attractive enough (or competent enough or smart enough or whatever). You want to be accepted, but you fear you're not good enough. You want respect, but you fear the other person will look down on you. You want to control your situation, but you fear you are powerless.

Do you see how your fears actually reflect your wants? When you feel your wants won't be fulfilled, you experience fear:

WE CAN'T LIVE WITHOUT . . .	SO WE FEAR . . .
Acceptance	Rejection
Grace	Judgment
Connection	Disconnection
Companionship	Loneliness
Success	Failure
Self-Determination	Powerlessness
Understanding	Being misunderstood
Love	Being scorned
Validation	Being invalidated
Competence	Feeling defective
Respect	Inferiority
Worth	Worthlessness
Honor	Feeling devalued
Dignity	Humiliation
Commitment	Abandonment
Significance	Feeling unimportant
Attention	Feeling ignored
Support	Neglect
Approval	Condemnation
Wanted	Feeling unwanted
Safety	Danger
Affection	Feeling disliked
Trust	Mistrust
Hope	Despair
Joy	Unhappiness

Even though we have listed twenty-five wants and fears here, Greg and Bob's team found that all of our deepest desires stem from our desires for connection and control. Our deepest fears, then, are the fear of losing connection and losing control.

4. You *react.* If you are like most people, you—consciously and unconsciously—fall into well-worn patterns of reacting when someone pushes your fear button. You'll do anything to soothe your hurt. You'll do anything to avoid the awful feeling of want. You'll do or say anything to calm your fear.

THE DAMAGING FEAR DANCE

When someone pushes your fear button, you tend to react with unhealthy words or actions calculated to motivate the other person to change and give you what you want. Often your reaction triggers the core fear of the other person, who then reacts with unhealthy words or actions to try to get you to fulfill his or her wants. And suddenly the two of you end up in a full-blown Fear Dance.

More often than not, your emotions and thinking result in behavior that damages your relationships. When you fear that your wants will not be fulfilled, you react. You may fear losing control, so you try to seize control.

You may fear losing connection, so you try to seize connection. Our team describes these reactions as your attempt to become the broker for your own wants. You desperately want your way—to be sovereign, to overcome your feelings of helplessness.

This means that it's not merely your core fear that disrupts and injures your relationships. It's how you *choose* to react when someone pushes your fear button. Most of us use unhealthy, faulty reactions to deal with our fear, and as a result we sabotage our relationships.

Is the Fear Dance All Bad?

Many people say to us, "The Fear Dance may not be the best dance, but sometimes it makes me feel better. How can that be bad?" Many of our unhealthy coping behaviors—our reactions—serve an "adaptive" purpose. While they may in fact damage the relationship, they do make us feel better, at least to a degree.

Take withdrawal, for example. Many men withdraw when their fear button gets pushed. They don't want to yell and scream, but they also don't want to allow their button to get pushed repeatedly. So what do they do? They leave. They hop on a motorcycle or head to the garage. Or maybe they just disappear behind a newspaper they've already read.

However they do it, they take themselves out of the conflict by fleeing, either physically or emotionally. By doing this, they're trying to protect themselves—but that very act harms the relationship and causes it to deteriorate. Withdrawing almost always taps a woman's fear of disconnection . . . and so the dance continues.

Withdrawal, of course, is only one of the ways we react when our fear button gets pushed. The chart shows some of the most common ways we react when we fear that our wants will not be met.

REACTION	EXPLANATION
Withdrawal	You avoid others or alienate yourself without resolution; you sulk or use the silent treatment.
Escalation	Your emotions spiral out of control; you argue, raise your voice, fly into a rage.
Belittling or sarcasm	You devalue or dishonor someone with words or actions; you call your spouse names or take potshots at him or her.
Negative beliefs	You believe your spouse is far worse than is really the case; you see your spouse in a negative light or attribute negative motives to your spouse.
Blaming	You place responsibility on others, not accepting fault; you're convinced the problem is your spouse's fault.
Exaggeration	You make overstatements or enlarge your words beyond bounds or the truth.
Tantrums	You have fits of bad temper.
Denial	You refuse to admit the truth or reality.
Invalidation	You devalue your spouse; you do not

appreciate who your partner is, what he or she feels or thinks or does.

Defensiveness . . . . Instead of listening, you defend yourself by providing an explanation.

Clinginess . . . . You develop a strong emotional attachment or dependence on your spouse.

Passive–aggressive . . . . . You display negative emotions, resentment, and aggression in passive ways, such as procrastination and stubbornness.

Caretaking . . . . You become responsible for others by giving physical or emotional care and support to the point you are doing everything for your spouse, and your partner does nothing to care for himself or herself.

Acting out . . . . You engage in negative behaviors like drug or alcohol abuse, extramarital affairs, excessive shopping, or overeating.

Over-functioning . . . . . . You do what others should be doing, and you take responsibility for them.

Fix-it mode . . . . You focus almost exclusively on what is needed to solve the problem.

Complaining . . . . You express unhappiness or make accusations.

Aggression or abuse . . . You become verbally or physically aggressive, possibly abusive.

Manipulation . . . . You control your spouse for your own advantage.

Anger and rage . . . . You display strong feelings of displeasure or violent and uncontrolled emotions.

Catastrophize . . . . You use dramatic, exaggerated expressions to depict that the relationship is in danger or that it has failed.

Numbing out . . . . You become devoid of emotion, or you have no regard for others' needs or troubles.

We All Do the Fear Dance

The Fear Dance happens in every relationship because all of us have inherited the sinful legacy of the Garden. And it doesn't take long to get going. The Fear Dance can move into full swing in mere moments. How quick and subtle it is!

A friend of mine, Scott, has a four-year-old daughter, Shelby, and a twenty-month-old son, Hayden. Even the youngest member of Scott's family has danced the steps of the Fear Dance.

"Right now," Scott says, "I am the 'flavor of the month.' People who have kids understand what I mean. Sometimes you're the flavor; sometimes your wife is the flavor; and sometimes neither one of you is the flavor (it may be the neighbor). Right now, I am the flavor for my son. Regardless of what happens—whether he gets hurt or if he's happy or if he feels sad—he comes to me first.

"My wife, Jen, has noticed this. She's aware, of course, that the 'flavor' choices ebb and flow. But she feels hurt when she wants Hayden to hug her but instead he just grunts—and then runs to me.

"Last night Hayden hit his head and ran over to me. Jen walked over and said to him, 'Oh, do you want Mommy to kiss it?'

"He grunted at her.

"'Do you want Mommy to give you love?' Jen asked.

"*Grunt!*

"In those few moments," Scott said, "I saw a dynamic develop between the two of them. They started into the Fear Dance. Now, what could a twenty-month-old fear? Well, already he's starting to get into little power struggles with his parents. He wants things *his* way. Last night he feared that he was going to have to do it his mom's way. He could feel the pull from Jen to get him to do what she wanted him to do, and he reacted against it by grunting. Notice that grunting is not on the list of reactions, but toddlers are creative, right? The more that Jen felt rejected, the more Hayden tapped into *her* core fear: 'My son doesn't love me.'"

Of course, no mom likes to feel rejected, whether with words or with grunts. And the more Jen felt that fear, the more she pursued her son to get him to fulfill her want and relieve her fear. So what did Jen do?

"Our daughter was walking by," Scott explained, "and Jen said to her, 'Shelby, do you want me to give you love?' Shelby's a sucker for that stuff. So our daughter dove onto Jen on the couch, and my wife started cuddling her. Well, when Hayden saw that, *he* wanted some Mom action too. He jumped down from my lap, ran over to Jen, and jumped into her lap—and my wife looked over at me, smiling. She had sufficiently manipulated Hayden into doing what she wanted."

What a very clever and funny tactic! Scott and Jen laughed about it afterward.

Do you see the Fear Dance this mother and toddler did? Hurt, want, fear, reaction. It was not a healthy dance, of course, and Jen realizes this. She realizes that if patterns like these never change, she and Hayden will be headed for trouble. If she continues to try to manipulate her son into acting in ways that she hopes will fulfill her wants and relieve her fears, then by the time he grows to be a teenager, they will have a very unhealthy relationship. Any parent who thinks *I'll feel good about my relationship with my child by getting him to do things that show me love* is setting up the relationship for hard times. Very quickly the child is going to look for more and better ways to avoid the parent's control. And one day the parent will say things like, "Now, why is it again that our child is so dead set on marrying someone so radically at odds with us?"

The Fear Dance can also kick in at work. When I spoke about this relationship-destroying dance on a recent live TV simulcast, for example, something I said pushed a colleague's fear button. The person reacted to it, but quietly. The next day, however, when the topic came up in a meeting, my colleague exploded. I had said that we were making some changes on our staff to improve our customer service. It was innocent to me, but not to him. He imagined that his job would be changed, even though I hadn't even mentioned who or what we were going to do. All night long, he dreamed with a sick stomach that he would be fired or reassigned. He just knew I was talking about him. So, he blew up at the meeting. Things quieted down quickly as soon as I asked him what he was feeling. I already knew his core fear (failure), so it was easy to watch him calm down when he realized I understood him. He instantly admitted his failure to recognize his button. If either of us had not understood this dance, his outsized reaction could have significantly damaged our relationship. When he learned that I had not even thought of his department, we both laughed and enjoyed the power of knowing our core fears.

I mentioned earlier that Greg and Erin realized that in many ways they had been having the same fight for years. That's true for many of us. As I worked on this chapter, I vividly recalled how I failed in two friendships with godly men. As I thought about what went wrong in those relationships, I remembered hurtful images of boyhood friends teasing me—way back in the second or third grade! The patterns of hurt, want, fear, and reaction that marked my schoolyard relationships still plague me as an adult. I keep doing the same dance.

I have two main core fears: being controlled by others and being belittled. I lost two great friendships by not understanding myself better in this area. Years ago these two friends on separate occasions said things that "made" me feel belittled and controlled. They didn't make me feel this way; I chose to hear their words as belittling and controlling. My past reaction has always been to verbally attack those who push my two buttons. I was really good at degrading people who tapped into my core fears. After those encounters, I was embarrassed and wondered who I really was as a person. It was as if I changed into someone else I didn't recognize. I didn't seem to have any control over my mean-spirited remarks. As I look back, I completely invalidated both friends, and I'm sure I tapped their core fears. Our relationships ended, and each of us developed a fear of just being together because we were not sure the whole situation would not repeat itself. We were out of touch for more than fifteen years. Last year I started e-mailing both of them, and to my surprise, both relationships were greatly repaired because we all started to better understand each other. By listening to each other, we started to reconnect.

When friends or couples don't understand how to change the hurtful patterns in their relationship, they will have the same fight for twenty years. Nothing ever gets settled. Nothing ever gets better. At best, they learn to "live with it," and never achieve the heart-to-heart connection they both long for. At worst, the fights escalate out of control and end up blowing the relationship to bits.

Give It Up?

When we describe the Fear Dance, almost everyone "gets it." They quickly see how destructive the Fear Dance can be. They grasp its dangers and recognize its sorry track record in their own relationships.

Yet some people don't want to give it up. They feel as if they just can't. Why? Because it's a "successful" system to keep them stuck, and it feels normal. By "successful," of course, I don't mean helpful. I don't mean pleasant. I don't mean beneficial. I mean that once it gets going, it gets the same result every time—even if it's exactly the result you don't want.

The Fear Dance works with guaranteed success every time it goes in motion. It doesn't matter what you throw at it; it works perfectly to get you right to where you *don't* want to be. And it does it every time, without fail.

But we shouldn't be too hard on ourselves. We do react in unhealthy ways, but we do it with a worthy goal of keeping the relationship going. You might call such a system "functionally dysfunctional."

It's *functional* in that it keeps two people bouncing off one another. It allows them to continue some sort of interaction, even if that interaction consistently hurts. It functions in a painful, crazy kind of way. At the same time, however, it's deeply *dysfunctional.* The relationships it creates bring tremendous pain. The Fear Dance "works" in that it allows the people involved to continue some sort of relationship, but it has no power to create the kind of relationship they really want.

Suppose you grew up watching your dad fix your bicycle. You didn't know it, but because he couldn't afford the proper tools, he always used whatever he could find—a chicken bone here, a bent tin can lid there. Your bike "worked," after a fashion, and over the years you got used to a handlebar falling off as you zoomed downhill or a tire bouncing away as you took a sharp turn. You retrieved the damage parts, took them back to your dad, and he "fixed" your rickety vehicle—at least well enough so that it could venture out once more. You didn't particularly like the way your bike rode, or the scars it put on your shins and elbows, but you couldn't imagine life without it.

What do you think would have happened if a bicycle repairman saw your bike and told you that he knew how to make it work much better? Maybe you'd go back home and tell your dad. And maybe he'd say, "Now Son, I used to watch my dad repair my bicycle, and he did it the same way I'm repairing yours. His daddy did it the same way, and so did his granddaddy. I think I know a thing or two about repairing bicycles. Don't listen to that man."

You could think of your bike as "functionally dysfunctional."

And if that's the only bike you knew, would you find it easy to risk your ride on something completely unknown? Probably not.

That's the problem facing many people today in their relationships. They may not like the way their friendships or marriages "ride," but everybody they know seems to suffer from the same wobbly wheels and bent-up handlebars. They may not like it much, but why risk what they have for something they can't imagine? Better to stick with the known, no matter how much grief it causes. It may not work well, but it works successfully enough to get the same (crummy) results, time after time.

It's a perfect system! It's just not a pleasant one.

One of the worst things about the Fear Dance is that, eventually, it makes us dependent on other people for our happiness and fulfillment. We look to our friends or family members or spouses to fulfill our wants. And there's something functionally dysfunctional about such a dependency.

God created us to depend on him, and as human beings we naturally gravitate toward being dependent. But there's a problem: such dependency was designed and reserved for God alone, not for our spouses or friends or bosses. So although the Fear Dance "works" after a fashion, it cannot bring us to where we want to be.

May I ask, do you want to enjoy everything that God meant for you to have? If so, you have to acknowledge that the unhealthy dance and the unhealthy reactions *will not* work. We usually tell clients, "I'm not telling you not to use them, but I am saying that if you continue to use them, you'll never reach God's best for you. The dance you've been doing has been successful for getting the results you've been getting. So if you want different results, you have to break the rhythm of the Fear Dance and learn a new dance."

Break the Rhythm of the Fear Dance

Do you see now how the Fear Dance has injured, crippled, and maybe even destroyed some of the relationships that mean the most to you? Perhaps you not only recognize the hurtful patterns but also feel compelled to change them. You don't want the Fear Dance to continue to ruin your relationships.

But what do you do now?

First, it amazes me how quickly many conflicts get defused once both people in the relationship recognize their part in the Fear Dance. Once both people identify their core fears, a solution often suggests itself. In many cases, all it takes is a true understanding of the *real* underlying problem.

Let's return one last time to Dan and Celeste. After Michael helped them to identify their core fears, it became very clear that the real problem was not about the move. Michael also helped them to see themselves in the picture; it's never just about the other person.

First, Michael asked Dan, "Are Celeste and her family responsible for your feeling controlled?"

"No, they aren't," he replied. "I've just never understood that my fear was feeling controlled."

"What should you do about it?" Michael continued.

"I need to do what's right and true, no matter how I'm feeling. I'll need God's help to do that, of course, but I want his peace to rule my heart. Finally, I want to stop reacting to others when I feel controlled. That's my problem, not theirs."

Michael turned to Celeste. "What could you do to help yourself feel valued and important?" he asked.

"I can remember who God says I am. I can spend time doing things I enjoy. And I can stop controlling Dan and become the wife that God created me to be."

Dan leaned toward her and said softly, "Thank you, honey. You are important to me." Then the couple hugged warmly.

But the exercise wasn't finished. Michael then asked Dan, "What could you do for yourself when you feel controlled?" Dan offered several ideas that showed he was placing the responsibility on himself, not others.

Now that the real issues had come out into the open, the pair started talking freely. Celeste opened up, and almost miraculously *she* began describing the boundaries they could draw around their family.

And no one talked about a move anymore.

"It was a very powerful moment when they got down to the real problem and their core fears," Michael said.

This couple enjoyed a huge breakthrough in their relationship because they finally stopped waltzing to the deadly rhythm of the Fear Dance. Once they determined the real problem, they could move on in their relationship.

So is that it? Are we done?

Hardly! It's one thing to identify the fear buttons that drive any particular conflict; it's quite another to break the rhythm of the Fear Dance. While I'm thrilled that this couple broke their stalemate about where to live, I believe they have a lot more work ahead of them. This was a great first step! But to continue down this satisfying road, they *have* to learn the new dance steps.

And that's what I want to show you in the next five chapters. The first dance step is my all-time favorite. More improvements in my life came from this one step than from all the other dance steps combined.

LIFE IS RELATIONSHIPS;
THE REST IS JUST DETAILS.

ONE-MINUTE REVIEW
THE DANCE THAT DESTROYS RELATIONSHIPS

1. **The external problem is rarely the problem.** What we think is the problem—finances, the other person—is not the core problem.

2. **The core problem is our fear.** The problem in nearly every conflict is that something touched each person's core fear. We wrestle with a core fear.

3. **Each of us is involved in a Fear Dance.** Triggered by a core fear, we get stuck in a destructive Fear Dance that involves our hurts, wants, fears, and reactions.

4. **Don't expect the other person to be the solution.** When we hurt, we want the other person to change so that we won't feel the hurt. But the solution is not to change the other person.

5. **The Fear Dance is functionally dysfunctional.** Because the Fear Dance is the only dance many people know how to do, they "function" in the midst of dysfunction. They adopt coping mechanisms, which often only deepen the problem.

6. **We can break the rhythm of the Fear Dance.** By identifying our core fears and by understanding that the other person isn't the problem, we can begin to learn new dance steps to healthier relationships.

PART TWO

NEW DANCE STEPS

4

THE POWER OF ONE: TAKE PERSONAL RESPONSIBILITY

My son Michael and his wife, Amy, also have been on the dance floor with their Fear Dance. And their reactions have not always been pretty.

One day Michael came home with a new cell phone and plan—about the sixth one in six months. He easily succumbs to the newest telecommunications gadget and the coolest "free minutes" plan. He was fully aware that Amy and he had recently discussed his cell-phone addiction and that he had promised not to purchase any new phones unless they discussed it. But he was confident that if he broke the news to her right, with humor, she would not be upset. He walked in the door, happy and enthusiastic about his new acquisition. "Hey, Baby, want my number?" he announced with a grin.

When Amy responded, "I already have your number," he thought he was home free. He smiled and proceeded, "Oh, you don't have *this* one," and showed her the phone.

The humor evaporated and Amy exploded. "You're so irresponsible!" she yelled. "How could you do this? We don't need another cell phone in this house!"

While Michael listened, Amy vented her frustration. Soon he noticed their young son, standing with them in the living room. Michael pointed to Cole, hoping Amy would take the signal not to display her anger or belittle him in front of their little boy. She noticed his signal, all right.

"Well, I *want* Cole to hear how irresponsible you are!" she fumed, and she continued her tirade.

Michael doesn't typically escalate an argument, but *that* comment sent him through the stratosphere. Amy had never done anything like it before—and Cole stood there, dumbfounded. You could almost see his bewildered brain wondering, *What is going on?*

Amy realized she had gone way over the line, and she fled into the bedroom. Michael ran right behind her, but not before he turned and instructed Cole, "You stay here!" Overcome by his anger, Michael started pointing at Amy and shouting, "This is all *your* fault!"

Of course, their problem had nothing whatsoever to do with his unwise purchase! After all, how could he be expected to control the way he used the family's money? After all, he was addicted. But none of that occurred to him at the time.

Amy responded to his barrage of accusations by retreating all the way into the closet. He followed right after her, pointing his finger at her. "What were you thinking, talking that way in front of our son, accusing me of being *this* and *that*?"

"Don't you point at me!" Amy shot back.

Michael sucked in his breath and retorted, "Oh *yeah*?" Then he began pointing at her in rapid-fire succession, with both hands, as if his fingers had become bullets from a machine gun. As he did, he says he saw himself as the smartest, coolest guy in the world.

Amy did not. She *laughed*. We'll tell you "the rest of the story" later, about how they came to a place where they stopped blaming each other and focused their eyes on themselves, taking personal responsibility for their actions. But what Amy did sent Michael into a completely different realm altogether. He could no longer contain himself.

Let me suggest that most of us are like Michael and Amy. Oh, you may be less explosive, but I suspect you do a destructive dance nonetheless. You do the Fear Dance in any number of ways. You may have tried to stop but can't. You wring your hands, thinking, *If only he would . . . If only she would . . . If only my daughter would . . . If only my neighbor would . . .* It's always the same dance, and it always appears to be the other person's fault.

How do you break the rhythm of the dance? If neither of you budges, the dance could go on forever. And for some people it does.

How do you stop the madness? It takes two to tango. It takes two to do the Fear Dance.

But it takes only one person to stop the madness.

I call that the Power of One. And this new dance step can revolutionize your relationships.

You Already Have the Power of One

Your fear buttons get pushed every day. Yet it's your *reaction* to those fears that determines whether you get stuck in the Fear Dance—and *you* control the thoughts that control your reaction, not your external circumstances.

Just pause for a moment and ponder this statement: *You can choose your reaction, and your reaction is based on your thoughts.* But from all of your thoughts will come your actions and your emotions, either negative or positive. Your thoughts are the basis for your feelings and reactions. That's awesome to me.

You have a choice about how you react when someone pushes your fear button. No one else controls how you think. No one else controls how you react. You alone do that.

Suppose you're walking down the streets of New York, and some guy you've never seen comes up and calls you a disgusting name. What do you do? Probably nothing. You keep on walking. You don't want a fight, and what some loon says on the streets of the Big Apple doesn't affect you. Let him blather all he wants.

What happens, though, if your wife or your boyfriend or your coworker calls you the very same name? It probably pushes your button. Why do you react differently? The name-calling itself hasn't created a button; the button was there in both cases. But in the second instance, the name-calling tapped your fear of rejection, failure, or disconnection (or whatever). In the first case, it didn't. This means that the Fear Dance *can't* be about the external; it *has* to be about the internal, about—what's in your mind. It's not about the existence of your button, but about the way you *choose* to think and react when it gets pushed.

Do you see how this empowers you? *You* control how you think and react. You can't control whether anyone pushes your button, but you can control how you think and react to its getting pushed. If this were not the case, then life would simply be an elaborate system of manipulation. But it isn't!

What's the Real Problem?

Most couples we see in our marriage intensives come with two very long lists:

> 1. *The specific problems they're having as a couple (finances, kids, sex, etc.)*
> 2. *All the behaviors they want the other person to "fix." In other words, "If my spouse would only change ___, I'd be happy."*

The couples are very clear about both things.

Is the problem the list of issues? Research over the past several years has consistently listed financial issues as the number one conflict that leads to divorce. But do you want to know something amazing? Financial problems never caused even a single divorce! They may provide the topic of angry discussion, but they don't *cause* anything.

Remember the relationship truth: The external problem is rarely the real problem. The problem is never about a list of issues. The issues themselves are just like the guy yelling at you in New York. And you have a choice about how you will react to them. You have the Power of One.

Is the problem the other person's behavior (or attitude or personality)? How many times do we hear, "My wife is always belligerent? I want her to quit yelling at me." "My husband spends too much time at work." Remember another DNA truth: It's never just about the other person. What these spouses really need to change, however, is almost always their *reaction* to the issues on the list. When we explain this, the guy usually says, "Oh, so I *don't* have to get her to stop yelling."

No, you don't. And in fact, you *can't* "get her" to stop yelling or to stop doing anything else without dishonoring her. But you *can* control your thoughts and how you react when your button gets pushed. You *can* choose to plug into the Power of One. You *can* take personal responsibility.

The problem is, most of us spend all our time and energy talking about what the other person is doing or not doing. We focus all our efforts on complaining or describing the hurtful activities of our friend or partner. Sue talks about what she doesn't like about Anne. Bill fumes about how Steve's actions drive him crazy. Roberta complains about Jim's handling of their money. But discussions like this go nowhere. They lead only to frustration and anger and disappointment. Worse yet, they merely keep the music going to the Fear Dance.

There is a better way. A *much* better way. We want to give you six steps to take control of your emotions and reactions to life.

1. Take Control of Your Thoughts, Feelings, and Actions

Whenever you focus your attention on what the other person is doing, you take away your own power. You make yourself weak. In focusing on the other, you try to control things you can't control. For that reason it's an exercise in total futility, inefficiency, and ineffectiveness.

How much better to have some say in the matter! How much more effective to take control of something you can actually control! When you focus on yourself rather than on the other person, you vastly increase your odds of being able to enjoy some impact and influence over the relationship problem that bothers you.

Remember when Michael's fear button got pushed? At that instant, he had a choice to make. He couldn't control that his button got pushed, but he could determine how he would think and react once it did. He couldn't control Amy or what she did, but he could control himself and what he thought and did. In other words, he could choose whether he would exercise personal responsibility for his own actions. He could choose whether he would take advantage of the awesome Power of One. But he chose what most people do: "Let's see if I can change Amy."

You and I have the same choice to make—and our choice will largely determine whether we enjoy deep, satisfying relationships, or fragile, disappointing ones. I can't stress enough how crucial it is that each of us takes personal responsibility for how we think and respond when our fear buttons get pushed.

By nature, most of us want to blame those who upset us. We work hard to try to get them to change how they treat us. We attempt in many unhealthy ways to manipulate them, to force them to quit pushing our buttons. But what usually happens when we take this approach? It succeeds only in pushing that person's own fear button, which in turn continues and accelerates the Fear Dance. We wind up feeling hurt, abused, estranged, and lonely—and yet another relationship takes a tragic turn for the worse.

To take personal responsibility means that you refuse to focus on what the other person has done. Too many of us think, *If only my friend would say this* or *If only my husband would do that*, rather than thinking, *I can't change him, but I* can *change how I react to him.*

Personal responsibility requires you to take a hard look at your own side of the equation. You might say to yourself, "You know what? My fear button just got pushed. Normally I would withdraw and run away, even though that solves nothing. But I'm not going to do that this time. This time I'm going to take responsibility for how I act, rather than trying to manipulate this person into acting toward me in a way I prefer."

Dr. Gary Chapman, author of the best-selling *The Five Love Languages*, highly endorses this strategy. He advises struggling spouses to keep doing what's in their power rather than focusing on what the other person should do. He helps husbands and wives identify their love needs and then counsels them to keep on loving their spouses, using the person's love language, for six months, regardless of how the person reacts. The spouses do this not to manipulate the other into acting the way they would like but to enjoy life more. And usually, in time, the relationship greatly improves.

Before we leave this step, I want to come back to a point I've been making throughout the book so far: *Your thoughts control your feelings and reactions.*

Think about that. If you want to control your reactions, you need to control your thoughts. You can take personal responsibility for all of your thoughts and actions and take your eyes off of blaming others for how you feel. This amazing truth has changed my life over the past two years more than anything else.

Dr. Archibald Hart's book *Habits of the Mind* has shaped my perspective about the power of our thoughts. He says, "Our body is the servant of the mind. It obeys the operations of the mind, whether they be deliberately chosen or automatically expressed. Disease and health, like circumstances, are rooted in thought."[1] He goes on to say that feelings are the consequences, not the cause, of our emotional problems. Our emotions are good sources of information about how we are thinking. We cannot control our emotions directly, but we can influence how we are feeling by changing our thoughts.[2] Change our thoughts first, and the desired feelings will follow. Our reactions, our emotions, our attitudes are the result of our thoughts.[3]

As I've said, this has changed my life. Just the other night my stomach was upset and nervous about something. I couldn't shake it. I felt discouraged about a situation, as if I had failed. *Why am I upset?* I thought. I went to bed, but the feelings wouldn't leave me. So I practiced Dr. Hart's principles. I reviewed the situation. I felt as if I was disappointing several key people in my life with one of the chapters in this book. But I also felt stuck and couldn't figure out how to improve it. Then the thought came, *God's power is made perfect within me through my weaknesses.* The truth of that promise changed my thinking, and my thinking changed my feelings. Instead of feeling discouraged, I felt grateful for the weak areas of my life that remind me of my dependence on God. I started thanking God for my weaknesses and cried out to him for his power to work within me and help me finish this book. I fell asleep instantly, at peace and with a grateful heart about being dependent on God. As soon as I changed my thinking, my heart reflected the corresponding emotion. I woke up the next day with an idea and started writing feverishly. Even my editor liked it.

YOUR THOUGHTS CONTROL YOUR FEELINGS AND REACTIONS.

What are the implications of Dr. Hart's insights for your relationships? How can you control your reactions by controlling your thoughts? This process underscores what we have been saying so far.

You must take your focus off the other person and look at yourself. Before you can control your reactions, you must control your thoughts. And when you do, you will find amazing freedom.

2. Take Responsibility for Your Buttons

It doesn't help a relationship—not in the least—to focus on all the "stuff" you think the other person needs to change. On the other hand, it's enormously useful to address what you are doing, to look at your own thoughts and reactions, and to ponder your own fears and emotions. It does help when you do your own personal work. It helps a lot.

"When my wife and I get into something," says one of my co-workers, "I have the ability to go off by myself and start thinking, *Okay. When I reacted that way, I wonder where that was coming from?* That's very productive. It's a waste of time, however, to talk about the other person's reactions. But it's very good to find out the other person's feelings and to express your own feelings. That's where you begin to solve conflicts."

Remember this: When your buttons get pushed, they're *yours*, and *you* are responsible for them. We often see people caught in pseudo-karate mode in which they spend all their time trying to keep the other person from pushing their buttons. They expend a lot of their energy on trying to control the other person's behavior. In their minds, it's all about the other person's not pushing their buttons.

How much more productive it is when they can honestly say, "Wait a moment! These are *my* buttons. It's *my* job to understand where my reactions come from, what they are about, and how to control them when my buttons get pushed."

→ YOU ARE IN CHARGE
OF YOUR BUTTONS.

And it doesn't matter what kind of buttons they are. We've all met people with sensitive buttons. You can't be around them a minute without pushing one of their buttons because they are very sensitive. It could be that you're such a person yourself. But if someone pushes your button, he or she pushes a button for which *you* are responsible and that *you* control.

I'm talking here not only about actions but also about thoughts. Many people easily understand that they make choices about their behavior. They don't always grasp so easily that they make choices about thoughts and ideas.

But if we had no ability to choose what thoughts we have, then why would God tell us, "Fix your thoughts on what is true and honorable and right. Think about things that are pure and lovely and admirable. Think about things that are excellent and worthy of praise"?[4] And how could the apostle Paul claim, "We take captive every thought to make it obedient to Christ"?[5]

You are emphatically *not* at the mercy of those who push your buttons. They do not have to control how you react. You do not have to give them the power to determine what you think or what you do. You must take control of yourself.

It's absolutely crucial to remember that when you choose to tap into the Power of One, you empower yourself. You begin to control what you can control rather than trying to manipulate what will always lie outside of your power.

Some adults remain childishly dependent, unnecessarily needy, and forever at the mercy of anyone willing to take care of them. Whether you're about to celebrate your eighteenth or your eightieth birthday, you can choose today to take responsibility for yourself. You can choose the Power of One.

Do you ever think that traffic makes you angry? It doesn't. What makes you angry is how you choose to respond to it. Traffic doesn't control how you feel. You have the power to take personal responsibility for your reaction to that stalled car in the express lane during the middle of rush hour traffic. You have the ability to tap into the Power of One.

Regardless of the size of your fear button, the Power of One gives you the ability to break the destructive power of the Fear Dance. This goes not only for trivial things like a reaction to stalled traffic but also to big things—even as big as infidelity.

A friend of mine was counseling a Chicago couple trying to weather the horrible storm of infidelity. The husband had begun an online relationship with a woman several states away, and eventually, while claiming to take a business trip, he met her in person. Later in therapy, the husband kept talking about how the affair never would have happened if his wife had taken care of his needs. He said to her, "If you had been more loving . . . If you had been more accepting . . . If you had been more physical with me and met my sexual needs." He continued to point the finger at his wife, refusing to take personal responsibility for his actions.

His strategy obviously didn't heal the relationship.

Meanwhile, the wife angrily blamed her husband for the affair, insisting that he hadn't been there for her and that he worked too many hours. She listed fault after fault, never once admitting that, in fact, she really had been neglectful and hadn't given herself emotionally or physically to her husband.

Her strategy didn't work especially well either.

"This couple didn't move forward in a productive way," my friend said, "until they started pointing their fingers back at themselves and saying, 'What can *I* do to change to make this marriage better?'"

Listen! Do you want great relationships? If so, then you need to learn this new dance step. You need to exercise the Power of One. It's the only way to experience the true freedom that all great relationships provide.

3. Don't Give Others the Power to Control Your Feelings

You'll never know real freedom in your relationships if you insist on letting others control how you feel and what you do with those feelings. Freedom and responsibility are merely two sides of the same coin. You can't have one without the other.

Imagine yourself in a power struggle, a conflict that really makes you upset. What can you do? If you want to remain powerless, you let the other person determine how you feel and how you react. You rant and rave and demand and bully, hoping to get your way. Unfortunately, you'll probably get the same kind of treatment in return. Michael and Amy found that out in the incident about the cell phone. So what happens? You end up with anger, frustration, and a bleeding, wounded relationship.

On the other hand, you could choose to exercise the Power of One and take personal responsibility. You could remind yourself that in a tug-of-war it takes only one person to drop the rope in order to end the power struggle. As soon as one person drops the rope, the game ends.

Most people don't realize that they have chosen to participate in the Fear Dance. You may be among them. You may be thinking, *What? Why would I choose to participate in the Fear Dance?* Remember the DNA truth: Not choosing is itself a choice.

Why don't *you* choose to drop the rope? Why don't *you* stop the Fear Dance? Why don't *you* take personal responsibility for your reactions? Why don't *you* tap into the Power of One?

Most people find it very encouraging to realize that they have the power to stop the dance at any point by choosing not to participate. They can choose. And when you choose to tap into the Power of One, you decisively break the power of the Fear Dance.

4. Don't Look to Others to Make You Happy

One of the things that will help you take control is clearing up a prevalent misconception. Many of us grew up believing a powerful but very deceptive myth. We completely bought into the idea that relationships are all about back-scratching. You know: "You scratch my back, and I'll scratch yours." Or, it's like the myth of the fifty-fifty marriage: "I'll go halfway if you go halfway."

YOU CAN STOP THE FEAR DANCE. ←———

Have you ever caught yourself or your friends making statements like the following?

- In a successful marriage, both spouses meet all the other's needs.
- The best relationships "complete" those involved; what was half becomes whole.
- The best way to find a best friend is to look for someone who can make you happy.

Do any of these statements sound familiar? They probably do. Yet despite what you may have been taught, all three statements are false. Myths. Deceptions. Lies!

And if you believe them, they'll end up costing you *big*.

The truth is, what we often call "needs" normally better fit the category of "wants." We want others to respect us, admire us, need us. But are those true needs? No one can meet all our needs aside from God himself. If you depend on a spouse to meet your "needs," you set yourself up for trouble. The relationship becomes an unhealthy, codependent one. Your fulfillment is emphatically *not* the job of someone else. God has given this job to you, and only you can shoulder it. God has promised to meet all of your needs.[6] You are the one who cooperates with him and receives his riches as he gives them.

The truth is, neither marriage nor any other human relationship makes one whole out of two halves. When you expect a human relationship to turn your half into a whole, you're headed for disappointment. Why? Because what really happens is that you believe that this other (flawed) person will make up for your personal deficiencies. This is when your heartache and disappointment and disillusionment double. It's not hard to see why. In your experience, do two unhappy people normally form one happy couple? Not usually.

The truth is, no one can "make" you happy. Not a spouse. Not a friend. Not a boss or a neighbor or a pastor. Abraham Lincoln spoke wisely when he said, "I reckon that people are about as happy as they make up their minds to be." You, and not someone else, choose how you will react to what life throws at you. You, and no one else, decide what you will do when someone pushes your fear button. The practical equivalent of "You will be about as happy as you make up your mind to be" is nothing but "Only by exercising the Power of One–by taking personal responsibility for your actions–will you find the secret to building strong relationships." Before you finish this book, I will show you how I recently used the Power of One to bring my own stress level to the lowest level of my life. Even my blood pressure dropped. I chose to think about life in a way that miraculously changed me. I share this here because we want you to know that the thoughts you have and your reactions to life determine your level of happiness and fulfillment.

In a passage full of insight about strong relationships, the apostle Paul writes, "If it is possible, *as far as it depends on you*, live at peace with everyone."[7] Paul knew that no one can "make" someone else act in a peaceful way. On the other hand, one person can choose to make the road to peace as smooth as possible. Even if the other person has no interest in peace, you can hold out the proverbial olive branch. And even if he or she doesn't take it, at least your own heart can enjoy a greater measure of peace than it had before.

This is nothing but the Power of One. And it's good news! If your entire well-being and delight in life depends on how someone else treats you, then you're in for a bumpy ride. But if you decide to take control of how you react to the challenges, insults, difficulties, and conflicts that inevitably come your way, then a whole new world opens up—a world marked by peace.

A world, by the way, available only to people who think like adults.

5. Become the CEO of Your Life

When did you become an adult? Don't answer too quickly! Bob Paul says he didn't grow up until he was in his thirties. And I didn't grow up until after I celebrated my fortieth birthday!

How can this be, you ask? Simple. An adult is someone who is fully capable of being responsible for himself or herself and who fully accepts that responsibility. A person who is capable of responsibility but doesn't accept that responsibility is functioning as a child.

When people take responsibility for themselves, they become empowered as adults. When I finally realized that my own thoughts and reactions were all mine and when I stopped giving others the power over my thoughts, I became an adult. A child is a person who remains completely dependent on others and blames others for his or her emotions or success. An adult is someone who is no longer a child.

By this definition, an adult is someone who takes personal responsibility. Taking personal responsibility, in other words, means accepting the job of an adult. If you refuse to take personal responsibility— if you reject the Power of One—then, in effect, you're refusing to become an adult.

That's why Bob can admit, "Not until my thirties did these ideas about taking personal responsibility start making sense to me. Only then did I start to make the transition to adulthood. All the way through my twenties, when my wife and I were having kids, I felt as if I was kidding everybody. I looked like an adult; I was doing adult work; but inside, I felt like an insecure little child."

In many ways I too remained a child until I was in my forties. Until that time, I looked to my bosses and my churches to take care of me. I'd whine and complain if they didn't care for me the way I wanted. I'd go home and tell my wife that they weren't being sensitive to me. I depended on them for all areas of care—until I finally took personal responsibility for my life. Only then did I start to grow up and become an adult. I didn't become an adult overnight. It was a slow process. I grew up more over the last two years than I have over the past fifteen years.

Does that make sense to you? Taking advantage of the Power of One really means accepting the job of being an adult.

So let's ask the question again. When did *you* become an adult? When did *you* begin taking personal responsibility for your own care? When did *you* start experiencing the Power of One? If you still expect others to make you happy, then you're still functioning like a child, regardless of your chronological age.

It's never too late, however, to take up the mantle of personal responsibility. At the moment you assume that mantle, you become an adult. You could, of course, remain a child in an adult's clothes for your entire life and never become a functioning adult. But why would you choose that?

Those who make the choice to leave childhood behind can expect to reap great rewards! Just as a reminder, I want to share again the following thoughts and choices that will determine your emotions, either positive or negative. These choices tend to lower stress and lead to more peace and joy.

1. Give up or give to God all your expectations that people, places, and things will bring you lasting happiness and fulfillment. Nothing outside of God can bring you life, joy, and peace. He gives to those who ask. This one step alone will reduce your stress level to almost zero. It's childish to think that something on this earth will bring lasting fulfillment and happiness. God is the source of life; people and things are overflow.

Stress is the gap between what we expect to happen and what is actually happening. Depending on the intensity of the expectation, we can be very or only slightly stressed. We again make that choice by placing value to our expectations. The more valuable an expectation, the more intense the stress. Just think about your own stress for a minute. The only time you get stressed is when an expectation is not being met as you had hoped. Whether it is driving, vacationing, working, studying, hiking, gardening, you name it, stress comes when things aren't working out as we planned. Drop those expectations, and see what happens to your stress.

As if I needed practice with this, I faced a dashed expectation just a few hours ago. I finished this chapter and was ready to send it off to the editors. I decided to move the electronic file to a different location in my computer. When a little dialog box popped up, I didn't bother to read it. (I know you know what's coming. You've probably done the same thing.) I clicked on yes before I realized it, and my chapter was gone. I lost all of my work! I called a computer expert, but after he tried a few things, he said, "Gary, it looks like it's gone." Gone!

That's when I had the choice: I could stew about the situation, or I could give up my expectation and move on. I chose to let go. In fact, I started laughing and thought, *Oh well, I'll just redo it.* Norma and I had planned a date, but she suggested I stay home and she would go with a friend. I finished the chapter a little before midnight. Even though my initial stress level went up to about a five, when I finished the chapter, it was back down to a one. In the end I'm very glad I redid the chapter because I had missed several very important points and ideas.

2. Realize that everything negative that happens to us can be reframed into something positive. I call this step "Treasure Hunting," and it really makes life's trials take on a different meaning. I have been learning that everything that happens to me can become a joy to me. That echoes what the New Testament says: "Whenever trouble comes your way, let it be an opportunity for joy."[8] I've seen the proof of this truth. I'll list two. Today my *thoughts* about trials are very positive.

- I was a very slow student in school and almost didn't make it to college. With low spelling and reading skills, I struggled my entire life at academics. These negative experiences became my greatest strengths and joy. Because I struggle in these areas, my books tend to be simple, practical, and easy to read. I hate reading boring books. People enjoy reading about my mistakes and the easy steps to follow. The steps have to be easy, or I wouldn't be able to apply them.

* In the past few years, I've had a heart attack, kidney transplant, and now diabetes because of the kidney medicines. These experiences have given me more understanding and empathy for what other sick people go through. I love these people a lot more now than before my illnesses. I have more compassion for hurting people in general. My love for God is stronger because of my greater dependence on him. All trials bring more love for God and others if we allow the trials to train us.

The list goes on and on. The key to joy and peace is deciding that trials are good for us and that we grow after we grieve for a while.

6. Recruit Assistants

When I insist that you have to take personal responsibility for how you react to the challenges of life, I don't mean that you're in this battle all by yourself. I don't mean that it's you against the world, come what may. I do mean that you are responsible for how you choose to act and react to those who push your fear buttons. I do mean that you are the chief executive officer of yourself.

But all CEOs have assistants! And you should have a few too.

What do I mean by choosing assistants? It's choosing people who agree to help you take care of yourself and stay responsible for yourself. But unless those people know what you need, they cannot help you appropriately.

Your need to take personal responsibility doesn't mean that you do everything by yourself or for yourself. While you'll never win by trying to manipulate others into doing what you want, you certainly can improve your relationships by recruiting willing assistants who, by their own conscious choice, partner with you in creating a stronger relationship.

In other words, unless you choose to tell your spouse what your buttons are, he or she might never know that part of you and can't help you. For example, if you tell your spouse that your core fear is rejection or being controlled, then he or she may choose to be your assistant and try to limit behavior that would push your buttons. But remember, your spouse is only assisting you. You still must be ready to respond in ways that benefit you in the long run.

The fact is, your relationships likely *would* give you a great deal more satisfaction if others didn't constantly put their sticky fingers all over your fear buttons. Life *would* feel better without the belittling and accusing and demeaning and abandoning. That's a no-brainer.

I recently got a reminder of the importance of recruiting assistants rather than trying to manipulate people into doing what I wanted. When I first called together some coworkers to discuss the content for this book, I felt as if certain family members weren't "doing" the message of this book. I wanted them to treat me a certain way, and they weren't doing it. But instead of taking personal responsibility, instead of realizing that I couldn't "make" anybody change, instead of going directly to my family members involved and asking them to be my assistants, I decided to go through the back door and make it look as if it were a staff meeting.

So I sent an e-mail to everyone in my family, instructing them to watch a three-hour video of Bob Paul teaching the material I'm teaching you right now. I hoped that by watching it, they would understand what I needed from them. Then I called together a big meeting, all the time saying, "We need to learn this new material. I don't feel like I understand it quite right yet."

During the meeting Michael finally called me on it. "You know," he said, "it's interesting. You're saying that you don't feel as if you quite understand this, and yet you're trying to make me and everyone else watch the videos and be here in a meeting to hear Bob explain the material. It seems to me that if you don't understand it, then you need to be having this meeting by yourself."

While Michael's comments irritated me, I finally admitted the truth: I felt certain family members hadn't been treating me right, and this was my attempt to manipulate them into doing what I wanted. The whole time I was not being honest. I was not taking personal responsibility. I had not tried to recruit any assistants. And my actions got us into conflict.

Things didn't calm down until I finally said, "All right, that's fair. I need to do the changing, and I can't make anybody else change." I also realized that when I feel hurt, I have to go directly to the people involved and be up front with them. In other words, I had to tap into the Power of One. And part of that involves recruiting willing assistants—not manipulated ones.

Here's what I could have done. My goal was to have my daughter, Kari, and her husband, Roger, learn about the DNA of relationships. Roger is one of the key staff members who will be presenting the material in this book to schools, churches, and businesses all over the world. So I wanted him to learn the material in his own life so he would be more effective in explaining the material to those he was recruiting to partner with us. I didn't feel as if I could be direct with them. I reasoned that Bob Paul's new teaching video on the subject would be just the ticket. I hid my intentions by inviting everyone in our family to watch the video. I should have just gone to Roger and Kari and discussed it with them, asking them to help me share this new message and suggesting that they watch the video with Norma and me. They would have gladly assisted me. Instead, they felt confused and manipulated.

You are the CEO of yourself. If you're smart, however, you'll openly recruit others as your assistants. These assistants, of course, are also the CEOs of themselves and therefore may ask you, in turn, to become their willing assistants. Is this manipulation? Far from it! It's cooperation, and there's a world of difference between the two.

I find it helps to work through a few important questions:

- For what things am I fully responsible?
- In what areas do I have a shared responsibility?
- In what areas do I have no responsibility?
- How can I learn to take the appropriate level of responsibility in any given situation?

I'm reminded of a few things as I work through the questions:

- I am fully responsible for my thoughts, beliefs, feelings, and behavior.
- I am not responsible for your thoughts, beliefs, feelings, or behavior.
- In a relationship I can influence—but not control—the thoughts, beliefs, feelings, and behavior of another.

When I'm the assistant, I have the privilege of helping my loved ones as they request (or as I see the opportunity). All the while, they remain the CEO of themselves. I'm not responsible for how they act or react; they remain responsible for themselves. But I can certainly do what I can to improve our mutual environment! Norma recently asked me to help her with an illness she is suffering from at the moment. She wanted me to call a doctor and find out some information for her. I responded, "My privilege." After I got the information, I passed it on to her. Now what do I do if she doesn't follow through with the information I gave her? It's not my responsibility to hound her about it. It's not my place to get angry if she doesn't use the information. It's her responsibility to do with it as she wishes and at her pace and on her conditions. She's the CEO of this situation; I'm her assistant.

As an assistant, you have the power to influence the environment in which your relationships grow, whether for good or ill. Your assistants have the same kind of power. They never take the job of CEO from you, and you never take the job of CEO from them.

But oh, what a difference a competent assistant can make!

The Power of Choosing Forgiveness

A big part of tapping into the Power of One involves forgiveness, both giving it and asking for it. It's not easy to do, but adults who want their relationships to flourish must become good at it.

Michael's wife, Amy, leads a small group of high school girls from her church. One night the girls started complaining that their pastor, Ted, never addressed the young people during his Sunday sermons. The fact especially upset them because their church has no Sunday-morning class for high school students. "We're not important to the church," they indignantly told Amy, "and to top it off, Pastor Ted doesn't even think about us when he writes his sermons."

Amy soon jumped on the bandwagon and unintentionally fanned the flame. When her students returned home, they got their parents all upset and cranky about Ted. The next thing you know, Ted got a few angry e-mails and phone calls from parents. It became a big mess, and then Ted found out about Amy's involvement. The two of them soon got into a conflict.

One day Ted—Michael and Amy's close friend—called Michael

and said, "I don't know what to do about this situation with your wife."

"I can't tell you what to do," Michael replied, "but you probably need to call her."

"Well," Ted answered, "if she'd just call and apologize, everything would be okay." They talked a little while longer and then hung up.

No more than ten minutes later, Amy called Michael. "I don't know what to do about this thing with Ted," she declared.

"I don't know," Michael replied. "Maybe you should call him and talk to him about it."

"Well," Amy answered, "if he'd just call me and apologize, this whole thing would be fine."

Michael started to laugh. "You will not believe this," he said, "but Ted said that exact thing to me about you, not more than ten minutes ago."

The situation did not get resolved until both Amy and Ted chose to take responsibility, apologize, and ask one another for forgiveness. They didn't say, "This is all your fault, you know," but instead admitted their hurt feelings, took ownership of their reactions, and confessed to one another what each had done wrong. In doing so, they followed some divine instructions given thousands of years earlier.

"If your brother . . . repents, forgive him," Jesus told his disciples. "If he sins against you seven times in a day, and seven times comes back to you and says, 'I repent,' forgive him."[9]

Much like us, the disciples wondered, *Who could possibly obey such a tough command?* So they pleaded with their leader, "Increase our faith!" Jesus replied, "If you have faith as small as a mustard seed, you can say to this mulberry tree, 'Be uprooted and planted in the sea,' and it will obey you."[10] In other words, "Gentlemen, I know that without God's help you can't forgive those who hurt you. But do you know what? You don't need more faith; you just need to exercise the genuine faith you already have. God already has given you what you need from heaven's Fort Knox of forgiveness. You already have the only key that opens the vault doors. Now use it. Take personal responsibility, and make the hard choice to forgive."

The truth is, the best of friends can hurt each other with unkind, stinging words. Partners in the best of marriages end some days sobbing into their pillows. In a broken world like this one, in which we end up deeply wounding one another—unintentionally at times, on purpose at other times—we have to make forgiveness a priority. We have to choose to exercise the Power of One and do what we can to make the wronged relationship right again. We must not wait for the other person to make the first move or take the first step. Being an adult means acting like an adult, taking charge of our clamoring emotions and making the difficult choice to ask for forgiveness when we wrong others and to forgive those who wrong us.

Forgiveness involves two actions. The first one is pardon. Basically, that is like erasing their offenses toward us. We immediately wash their offenses away like a wave washing away a message in the sand. Second, forgiveness involves caring for the offending person because most people who offend us have something in their own heart that needs healing. When we forgive others, they are released and healed, but we are too. If you remember the Lord's Prayer, one of the petitions is, "Forgive us our sins [trespasses], just as we have forgiven those who have sinned [trespassed] against us."[11] It suggests that if we forgive others (pardon and help release them), then our Father in heaven will forgive us (pardon and release us).[12] Forgiveness helps the offended person as much as the one who offends. Taking personal responsibility means accepting our part of the offense and seeking forgiveness for where we are wrong. That completes the dynamic in this part of the Lord's Prayer.

FORGIVENESS HEALS ← RELATIONSHIPS.

But you want to know something else? *You* will also hurt others in your relationships. And that means you need to cultivate the habit of asking others to forgive you.

Several years ago I had a very embarrassing experience. Greg and I took a faulty refrigerator part to the repair shop. I wanted the part back quickly and got frustrated when I didn't hear anything about it for several days. I called the repair place several times to find out if the part was fixed. Finally I had had enough. I called again and yelled at the guy on the other end of the phone: "I've had it! Do you think it's good for a customer to wait several extra days for a part to be fixed? Is this how you normally run things—lie to people about when they will be serviced? I'm coming down right now to pick up the part, fixed or not." After saying several other dishonoring things, I slammed down the phone.

"Wow!" Greg said in disbelief. "Dad, you really let that poor guy have it!"

When we arrived at the store, I discovered some distressing news. Not only was the part fixed but the company also had been waiting several days for me to pick it up.

"What happened here?" I asked in bewilderment, looking at Greg. "Are we in the twilight zone or something?" Of course, I was already embarrassed by my actions on the phone.

I soon realized my mistake. I had lost the phone number to the store, and by accident I had looked up the wrong number and had been calling the wrong company. The poor guy I annihilated on the phone had never *had* our damaged part. No wonder he'd acted so confused!

Smalley, I thought, *pack your bags—you're about to go on a guilt trip!*

With Greg listening, I called back the store (the one that never had my part).

"Hello," I said to the employee, "this is Mr. Smalley."

"Sir," the poor guy started to say, "I'm sorry, but we've lost your part. . . ."

I must admit, I felt tempted to go along with his story. It sounded so much better than the one I was about to tell. But I didn't.

"Speaking of things being lost," I said, trying to be funny, "I've actually lost my mind."

Greg laughed.

"Sorry, sir," the employee said, obviously confused. "I'm not following you." When someone begins to eat humble pie, the sound coming from his mouth often confuses the listener.

"Never mind," I explained. "I just needed to tell you that I was wrong to treat you so ugly when I called a few hours ago. As it turned out, I got your company mixed up with the company that actually had my part. They finished the work days ago, but somehow I copied down your phone number from the yellow pages. I'm very sorry for the way I talked to you," I said, "I apologize. Will you forgive me?"

Although I'm sure the employee wanted to let me have it, he accepted my apology and then hung up.

Is it easy to ask for forgiveness? No. It never is. Not even when you're talking to a stranger on the other end of a telephone line. But it's absolutely necessary if you want to pave the way for good relationships. We all have to learn how to tap into the Power of One and choose both to forgive and to ask for forgiveness.

"Be kind to each other, tenderhearted, forgiving one another, just as God through Christ has forgiven you," the Bible tells us.[13] Did God forgive you? Did Christ give you a full pardon? If so, then he calls you to tap into the Power of One and take the first step toward reconciliation with the ones you love.

"I don't have that much faith!" you cry. But if you're a Christian, you already have enough of it to meet the challenge. God has given you what you need. You just need to start moving to the cadence of this first dance step, the Power of One. Let God do the rest.

The Best Medicine Is Not Always Laughter

Remember the out-of-control conflict between Michael and Amy described at the beginning of this chapter? The fight began when Michael came home after buying yet another cell phone. We last saw them in the bedroom closet, where Mount Saint Helens had erupted in a series of superheated lava flows.

We probably ought to get them out of there!

After Amy stopped laughing at Michael's rapid-fire finger pointing, she took control of her reactions. "We've got to settle this; this is out of control. Michael, I'm sorry I blew up at you."

Then she got up, left the closet, and headed straight to their bewildered son still standing dazed in the living room. She spent several minutes apologizing to him and reassuring him that she would never again talk like that about his daddy.

"I was wrong, sweetheart," she said, stroking his hair. "I never should have acted that way."

A few hours later, Michael also tapped into the Power of One. He apologized for buying a cell phone they didn't need and that they had not agreed to purchase.

"I couldn't focus on Amy's behavior. I had to focus on my own feelings and behavior," Michael says. "When I did that, the whole mess got defused. I apologized for the cell phone fiasco, asked her forgiveness for my out-of-control reaction, and we got back to living on the same page."

Oh, and one other thing. Michael returned the cell phone. It seemed the personally responsible thing to do.

You'll never have your desired satisfying relationships unless you and your loved ones feel safe around each other. The next chapter gives you five ways to create a safe place for love to flourish.

LIFE IS RELATIONSHIPS;
THE REST IS JUST DETAILS.

ONE-MINUTE REVIEW
THE POWER OF ONE

1. **Take control of your thoughts, feelings, and actions.** You are part of the picture in every relationship, in every Fear Dance. You can choose to do something. Remember that your thoughts determine your feelings and actions.

2. **Take responsibility for your buttons.** You have a choice about how you react when someone pushes your fear button. No one controls how you react. You alone do that. You are in charge of your buttons.

3. **Don't give others the power to control your feelings.** Focus on the right person. Personal responsibility means refusing to focus on what the other person has done. The only person you can change is yourself. You can stop the Fear Dance. You control whether you get stuck in the Fear Dance. It takes only one person to stop the destructive dance.

4. **Don't look to others to make you happy.** Don't fall into the "If you scratch my back, I'll scratch yours" myth. Come to relationships with realistic expectations.

5. **Become the CEO of your life.** You can't force people to meet your needs, but when you express legitimate needs to others, they can choose to step in to assist you.

6. **Forgiveness heals relationships.** Taking personal responsibility means you confess your wrongdoing and ask for forgiveness. You also forgive others.

5

SAFETY: CREATE A SAFE ENVIRONMENT

In how many of your relationships do you feel safe to open up and re veal who you really are? How many people do you share your deepest thoughts and dreams with? In most of your relationships do you feel close to or distant from the other person? Do you feel deeply connected, or are you engaged in some form of the Fear Dance?

Unfortunately, my wife has not always felt safe around me. Some people refer to me as one of the relationship experts, but in my younger years I was an expert only of myself. In the early years of our marriage I tried to change Norma to be more like me. I was so blind to what builds a great relationship. She did not feel safe around me. Listen to her reflection on those years: "From the beginning, you were so critical of me. You set too high a standard for me to live up to. I felt so controlled by you. I believed in you, so I let you overwhelm me. It worked for a while, but it eventually shut me down. And in the long run, it really didn't work for either of us. You constantly put your work and others in front of me, so I felt inferior to your employees and your dreams. I loved all of your dreams, but they swamped me in the beginning."

I've been married to this wonderful woman for more than forty years. I regret having created an environment that shut her down, that did not honor and value her. Today, however, after I have practiced many of the concepts outlined in this chapter, Norma feels much safer. "Because of the past, I now feel about 95 percent safe," she says. My prayer is that by committing to the principles you're about to read, I will create an environment in which Norma will feel 100 percent safe.

If you are like me, you long for relationships in which you feel completely safe. You want to feel free to open up and reveal who you really are and know that the other person will still love, accept, and value you—no matter what. But too often you and I are hopelessly stuck, afraid to open up with others because we're not quite sure what they will say or do or how they'll use what they learn about us. Or we're stuck in the Fear Dance, crippled by our fear and reactions, exhausted.

Why are we exhausted? Because we spend so much energy trying to hide. We put up walls and try to project an image we think people want so that when they look at us through the camera lens, they like what they see. That's a problem, of course, because it's hard for people to get close to us if we're standing on the other side of a thick wall or a false mask.

The good news is that you can create an open atmosphere that will allow you to be your true self. You can choose to exercise the Power of One and take personal responsibility to break the rhythm of the Fear Dance with a new dance step: Safety.

This second new dance step will help you create a safe climate in which you can build open relationships that will grow and flourish. It will help you build relationships in which you and the other person will feel cherished, honored, and alive. It's almost as if this step changes the background music to your dance, setting a soothing tone that will allow you to feel relaxed in your relationships.

If that sounds like paradise, it's maybe because Eden was a supremely safe place. Adam and Eve felt no fear there. Before their sin, they enjoyed an amazingly intimate relationship with God, themselves, and each other. The couple felt so close to one another that

God described them as "united into one."[1] Nothing came between Adam and Eve—not insecurities, not sharp differences of opinion, not even clothes! They were completely open with each other—no walls, no masks, no fear. Their relationship blossomed.

By learning the steps to safety, you can experience that same kind of relaxed openness in your relationships. You can learn a new dance.

> **STEPS TO SAFETY**
> 1. Respect the wall
> 2. Honor others
> 3. Suspend judgment
> 4. Value differences
> 5. Be trustworthy

1. Respect the Wall

None of us likes a relational wall. It keeps us from feeling close to the other person. We want to destroy that wall, to break down that wall.

Before you head toward the wall with a sledgehammer, however, think about why that wall got erected in the first place. Walls are *always* built by people who feel threatened. Behind every wall we find a person who feels unsafe. That person doesn't want to stay closed and defended, but because the environment feels unsafe, he or she builds the wall for protection and self-preservation.

You may know people who erect these kinds of walls. They may have been abused at some point and have a general distrust toward everyone. If that person is your spouse, it is valid to understand why the walls are up. Over time your spouse will start trusting you if you can create a safe place for him or her.

Greg and his wife, Erin, learned about protective walls early in their marriage. For the first few years Greg kept a nest egg of money hidden from Erin. Occasionally he would use the funds to buy antiques or something else he wanted.

One day an antique dealer with great sporting items called the house and told Erin, "I have a neat item for Greg."

"That's great. I want to get him a present," she replied. "What is

91

it?" The man described an old laced leather basketball, something Erin knew Greg would love. "Yes, I'll take it!" she said excitedly.

When the dealer called back the next day, Greg picked up the phone. Erin hadn't told the dealer that she wanted to surprise Greg with the basketball, so the man told Greg all about it, never mentioning his conversation with Erin. Greg quickly hopped in the car to meet the dealer and buy the ball, using his secret stash of funds.

The following day Erin called the man and asked, "Can we meet so I can get the basketball?"

"Actually," he replied, "your husband already came by yesterday to buy the ball."

Not only was Erin disappointed that she couldn't surprise Greg with the basketball, but she was also puzzled about where Greg had gotten the money without her knowing about it. She visited the bank, and when she found no withdrawal, she started getting suspicious. She confronted Greg with her suspicions, and he finally admitted his secret stash.

Greg's deception deeply hurt Erin. It made it difficult for her to trust her husband on financial matters. She erected a thick wall between them in one day, trying to protect herself from other possible deception.

This situation greatly frustrated Greg. "Things would be going great, and then she would come at me with receipts and demand, 'What are you doing? What's going on?' I continually tried to knock down the wall. I bullied her and tried to strong-arm her into dropping the matter and just trust me." The more Greg hedged, the more Erin distrusted. Their Fear Dance was in full swing.

Nothing improved until the couple spent some time with one of Greg's mentors, Dr. Gary Oliver. When Greg and Erin described their struggle, Gary said, "Greg, you need to honor the fact that she needs this wall up right now. Your deception threatened her. She doesn't feel safe. You have to seek to understand her and value her concerns."

Instead of trying to break down Erin's wall, Greg honored her need to protect herself. Instead of insisting that Erin just trust him, he tried to create an environment of safety. With time and Greg's consistency, Erin eventually felt safe enough to take down the wall and trust her husband again.

When I see a wall separating me from a loved one, it's natural for me to think, *I have to get rid of that wall.* But as soon as I take out the jackhammers or call out the bulldozers, I confirm myself as a dangerous threat, forgetting that the reason the wall went up in the first place is that the person didn't feel safe with me.

So does the wall help build the relationship? Not really. At some point, if the relationship is to flourish, it has to come down. What, then, can you do to encourage the person to take down the wall, brick by brick?

First, the person needs to know that you understand the wall is there for a reason and that you accept its presence. The person needs to know that his or her well-being is the most important thing to you; therefore, the wall can stay as long as it is needed.

Second, let the person know that you're not going to require him or her to be open with you or break down the wall until he or she feels safe. Your job is to give the other person every reason in the world to feel safe, while still honoring the right and responsibility of that person to take care of himself or herself.

You can even imagine stationing yourself as a sentry. Let the person know, "I understand that the wall is there because you feel unsafe. And I want you to know that I am going to stand outside this wall and work on myself so that you can eventually feel safe. I'll try to keep my mouth shut and start discovering what I've done to create such an unsafe place for you. I won't rest until you finally feel relaxed to open up and be yourself around me. I'll even try to protect you from others who create the feeling of apprehension."

During the first thirteen years of Bob and Jenni Paul's marriage, Bob was a real bulldozer. When he wanted his way, he demanded it. And when Jenni resisted, when she said no, he would just rev up his engine and push harder. Bob admitted. "She would say no, but I would think, *Oh yeah, but . . .* and I would find ways to try and get around it or try to change her mind. But it was like hitting my head against a brick wall."

Then one day Bob realized that the wall Jenni had erected was one of self-protection. She felt threatened by his forceful way with her. He also realized that using a battering ram was not an effective way to remove the wall. He needed to create a safe environment that would allow Jenni to take down the wall when she felt ready.

He knew the wall was starting to crumble one weekend when he asked Jenni to accompany him to a seminar. "No, I don't think so," she had responded.

He felt disappointed with her resistance, but he realized she needed to know she was free to say no to him and that he would not pressure her. Bob told his wife, "Okay, Jenni. I respect your decision."

Jenni walked away, but about twenty minutes later she came back to Bob and said, "You know, I changed my mind. After you said you respected my decision, I saw you really meant it. I realized that was all I really needed. I would like to go with you to the seminar."

Respect the wall. The other person has built it for a reason. And when you create a safe environment in your relationship, when the other person no longer needs to protect himself or herself from you, the wall will eventually come down.

2. Honor Others

A second step to safety is learning to honor the other person as valuable. Honor is a way of accurately seeing the immense value of someone made in God's image. God created each one of us as a one-of-a-kind person, with unique gifts and personality. He sees us as precious and valuable. When we see others as God sees them, when we recognize and affirm their value, we help create a safe environment that encourages relationships to grow.

→ SEE OTHERS AS GOD SEES THEM.

But you can't affirm that value if you don't first recognize it. My son Greg learned that in the middle of a pressured day with his family.

Nothing seemed to go right that morning. The family was rushing around the house, getting ready to fly to Disney World. Everyone was running late, and it looked as if they had more luggage than the airline would allow. Finally Greg thought he had everyone in the car, with every conceivable space filled with luggage. But where was his daughter Maddy?

Maddy was in the house frantically searching for Gracie, her favorite Beanie Baby. The little yellow rabbit was the toddler's most valuable possession. Maddy wouldn't go anywhere without Gracie. The trouble was, Maddy constantly lost Gracie, and when she did, it triggered a crisis of major proportions. When Maddy finally located her rabbit, she came running out to the car, sweating profusely.

Oh, no, Greg thought, *I know she's going to lose Gracie on the trip. I don't want to go through this on vacation!* So he said, "Maddy, hold on. Actually, Mommy and Daddy need you to leave Gracie here. We need someone to watch the house. So why don't you put her back in your bed, and she can take care of the house?"

Greg's words totally destroyed his daughter. She gave him a look that said, *Are you crazy? Leave Gracie behind? What are you talking about?*

Greg kept trying to give logical reasons to leave the doll behind. Despite his arguments, Maddy made no move for the house. Finally Greg got very stern and said, "Go right now, and put her back in your bed!"

Maddy turned around, her little head down, tears flowing, and slowly walked back to the house. A few minutes later Greg yelled, "Come *on*, Maddy! We're going to be late!" Finally she reappeared . . . still holding Gracie.

At that point it became a battle Greg felt he had to win. So he said, "Honey, you're disobeying me," and he launched into a lecture about the consequences for disobedience.

Maddy listened for a while but then pushed through Greg's words and said, "Daddy, wait a minute. Going to Disney World, is that really going to be lots of fun?"

"Oh, man, going to Disney World is going to be the best time we've ever had. But we have to go!"

Maddy put her little head down, teared up again, and slowly handed Gracie to her father. "Daddy," she said, "if Disney World is going to be so much fun, I want Gracie to go in my place. I'll stay home and watch the house." She was dead serious.

Greg, of course, instantly felt like "the biggest heel of all time," in his words. He recognized Maddy's sacrifice and understood the enormous value that his daughter placed on her yellow Beanie Baby. Maddy had acted in a way completely consistent with her belief–and Greg realized that he also had to act in a way completely consistent with his belief that his daughter was a person of limitless value, made in God's image and worthy of greatest honor. So Greg loaded up Maddy and buckled Gracie in her special seat, and the family drove off to the airport in its bulging, overstuffed car.

If you want to create a safe environment that encourages healthy relationships to grow, then start by honoring those around you. Picture those individuals as people personally autographed by God.

Wouldn't you feel thrilled to be seen with someone who bore God's personal autograph? Wouldn't you want to have your picture taken with such a person and hang that picture in a prominent place on your wall? Or imagine yourself bowing in front of those whom you honor, bending your knee in their presence. Or imagine giving those people a standing ovation, like the one you would give to someone on a stage finishing an outstanding concert. Find ways to honor the people you love.

Another practical way to recognize value in another person—and to create the safety you need in your relationship—is to keep a list of all of the good qualities of that person. I keep several such lists in what I call my Honor Journal. In it I have several pages of things I find valuable about my wife, children, and grandchildren. Sometimes when I feel frustrated with one of them, I read the Honor list rather than read them the riot act. That way I can see them as God sees them, and my perspective changes.

Sometimes we play a game that makes use of this information. We call the game Bombardment. One person is the designated honoree, and each of the others takes sixty seconds to say, out loud, every valuable thing that comes to mind about the designated person. You can play Bombardment at dinner, on a date, or whenever.

I love the story of Armon, a six-year-old who was trapped in six feet of rubble and bricks after an earthquake in Turkey. His father knew the location of where Armon's school class should be, and the man started digging and lifting broken bricks off of the spot he thought his child might be. Friends and rescue workers kept trying to persuade Armon's father to give up the dig. He would always say, "Either join me or leave me alone." After forty-some hours and bloody hands, the father heard a faint voice. It was Armon, "Daddy is that you?" Then Armon shouted to the other trapped kids, "See, I told you my daddy would find us!" Wouldn't it be great to have people like Armon's daddy spending every day looking for the value in us and never stopping until they found all of it? If we or others try to dissuade them, they'd say, "Either join me or leave me alone."

Of course, none of us honors others perfectly. We all say or do hurtful things that dishonor the ones we really love. When I mess up like this, I try to say, first to myself and then out loud, "You're too valuable to treat like this." I can remember getting on my knees as a parent and saying to my kids, "I love you so much, and you're so valuable to me. I'm so sorry that I just said that or just did that. Would you forgive me?" I sought their forgiveness because I recognized their enormous value to God. They are precious—and what I said or did degraded and dishonored them. When I said or did hurtful things to them, I actually took value away from them, which is the opposite of honor. My confession motivated me to treat them in a more loving way, which helped to create safety in our home.

Choosing to honor others is important in all kinds of relationships. Dan's boss, Lee, is a micromanager. As a result, the pair frequently finds themselves in conflict. Dan struggles with resentment and impatience toward Lee, but he can't figure out how to turn things around. In his frustration, Dan complains to his colleagues about Lee, belittling him. "You wouldn't believe what he did this morning. What a control freak. I wonder if he watches his children brush their teeth in the morning, just to make sure they do it right. I'm glad I didn't grow up in his household."

Remember that all relationships involve choice. What if, instead of doing the destructive dance with Lee, Dan chose to honor his boss? What if Dan began by choosing to note every time Lee did something well and by periodically reviewing that praiseworthy record? "When Lee says he'll get back to me with his response by a particular time, he consistently comes through." "Lee has a great eye for detail." "Lee kept me from making an expensive error that almost slipped through the cracks."

Next, Dan could start to look for opportunities to honor Lee verbally—however difficult that might feel, at first. "Lee, I just want you to know that I appreciate your commitment to doing a thorough job." "Thank you for expressing such a clear vision for this project." "I know how hard it must be to keep all those balls in the air, Lee, but I think you do it very well."

What if Dan would honor Lee when talking with his colleagues? "Lee really came through on that last project." "Lee gave us good direction on that proposal."

If Dan really believes that Lee is a person made in the image of God, as the Bible tells us, then he will take care not to demean him or to slander him in any way. If Dan respects and honors his boss, he may find that over time, Lee will become less difficult and more open to discussing Dan's legitimate concerns. But even if he doesn't, Dan can know that he is doing the right thing.[2] I actually did this exercise with one of my bosses, and he said to me after a year, "I feel closer to you than to my own son." I could see in his eyes a deeper love and appreciation for me. I would never have dreamed our relationship would turn in this direction.

We honor others when we see them—and treat them—as incredible gifts of God. Each of them has immeasurable value as a unique, divine creation.

3. Suspend Judgment

When Jolene and her older sister, Patty, get together, the sparks really fly. Inside of ten minutes, Patty usually starts asking Jolene barbed questions about her current dating relationship.

"Is Rick just a poorer version of Josh?"

"It's probably a good thing Mom isn't around to see this, isn't it?"

"Do you think it's a wise idea to let Bill stay over at your place like that?"

Jolene bristles at the judgment not so well hidden in her sister's questions, and as a result, the two women almost always end up in a heated argument that leaves both feeling hurt, attacked, and alone. The ironic thing is that both sisters care deeply for one another. If they didn't, Jolene wouldn't care what Patty said, and Patty wouldn't care how Jolene lived.

How can these two women create a safe environment, where neither feels attacked and both feel loved and cared for? If they came to me, I would recommend that they learn to suspend judgment and instead to adopt an attitude of curiosity—even fascination—into what makes the other "tick."

Judgment closes people up and shuts them down. When people feel judged—as Jolene does when she talks to Patty about her relationships—they usually want to defend themselves and maybe even go on the attack. Why? Because they feel unsafe.

Much better things tend to happen when we suspend judgment (on both ourselves and others) and replace it with a genuine interest in the other person.

People usually act and feel the way they do for good reasons. Perhaps Jolene really does tend to pick "loser" boyfriends—but maybe she does so because she feels like a loser. Maybe she sees herself through a distorted lens. What if, deep down, she tells herself, *I don't deserve anyone better because I made such a mess of my life in college?*

Imagine what might happen if Patty expresses interest in Jolene rather than judging her. The two women get together for coffee at a local Starbucks. Jolene says, "Bill and I had a disappointing time last night."

Instead of pouncing on Jolene for letting Bill stay the night, which she usually does with her words or with her facial scorn, Patty says, "You and Bill really enjoy hiking together, don't you? What other things do you like about him?" After Jolene mentions Bill's love for art, Patty expresses genuine interest in her sister. "You used to paint when you were in college. You are so creative. Do you still have your oils?"

Jolene is surprised by her sister's interest. She talks about how she has given up on her painting—and feeling safe with Patty, she finally talks about her feelings of failure.

Do you see what would happen here? When Patty suspends judgment and expresses a genuine interest in her sister, she creates an environment of safety. When she hears Jolene's view of herself, she can begin to understand Jolene's poor dating choices. That discovery most likely will lead Patty to feel compassion toward her sister, not judgment. And you know what tends to happen when people sense compassion, don't you? They usually open up.

Compassion and understanding create a tremendous amount of safety. When a person refuses to judge my motives and instead tries to understand why I did some foolish or hurtful things, that person's compassion encourages me to open up—and our relationship grows. The wall comes down, and the conflict ceases.

Judgment results in defensiveness and closes down relationships, while curiosity results in openness and safety, giving life to relationships. When we express our interest in someone, something energizing occurs. Have you ever met people who are awesome listeners? They seem fascinated with everything you say. They hang on every word. They ask good questions and clearly express an interest in getting to know you. You almost can't help but walk away from people like that without thinking, *Gosh, I really like them! I felt so cared for. They seemed so interested in me.* You might not even remember the people's names, but you've already decided they are great. Why? Just because they seemed curious and interested in you.

Judgment writes people off, bangs the gavel, and sentences them to fifty years at hard labor. That kind of judgment shuts off discovery. It's as if you've already heard everything you need to hear in order to render your verdict: "That's it. You're finished."

Curiosity says something quite different. It says, "I don't know enough yet to render a verdict, so I'll forget about sentencing for a while. It's true that I don't like what has happened. But I still need to open the door to discovery." One lifetime is not long enough to really know the true beauty of another person. Besides, everyone changes inside every year, so you'll never be able to really know everything about one person. Stay curious.

The process of discovery gives life to relationships. If you stay fascinated with your spouse, your friends, your children, your colleagues, your neighbors, you'll never find the end of your opportunity to learn—both about them and about yourself. When you choose to suspend judgment and foster a spirit of curiosity, you keep the relationship safe and alive. You encourage it to grow and deepen.

4. Value Differences

A fourth step to safety is learning how to deal with our differences. When two people are in conflict, they often point to their differences as the problem. But that's simply not true. Differences are actually a blessing *if* you know how to deal with them and capitalize on them.

Jim and his wife struggled for years over how to do vacations. Her idea of a great vacation was to cram as much into their time as possible. They saw as many sights and did as many tourist activities as they could manage. Only then, when they had seen everything there was to see, had they really "succeeded."

Jim's ideal vacation, on the other hand, took him completely away from his busyness and hectic schedule. He wanted to lie on a deserted beach for a week, doing absolutely nothing.

One year Jim told his wife that he just couldn't do her type of vacation anymore. He also recognized that she couldn't do his. So they agreed to alternate his pattern with hers. One day they would see all the sights and keep a really busy schedule, and the next day they'd lounge by the pool. The following day they'd scurry around like ants, and then the next, plop down at the beach.

They had the best vacation ever "because by working *with* our differences," Jim said, "we both felt like we were winning. And to top it off, we found that the balance was much healthier for both of us. It increased our ability to enjoy our vacation more than we ever had."

By valuing his wife's differences rather than resenting them, Jim also found a valuable side benefit. He has discovered many important things about his wife: her knowledge of history and art, her ease with strangers, her appreciation for beauty. But he also has made surprising discoveries about himself. And he would have remained in the dark about both had he not begun to value the differences he saw in his life partner.

If a relationship is to feel like a safe place, it must make room for *all* of both people. None of us has the option of getting rid of some part of ourselves. Wherever I go, I carry all of me with me. And if certain parts of me (or certain parts of you) are not welcome in our relationship, then we no longer have room to be who we are. And what's safe about that? Nothing! In such a case, you *have* to put up walls or use energy to pretend to be someone you aren't.

Think about the current relationship conflicts you face. What differences in the other person bother you? How can you value those differences? And how can you make those differences work *for* your relationship?

Think of two people who irritate you. Then think of their specific behavior that irritates you. Now, try to think of at least one good thing about that irritating behavior. It won't be easy, but it can be done. Here's what I mean. When my son Michael was younger, I was always irritated when he ate cereal. He would rub his spoon over his chin and scoop up dripping milk. That bugged me. What's good about this irritating behavior? One day I realized that I eat cereal the same way. What irritated me about Michael's behavior is something I do myself. He was a mirror of my own behavior. I have learned that when someone's behavior irritates me, I look inside myself to see if I am guilty of doing a similar thing. I now know that I tend to get irritated with others when they reveal my own imperfections. That realization is a good thing that came from my irritation.

What if your irritation is with your spouse? What if he or she is just plain lazy and never helps around the house? What if your spouse mismanages the household money? Then what? You can choose to value the person. Try to understand what causes the behavior, what past damage may be responsible for the irresponsibility or laziness.

Your partner may be so wounded that he or she can hardly function. Be careful to suspend judgment. Value the good. As you honor the other person's uniqueness, as you value his or her differences—even the traits that irritate you—you create a safe place for your relationship to grow.

5. Be Trustworthy

When Bob Paul was eighteen years old, he worked as a handyman for a rich, eccentric psychiatrist. One day Bob's boss sent him up to clean a skylight. Despite the tight fit, Bob dutifully started cleaning, armed with some noxious chemicals and a rag.

A short time later, the psychiatrist called Bob downstairs to help him move some things out of the living room. Bob woozily picked up a clay figurine to take it to another room, but he accidentally hit the toe of the statuette on a doorjamb. The leg fell off, *clunk*, and hit the ground.

The psychiatrist started waving his arms and screaming at the top of his lungs. "Do you have any idea how much that thing is worth? It is *thousands* of years old, and it's worth *thousands* of dollars! Do you realize that one of the things that made this so valuable was its perfect, flawless condition? I can have this leg glued back on. But now, just by virtue of the fact that it has a crack, the piece has lost thousands of dollars in value!"

Because Bob did not see the figurine as valuable, he treated it carelessly and broke it. How much better it would have been to realize both its value and fragility than to act carelessly and thus cause irreparable damage!

The fifth step to safety in our relationships is to make sure that we are trustworthy in handling the delicate and valuable men and women with whom we want to deeply connect. In each of us lies something of staggering worth and value—yet that something is very vulnerable, easily damaged or devalued.

Trustworthiness is recognizing the value of someone and then treating that person accordingly. When we treat someone in a way that shows that we recognize both their *incredible value* and their *vulnerability*, we demonstrate our trustworthiness.

The kind of trustworthiness I have in mind has two parts:

- Be trustworthy with others.
- Be trustworthy with yourself.

BE TRUSTWORTHY WITH OTHERS

When you are trustworthy with others, you dedicate yourself to treating them as the valuable and vulnerable people that they are. When you are trustworthy with yourself, you act in ways consistent with your own value and vulnerability. So when others, at some point, show themselves as untrustworthy in dealing with you, you have to act in a way that is trustworthy to yourself, that safeguards your own value in view of your own vulnerability.

My sons learned this lesson in the mountains of Colorado. One winter Michael visited Greg in Denver. To satisfy his new interest in photography, Michael begged to find a scenic location suitable for a great picture. About an hour out of Denver, they found the perfect spot. They parked on the side of the road and hiked down to a river, where they found a gorgeous frozen waterfall.

Michael carefully tested the river to see if it had frozen over. He walked out a few feet and judged that it would support the weight of both brothers. He planned to briskly walk out to the falls, snap a few pictures, and then return to the bank. The plan sounded insane to Greg, but Michael talked him into it.

"Trust me!" he said.

Although Greg felt nervous about it, he followed Michael toward the falls, "like a sheep being led to slaughter." Suddenly they heard loud cracking sounds, and Michael fell through the ice.

"Mom is going to kill me!" Greg blurted out, starting to panic.

But then he noticed that the river was only about three feet deep where Michael had fallen in. The icy water reached only up to his waist.

"Get me out!" Michael begged as the shock of the frigid water hit him.

"But I thought you said, 'Trust me,'" Greg replied, trying not to fall over from laughter. Moments later Greg realized he shouldn't have laughed. As soon as he reached for his brother, he also fell through the ice. Now they both stood waist-deep in freezing mountain water. After a few agonizing minutes, they managed to pull each other to shore. But then they faced the real challenge.

Darkness was about to fall, and they hadn't dressed for a dip in freezing water. Greg's truck sat about a quarter mile up the trail from where they had fallen in. As Michael surveyed the situation, he noticed a small opening in the surrounding cliff; it looked as if they could hike straight up to the truck.

"Trust me," he said again, "the shortest distance between two points is a straight line."

"I'm not sure who was more of a nitwit," Greg says today, "Michael, for concocting this plan, or me, for trusting him again."

As the shivering pair started scaling the cliff, Greg realized that Michael's math teacher must not have explained that the "straight line" principle neglects to take into account hazardous terrain. Without gloves, it took them about an hour to ascend the snow-covered cliff. When they finally reached the truck, their hands felt completely numb and they couldn't get the key into the door. They started imagining the newspaper headlines: "Two boys freeze to death with truck key in hand."

Finally, after rubbing and blowing on his hands, Greg managed to get the door open. He had to repeat the process to turn on the engine. It would be awhile before he would trust his brother again.

Unfortunately, this lighthearted story reflects what happens every day with couples and friends. Trust is a key ingredient when it comes to safety, openness, and intimacy in all relationships.

What about more serious situations? What about the pregnant young woman who believed her date when he said, "Trust me. You won't get pregnant if we do it just this once"? What about the son who believed his father when he said, "Trust me. My company won't know that I haven't reported this money"?

These people were not trustworthy because they did not take into account the value and vulnerability of the people who they asked to trust them or their own faults and inconsistencies. And like the chipped figurine, the young woman felt her value sullied and the son felt his worth diminished.

What would trustworthiness look like in these situations? The young man would realize the value and vulnerability of his date, and no matter how much he felt tempted, he would value her trust even more and so would choose not to convince her to have sex with him. The father would value his son so much that he would choose not to embezzle funds from his company. He would recognize that his trustworthiness was far more important than any amount of money he would have gained through his deception.

Being and staying trustworthy is an ongoing responsibility and choice. But when other people see us as trustworthy, they feel safe with us. They have no need to build walls of protection.

BE TRUSTWORTHY WITH YOURSELF

The second part of being trustworthy is remaining trustworthy with yourself. When you stay trustworthy with yourself, you act in ways that express your value and vulnerability.

Whenever you let someone have access to the most sensitive part of you and they start getting careless, you must take back that part of yourself and think, *Excuse me. Apparently, you've lost track of how valuable and how vulnerable I am. But I haven't, and I can't let that happen.*

If the young woman in the previous illustration would have remained trustworthy to herself, she would have stood up to the young man: "I am not going to let you push me into an action I think is wrong. I am too valuable for that." The son would have said to his father, "Dad, I feel uncomfortable getting involved in this kind of scheme. I do not want to go down that path." Do you see how these two people had a healthy view of themselves? They saw themselves as God sees them—valuable, precious—and they had no intention of letting anything damage that. So they safeguarded their value by remaining trustworthy to themselves. Sometimes taking a stand about our own value could create conflict with others. We need to reassure others that our love is still the same for them but state that we don't feel comfortable about joining them in any activity that may diminish our own value.

All relationships involve choice. When people treat you badly, you can choose to be trustworthy in a couple of ways. You may need to build a wall and shut the person out, at least for a time. That can be very appropriate. Some people have no clue and are not likely to get a clue anytime soon. Therefore you can treat them cordially, but you don't need to give them access to the most vulnerable part of you. They can shout over the wall, but that's it. The problem with this tactic, of course, is that it hinders a deep relationship. It makes connection impossible. You simply can't hug someone standing on the other side of a wall.

The other alternative is more like drawing a line in the sand. You say, "Hey, I'm safeguarding that part of me because I can't trust you with it right now. But I want you to know that I want this relationship with you. Therefore, I will give you repeated opportunities to try again. But I need you to know that the next time I let you in, and every single time thereafter, I'll be requiring the same thing: that you show me, through word and deed, that you understand how valuable and vulnerable I am and that you act accordingly. To the degree that you do this, let's be friends. But when you forget, I need you to know that I will protect myself."

Your ability to feel safe in a relationship depends more on the second part of trustworthiness than on the first. If I can't trust myself to remember how valuable and how vulnerable I am, then my whole well-being depends on other people's remembering. To the degree that they remember, I'm safe; but to the degree that they forget, I'm not. In that case, I'm helpless and have no say.

But when I remain trustworthy to myself, I can afford to give others a whole lot of freedom in relationships. I know that others *are* going to forget, that they *are* going to have moments where they stop being trustworthy. I can live with that, however, because there's always someone taking responsibility—me. When other people act in unsafe ways, when they get caught up in themselves, I take the most vulnerable part of me back, and I protect it. And when they regain their trustworthiness, I can say, "Let's try this again."

Create a Safe Haven

A family in deep crisis once sought out Michael for counseling. The family's sixteen-year-old daughter had gotten pregnant, throwing the entire household into an uproar.

Michael first asked to see the father and mother, without their daughter. He wanted to figure out what was happening under their roof. He quickly discovered that hate had taken over.

"My daughter knows that we're a good Christian family," the father fumed, "and she knew that if she ever got pregnant, she'd be kicked out of this house!"

When this man discovered his daughter's pregnancy, he lost his temper. He yelled, he screamed, he turned over furniture in her bedroom, he tore out her phone and grounded her from everything but breathing. He lost all control and threw the house into total chaos.

And then, amazingly, he couldn't figure out why his daughter had tried to run away and elope with the boy who made her pregnant.

Michael tried to help this father understand that he had created an unsafe environment in his home. His ranting and raving and unrestrained fury did not create an environment where his daughter felt inclined to come to him with her problems.

"Look," Michael said, "every kid is going to make mistakes. Every child is sinful. It's not our job as parents to shame them, yell at them, belittle them, or threaten them. It's our job to love them and lay out clear boundaries and give them healthy rules. But even when those rules get broken, we *have* to maintain a safe environment. And if we don't maintain a safe environment, then we're the last place our kids are going to go to in a crisis—and that's the worst thing that can happen. When our children don't feel that they can come to their parents with their mistakes and still be loved no matter what, we get chaos."

When my children were growing up, I did my best to create a safe home environment. To reinforce my pledge, I hung a plaque in the hallway that said, "To Norma, Kari, Greg, and Michael: In assurance of my lifetime commitment to you."

My kids' friends sometimes made snide comments about my little message, but my children have told me how much that plaque meant to them. They knew they could count on me, not to be perfect, but to stay committed to them, no matter what. And they tell Norma and me today that our home felt like a safe haven.

And the tradition continues. These days, every night when Michael puts his own kids to bed, he tells them, "Now remember, Daddy loves you!"

"I know," his children say.

"But I love you no matter what," he replies. Those kids hear the same reaffirming words every night. "There's nothing they can do that will ever make me stop loving them," Michael says. "I want to create a safe environment for them." He'll sometimes ask Cole, "Is there anything you can do that will make me stop loving you?" He'll give his son some examples, and Cole will mention a few. After each example Michael will say, "Nope, I'll still love you even after you do that."

You can do the same thing. Whether you're a parent, a friend, a spouse, a member of a team, or a part of an organization, you can create such safety around you that people will naturally feel drawn to you. You can choose to create an environment in which healthy relationships have a chance to grow. Or you can choose to shut them down before they get a chance to start. The choice is yours.

We know a young single man who feels so anxious, so stressed-out, so fearful of being rejected, that he creates a powerfully toxic environment wherever he goes. His fear of rejection leaks out, and when young women try to approach him, they see the relational smog clinging to him. *Eeuuu,* they think, *I don't want to be a part of this.*

You know what happens, don't you? He ends up rejected and alone, the very thing he most fears. Why? It's sad, but simple: He has not yet learned to create a safe environment that invites others into a relationship with him, where they can feel safe and confident and secure. He's looking through the wrong lens. He fails to see himself as God sees him: a valuable, precious person.

When people feel safe in our presence, they naturally open up. And when they open up, connection naturally occurs. You don't have to force it. You don't have to coax it. You don't even have to encourage it. It just happens.

Do you want it to happen in your own life? Then get to work at creating a safe environment. And get ready to discover how to love yourself the way God loves you.

LIFE IS RELATIONSHIPS;
THE REST IS JUST DETAILS.

ONE-MINUTE REVIEW
SAFETY: CREATE A SAFE ENVIRONMENT

1. **When you create a safe environment, relationships flourish.**

2. **Respect the wall.** When people are threatened, they build a wall. Instead of trying to knock down the wall with a sledgehammer, respect the wall. Create a safe environment in which the other person can gradually take down the wall.

3. **Honor others.** When we honor others, we see them as valuable. We see others as God sees them. Honor creates a safe environment in which people can come together.

4. **Suspend judgment.** When we express genuine interest in people rather than judge them, relationships have a better chance of growing.

5. **Value differences.** When we value our differences rather than make them the focus of our conflict, we create safety.

6. **Be trustworthy.** When we are trustworthy with others, we dedicate yourself to treating them as the valuable and vulnerable people that they are. When we are trustworthy with ourselves, we act in ways consistent with our own value and vulnerability.

6

SELF-CARE: KEEP YOUR BATTERY CHARGED

Several months ago I tried something that appeared to be very safe and fun, but I almost lost my life. Norma and I took a vacation to Mexico. We rented a great little place right on the beach, where we could feel the cool ocean breezes and stretch out in the warm, sub-tropical sun. It provided the perfect setting to unwind and recharge.

One day I decided to go swimming. As I walked toward the sea, I looked around and saw no one else on the beach. No tourists, no surf-ers, no beachcombers. No one, not even a lifeguard. I had the whole, glorious, sparkling sea all to myself!

I plunged into the inviting waters and started playing in the gently rolling waves. The sand felt good between my toes, but I wanted nothing more than to swim for a while in the gorgeous, azure waters. So I headed out a little distance from shore—not too far—to get some good exercise. As I swam, I wondered about the red flags planted prominently on the beach, but I disregarded them. *Must have some meaning to the locals,* I thought. *Or maybe some family left the flags behind.*

It never dawned on me that the flags might have been meant for people like *me.*

Before I understood what had happened, a swift-flowing undertow swept me out into the open sea. I had been having too much fun to notice that powerful forces had sucked me far out from shore. Fortunately, I could still touch the bottom, but I finally noticed how small and distant the beach appeared. I thought, *Hey, this looks dangerous.* So I started to swim back—but no matter how hard I tried, I couldn't get any closer to shore. In a few minutes I could feel my muscles growing weary and my lungs giving out as I struggled against the force of the tide. But nothing I did seemed to make any difference. And I could no longer touch the bottom.

Before long, I lost all my strength and slipped beneath the waves. Moments later I popped back up, sputtering, gasping, and waving my arms wildly—but still I saw no one. As I started going down again, I thought, *I'm done! Here I've changed my eating habits, I'm exercising every day, I've done whatever the doctors told me to—and now I'm dying in this water. And nobody even knows where I am!*

(Later I found out that Norma had taken a break from reading a novel and, at that very moment, was watching me struggle—although she had no idea that I was the one struggling.)

I went down again, bobbed up, and frantically waved my arms. Just before I sank for what probably would have been the last time, I saw him. Somehow a burly lifeguard had seen me in the throes of drowning and had raced to my rescue. I have to tell you, while I like lifeguards, I absolutely *love* this one. Had he not been there that day, I would not be here today. He quite literally saved my life. (Incidentally, his name was Jesus—pronounced *Hay-soos.*)

But you know what? As grateful as I feel for his heroic work, I never should have met the guy. He never should have had the opportunity to become my personal hero. Why not? If I had taken the time to find out what the red flags meant, I wouldn't have needed a rescuer. If I had made the effort to learn about the dangerous ocean currents in our Mexican paradise, I never would have found myself exhausted, gasping for air, and drowning within sight of my almost widowed wife.

In other words, if I had noticed the red flags and taken appropriate care of myself, I could have avoided my near-death experience.

Good self-care makes sense not only for me but also for all of my loved ones and for everyone else around me. The same is true for you and all your relationships. Good self-care is vital for satisfying interpersonal connections. Ignore it, and in no time at all you'll find yourself sinking and gasping for relational air.

Take the word of someone who knows!

A Revolutionary Way of Thinking

Self-care is one of the most powerful dance steps that Greg and Bob teach couples in conflict. Without the least bit of exaggeration, I have to tell you that the practice of self-care has had a profound impact on our staff and the whole Smalley family. In fact, this dance step is quite literally saving my life. It is my personal lifeguard. In a few pages I'll tell you more about my own life, but for now, I want to emphasize the crucial place of self-care in creating, sustaining, and growing healthy relationships.

What is good self-care? Picture yourself as a large battery. Pretend you have two terminals on the top of your head and several sockets on your sides, where people can plug in to you for their own needs. You get fully charged as you carefully maintain those top terminals and get regularly connected to God through them. As God's love recharges you daily, you in turn can relay that love to others. You could even put a sign on yourself: "Plug into me. I'm here to show my love for you."

If, however, you allow anger or resentment to corrode your supply line to God, or if you get so busy caring for others that you forget to connect regularly to the power and wisdom of heaven, what happens? You soon become a dead battery, of no use to anyone. Good self-care ensures that your power levels stay high, making it possible for you to continue to bless others.

Far and away, good self-care is the dance step that most profoundly changes the people who come to the National Institute of Marriage. While they benefit tremendously from understanding and putting into practice the other four dance steps—the Power of One, Safety, Communication, and Teamwork—it's this one, self-care, that most often stops them in their tracks. It truly is a revolutionary way of thinking for many people; they almost never anticipate it. In fact, they almost always "trip" when we start talking about good self-care.

Many people react strongly (at first) against the idea that in order to enjoy healthy relationships, they first have to keep themselves healthy. "That is so contrary to what I've been taught all my life!" they tell us. But once they "get it," once they see why and how good self-care sets them up for relationship success, they almost invariably say something very different: "Why hasn't anybody ever told me this?"

Self-Care and the Great Commandment

I'd like to start our discussion about self-care by rehearsing what Jesus called the greatest commandment: " 'You must love the Lord your God with all your heart, all your soul, all your mind, and all your strength.' The second is equally important: 'Love your neighbor as yourself.' "[1] You might not realize it, but these words point us to the heart of good self-care.

Take a look at them again. First, Jesus teaches us to value God above everything else. We are to love him with all our *heart*, all our *soul*, all our *mind,* and all our *strength*. Jesus refers to the four key areas that make us human: the spiritual, the emotional, the intellectual, and the physical. More on that in just a bit.

In the same breath, Jesus also teaches us to highly value our neighbor *in the same way* that he expects us to highly value ourselves, as God's very special creations. Jesus assumes that we want the best for ourselves; that's how he created us. He instructs us to pursue the best interests of others with the same energy that we pursue our own best interests.

When you love God with every part of your being, he fills you up to overflowing with his amazing love. Out of that overflow, you give to others. This is the balanced life, the only kind of life worth living.

But notice something crucial: If you don't take care of yourself, you have no overflow. Without an overflow, you find it very hard to take care of others—and almost impossible to obey Jesus' command! If you and I want a healthy and satisfying life, all three pursuits must remain in balance: loving God and loving others with the same energy that we love ourselves.

What Does It Look Like?

Since Jesus closely linked loving God with loving others as we love ourselves, it makes sense that in your self-care you need to pay close attention to the four areas he explicitly mentioned: the heart (spiritual), the soul (emotional), the mind (intellectual), and the strength (physical). In a word, God expects you to attend to your whole being.

Most people have a pretty good idea of what attending to their body means, even if they don't do it well. They have a general idea, at least, of what it ought to look like: regular exercise, eating right, getting enough rest. And even if they're not attending to the physical side of things as they know they should, they still recognize its importance.

Most people also acknowledge the necessity of keeping a sharp mind. They recognize the importance of a good education, of developing strong thinking skills, of a regular reading program. Again, they may not follow through on their good convictions, but they freely admit the importance of the intellectual part of themselves.

Most faith-based people also have a basic idea of what it means to attend to their spirit. They admit the importance of prayer, of regular Bible reading, of getting involved in church, and of developing sensitivity to spiritual things.

When it comes to the emotions, however—the soul—people tend to go totally blank. Most have no clue what this means. And so they do a lousy job of caring for themselves emotionally. I know I did.

Most of us simply do not understand the role that emotions are supposed to play in who we are. We do not appreciate how God designed us to function as fully emotional beings.

Why are the emotions so important? Think of your emotions as God's information system. They inform you about your needs and your deepest beliefs. When you feel a strong emotion—fear, let's say, or grief—your body is trying to tell you something important. Without your emotions, you're like a bicycle trying to function on only one wheel.

Look at it this way: Your brain is the processor, the decision maker. But without the good data supplied by your emotions, the processor has little to work with. And of what use is a processor without good data?

God designed you to work best when your mind and your soul work together. You make the best decisions when you use your feelings to inform your brain. To get the best result, you need both your emotions and your intellect.

Yet it's here the problems often surface. What if you have been ignoring this major part of who God created you to be? What if you don't know what to make of your emotions, or even how to tap into them? What then?

Listen to Your Emotions

If you're not sure what to do with your feelings, a good place to start is to simply ask yourself, "What am I feeling?"

Since emotions always have a physiological expression, try to name the feelings in your body. Do a total body scan, starting from the top of your head, and think carefully about what you are feeling. Do you feel any tension anywhere, any butterflies?

As you do this, remind yourself that you're after information. Don't judge your emotions; just see them as information. What is your body trying to tell you? If your chest feels tight, if your stomach feels in knots—what could it mean? What is your body trying to tell you? Just look and listen, without chiding yourself, "I really shouldn't be feeling this way."

IDENTIFY YOUR EMOTION

Suppose that my stomach is in a knot and full of butterflies (believe me, I know the feeling!). Since I choose to see such emotions as data, I ask myself, "Okay, what are these emotions trying to tell me? I *am* feeling kind of nervous—but what am I feeling nervous about?"

I might be worrying that I'm about to let a whole lot of people down at work, that some of my ministry plans might fail miserably. I might be questioning whether I really heard from God. I might be nervous that people will see me as a phony.

Once I identify the feelings, I ask myself, "So, what am I needing right now? What do I need from others? What do I need from my-self?" I also want to ask, "What am I doing that might be causing this? Am I doing or thinking anything that could be prompting these feel-ings?"

Let me give you an example. Suppose that you're married to a man with a terrible sense of time. He tells you that he's going out to the store to get something and will return at eight o'clock in the evening. Soon eight o'clock rolls around, and no husband. He doesn't call to say he got delayed.

For a while, you feel fine. But when another hour goes by, you start to get a little irritated. Then you feel angry. *He is so inconsiderate!* you might think.

But when another half hour creeps by, you start to feel afraid. You wonder if something terrible happened. You begin to rehearse all of the awful possibilities. And by the time he finally gets home, you are about to burst. As soon as he walks through the door, you blast him.

"You are so inconsiderate! All you had to do was call! Do you realize that I have been sitting here, worried sick that you were lying in a morgue somewhere?"

Do you want to know the truth? You really should have said, "Do you realize that I was sitting there, *terrorizing myself* into imagining all the horrible things that could have happened?" Yes, your spouse should have called to say he would be late. But did you really have to terrorize yourself into worrying about tragedies that have practically no chance of occurring?

EVALUATE THE TRUTH OF YOUR EMOTION

Good self-care notes troubled emotions, but it also does something more positive with them. You need to determine, "Am I telling myself the truth, or am I just terrorizing myself?"

Once you identify what you're feeling, the next step is to take it to God and say, "Okay, God, is this truth? If it is truth, I want to act on it. But if it is not the truth, I need to move on to something more productive." It's not wrong to feel afraid, but it is most unfortunate to live in fear of something that doesn't exist.[2]

I used to get fearful before almost every speaking engagement. I would start thinking of all the negative things that could happen. Would the crowd reject me? Would I be any good? Would the audience rank me lower than the other four speakers? I could work myself up into a real lather.

For years I would list all the negative things that could happen. "I could be embarrassed. I might not be asked to return. I could lose an opportunity to write about my insight because nobody seems interested in it."

Eventually I learned to reframe these possible responses. "If I am embarrassed," I might say, "If they never ask me back again, God is the one who opens doors; he is the one who takes care of my reputation. I do not want to be invited back in order to get something out of life. I want *him* to be my satisfaction. So if I don't get invited back, fine. And if I do get another invitation, that's fine too. Either way, it has nothing to do with my level of fulfillment."

Remember, God made you to sense emotions. He has deep feelings himself, and he created you to have them, too. Emotions exist to give you important data about the world and how you fit into it. Treat your emotions as a valuable stream of information—and then use the information wisely.

Is Self-Care Selfish?

If you're like many people who come to visit us for counseling, you're feeling some very specific emotions right now.

Annoyance. Confusion. And maybe a little alarm.

"I see what you're saying," you might begin, "but isn't all this talk about self-care a little, well, *selfish*? And doesn't the Bible condemn selfishness?"

Good question. The short answer is this: Far from being selfish, good self-care is a godly thing. The truth is, Jesus practiced good self-care, as did Paul and the other apostles. Let me show you what I mean.

Throughout the Gospels, we find that Jesus tended to his own needs. When he needed some alone time, he took it.[3] He gratefully allowed supporters to meet his physical needs.[4] He made it no secret when he felt hungry or thirsty.[5] He did not allow others to control his agenda.[6] He didn't shrink from asking his friends to support him in a dark time of need.[7] And he didn't hesitate to remove himself from danger before his God-ordained appointment with a Roman cross.[8] In short, Jesus practiced excellent self-care, yet he never allowed it to degenerate into selfishness. That's how he could eventually march without hesitation to his crucifixion.

If Jesus wanted us to overlook our legitimate needs, it's hard to see why he would tell his disciples, "Your Father already knows your needs" for things like clothes and food and drink.[9] And why would Jesus have instructed them to come to him for rest, if he didn't think they needed any?[10]

Second, consider the godly counsel of the apostle Paul. If Paul had really meant to condemn good self-care, he never would have written, "No one hates his own body but lovingly cares for it, just as Christ cares for his body, which is the church."[11] The apostle commends those who feed and care for their bodies; he doesn't denounce them. And that's nothing but good self-care! No wonder he could tell his young protege Timothy to "stop drinking only water, and use a little wine because of your stomach and your frequent illnesses."[12] It's as if Paul said, "Timothy, I want you take better care of yourself. I'm concerned for your health, and I think you can do some things to avoid getting sick so often. It concerns me that your stomach causes you so many problems. Don't ignore it or try to 'tough it out.' How can you be of any use to others if you're constantly feeling ill? So let's make some changes in your diet, okay?"

It's only when you allow your cup to be filled that you can fill the cup of others. If you have nothing in your cup, you can't give anything away. Or consider another illustration, familiar to anyone who has done some flying.

What do the airlines tell adult passengers traveling with children? In case of an emergency, the adults are first to take care of their own needs—by firmly strapping an oxygen mask over their mouths—before attending to the needs of their children. Why? Because the airlines like to encourage selfishness? Because they want squealing kids to suffer oxygen deprivation? No! They give these instructions because they know a functioning adult can help a child better than an unconscious or dead adult. What if all the adults on a plane blacked out due to a mistaken bias against good self-care?

In fact, healthy self-care sets you up to give generously. If you take seriously God's direction to "be filled with the Spirit,"[13] you don't have to worry that God will drive you to give until nothing's left. And you don't have to wait to give until somebody does something for you. If you take responsibility for yourself and attend to your own self-care, you can act from a position of wholeness, not neediness. And that sets you up for relationship success.

Good Self-Care Blesses God

What would you say if I told you that good self-care not only travels in the opposite direction from selfishness but that it actually *blesses* God? That, I believe, is the absolute truth. And I think I can prove it without much trouble.

Imagine for a moment that you're a parent of small children.

Now, do you love those children? If you saw your children getting mistreated, how would you feel about that?

"Oh, I would hate that," you say. "I would passionately hate that!"

I'm sure I would. How about if you saw your children full, alive, happy? How would you feel about that?

"I would love that!" you say.

I agree. So let me ask you one final question: Is there *any* possibility that God loves you less than you love your children?

I didn't think so.

God loves to see his children full, alive, content. God feels blessed when we feel full. That is why the Bible says, "For the Lord delights in his people."[14] That is why Jesus announced, "My purpose is to give life in all its fullness."[15] Good self-care blesses God.

Think of it this way. Imagine yourself in the psalmist's sandals for a moment. While walking around the beautiful Temple courts, you excitedly shout, "Bless the Lord, O my soul: and all that is within me, bless his holy name."[16] It's a good blessing, isn't it? But what if you haven't been taking good care of yourself? What if the "all that is within me" amounts to an empty tank, a dead battery? How much can you really bless the Lord when you feel totally drained? On the other hand, what if you've been practicing good self-care? What if you're full? In that case, when you summon "all that is within me" to bless God, you can offer God a full blessing.

Taking good care of yourself is actually a godly thing. It's always in the best interest of all parties involved. Why? Because only when you're full do you have the resources to care for others. You cannot fully extend yourself unless you operate from fullness. And you never will get full unless you take good care of yourself.

Sometimes good self-care is interrupted by an emergency, and you may be required to sacrifice your priority for a short period of time. Your neighbor was in a car accident, and you help out for several days. You get very little sleep. You know you're not taking good care of yourself at the time, but the emergency won't last forever. My own daughter, Kari, had to take two years away from her friends, church, and almost everything she enjoyed to care for her infant who weighed only around two pounds at birth. After those years, I saw Kari come back to life again, but it was gradual. Sacrifice is sometimes exactly what God wants for us. But if that's all we do, all the time, it will wear us out—and everyone loses.

We have to be careful not to get out of balance, even when good things require extraordinary amounts of physical and emotional energy from us. We must not be blind to the importance of self-care. In places like our churches or charities, sometimes even our families, we can unnecessarily wear out. As loving members, we need to remind each other that even Jesus took time to rest and get away from the crowd.

You Are Valuable

I believe there's another reason why many people neglect to take care of themselves. They push self-care way down the list of their priorities because they have never seen themselves as valuable. While they often wear themselves out caring for others—whom they regard as highly valuable—they consider taking care of themselves a burden or a chore.

If these misguided people have children, I like to ask them, "How do you view your sons or daughters?" Most often they respond with words like *precious* and *awesome* and *beautiful*. They look at their kids through the eyes of wonder. When their children need something, the parents respond with all the energy required to meet that need. While it can be frustrating, tiresome, and difficult to meet children's needs, most parents never question whether the children deserve their care.

When these same parents consider their own needs, however, they often flip a switch. Since they do not see themselves through eyes of wonder—they do not put the same value on themselves that they give their children—they do not feel motivated to energetically respond to their own needs. Some even consider self-neglect a virtue, so they wear themselves out caring for others, whom they deem as more worthy of attention. They forget one of the truths about our relationship to ourselves: We must see ourselves as God sees us.

I encourage such worn-out moms and dads to discover the truth about who they really are, who God made them to be. I encourage them to prayerfully see themselves through God's eyes—and the Bible tells us that he sees all of us through the eyes of a loving and compassionate Father. Choose to see yourself with wonder and as precious, awesome, and beautiful.

How do you see yourself? Do you think others are uniquely created—but not you? Can you rejoice in the gifts and talents of others—

but not in your own? Do you value and esteem your friends and family—but not yourself?

A counselor friend of mine used to work with a young woman who battled severe depression. She would plunge into a deep despair that she described as a dense fog or a black cloud. She would remain in this dark abyss for weeks on end. She never knew when it was coming.

My friend worked with her for weeks, to no avail. He simply couldn't find any pattern to explain the cause of her depression. So he asked her to notify him as soon as she felt the next depression coming on.

One day during a weekly therapy session, she said she could feel the fog rolling in. My friend and this woman then carefully traced the first stages of her depression to three days earlier. On that day, feeling fine, she had visited the beauty salon to get her hair done—but by the time she left, she felt the fog descending. What had happened?

It turned out that the woman had looked at a poster of a well-coiffed model, then at herself in the mirror. And she thought, *I am so fat, so ugly—I am disgusting! Why would anybody love me?* And so a deadly conversation ensued in her head. By the time she walked out of that salon, she felt the dark cloud shrouding her, never noticing that she had unconsciously kept up the conversation as she went about her normal business. Her negative self-talk had become so constant, it was as if she lived by a busy road. After a while, she no longer heard the cars.

My friend had to get this woman to stop her negative self-talk and replace it with the truth of how God saw her. This took some time, but once she began to embrace God's picture of her, things started turning around. "Today," my friend says, "you would not believe this woman. She is a different human being."

What we see as valuable, we tend to honor. In fact, Jesus said that whatever we treasure, we'll have positive feelings about that treasure.[17] The opposite is also true. If we see something as worthless, we lose our positive emotions toward it. When God looks at his children—all of them, including you—he sees you as precious, worthy of honor and love.[18] He sees you as strong and wise.[19] He sees you "shine like stars," "a letter from Christ," and as "members of God's family."[20] If you belong to Christ, don't try to exclude yourself from these awesome descriptions. They truly picture *you*, not only your kids or your friends or your heroes.

When you begin to see yourself as valuable, when you start to look at yourself as God sees you, you find the motivation to attend to yourself in a way worthy of the real you. You begin to honor your body by taking good care of it. And God is pleased! We've seen many people experience a life-changing paradigm shift when they finally start to see themselves as valuable and worthy of care. This dance step revolutionizes their relationships—and it can do the same for you.

The Place God Lives

For those who still struggle to believe that they could be worthy of good care, I try another tack. I like to remind them of a temple. Not a building of marble and gold, but a temple made entirely out of living flesh and blood. Yes, that's right, I'm talking about *you*—if you are a believer in Christ, the Bible calls you the temple of the Holy Spirit: "Don't you know that your body is the temple of the Holy Spirit, who lives in you and was given to you by God? You do not belong to yourself, for God bought you with a high price. So you must honor God with your body."[21]

The Bible insists that every Christian—more specifically, the *body* of every believer—is a divine temple, holy to God. So I have a question: Do you not have a solemn responsibility to take care of the *only* place where God has chosen to dwell among his people?

Have you ever thought about the personal implications of being made into a "holy temple," a "dwelling where God lives by his Spirit"?[22] Have you pondered what it means to "honor God with your body"?

Too often we limit our thoughts on this topic to the obvious: We shouldn't sleep around, we shouldn't smoke, we shouldn't take drugs, we shouldn't get drunk. Rarely do we focus on all the positive things it takes to care for and maintain these temples of ours.

That's exactly where good self-care enters the picture.

When you take good care of the temple God has loaned you, you honor him. When you do not take good care of yourself—when you constantly get to bed late because you're too busy taking care of others, when you ignore the warning signs your body sends you, when you wake up feeling terrible and tell yourself it's the price you pay for serving God—then you dishonor God and disobey his commandment. As far as I know, no one has yet to discover any Bible verse that commands us to "stay fatigued for Jesus!"

One woman who just went through a marriage intensive finally understood that she did not have to feel constantly depleted and ignore her own needs in order to honor God. Once she began to grasp this concept, all the things that had stood in the way of her taking good care of herself suddenly evaporated. She looked at us, full of surprise and joy and hope, and said, "You mean, I could do this and actually honor God?" She paused for a moment, smiled, and declared, "I can get behind this!"

Can't we all?

Three Components of Good Self-Care

Good self-care has three main components, and every one is important. Neglect or overlook any of the three, and you'll soon be heading for trouble. When you keep close tabs on each component, you'll vastly increase your chances of strengthening and deepening the relationships that mean the most to you.

1. Receiving. To stay healthy, you have to receive from others. You need the resources that God wants to give you as well as the help and assistance he wants to provide through others. You must open your heart to God and to others in order to receive what you need. To practice good self-care, you must learn to let the love of God and others penetrate. You must allow God's love to sink into your soul. You must receive.

2. Attending. Good self-care means that you must learn to attend to your own legitimate needs. That means that you have to understand what your emotions are telling you about your circumstances. Remember, your feelings provide information essential for effective self-care.

Jesus himself, you'll remember, "grew both in height and in wisdom, and he was loved by God and by all who knew him."[23] Christ grew up and matured as a whole man. His body grew. His mind grew. His heart for God grew. His relationships with people grew. He allowed all the "data" he received from his environment to help him grow into a mature person.

All of these sources—signals from the body, mind, and heart—provide helpful information that can guide and direct your self-care process. Do you want personal harmony in your life? You'll get it only by paying balanced attention to all of them.

3. Giving. When you keep in mind that God made you for relationships, you stop self-care from degenerating into selfishness. Why? Because you realize that you take care of yourself so that you have something to give to others.

Let me say it as strongly as possible: there's no way that you can really take care of yourself without truly giving and serving others. If you're not giving—if you're focused only on receiving and getting full—then you're working against your own best interests.

You are like an open, rooftop water well. Although in our country we don't rely on open wells for water, many people in arid countries around the world still get their water from cisterns—large catchments that hold water from rainfall or other sources. The well is useless if it has no water in it. But the well is also unhealthy if the water in it becomes stagnant and stale. That happens when the water just stays in the well and never flows out. Only when water flows out can new, fresh water come into the well and keep the water healthy. Your goal must be to get full, get poured out, and get full again, in a never-ending cycle of giving and receiving God's love. This is the essence of good self-care. By caring for others, you care for yourself.

Receiving, attending, giving—if any of these is missing, you'll develop a big hole in your self-care. But when you pay careful attention to all three, you set yourself up to develop deep, lasting, fulfilling relationships in all walks of life.

How Do You Show Up?

How do you show up for your relationships? Are you healthy or crippled? Are you prepared or needy? Are you ready to give or too tired to talk? Solid relationships require the old Boy Scout mentality: Be prepared!

My friend Scott Sticksel comments about being prepared: "When my dad and I would go on fishing trips, he would show up prepared. He'd have all our fishing gear, food, even a good first-aid kit containing everything in it: needle and thread, scissors, matches, gauze. He was ready."

Then Scott adds, "That's how I think we need to show up for our relationships. That way, when unexpected stuff happens, we're ready and prepared to do something about it."

Believe me, I know the wisdom of Scott's words, because recently

I got a wake-up call that showed me I *wasn't* ready and I *wasn't* prepared. And it almost cost me my life.

A Wake-Up Call

In November of 2003 I underwent kidney transplant surgery. A few days after the operation, I started reading a book that prompted me to completely retool the way I operate.

Dr. Don Colbert's *Deadly Emotions* helped me to see what may have contributed to the heart attack I suffered a couple of years ago and to the autoimmune disease that destroyed my kidneys. Without realizing it, for the past ten years I regularly allowed myself to get upset, frustrated, and even hostile about everyday events. My stress level skyrocketed and remained at perpetually high levels. I continuously pumped into my body two major stress hormones, an unwise action that, according to Dr. Colbert, "has a very damaging effect on our body."[24] In fact, "If left unchecked, the perpetual release of the stress hormones adrenaline and cortisol can sear the body in a way that is similar to acid searing metal. Even hours after any immediate stress producing incident has subsided, these hormone levels can remain high and can continue to do their damaging work."[25]

My unrelieved stress placed my immune system on hyperdrive. It finally turned on my normal cells, no doubt significantly contributing to my heart attack and kidney disease. The biggest problem with what I was going through is that I didn't recognize what was happening to me. I didn't even see my high level of stress. I thought it was normal and that everyone has this level of stress. *Gut it out, Smalley,* I told myself.

Do you see what happened? I had not been taking care of myself: listening to my emotions, letting them inform me of situations that needed my attention. I had allowed stress to hijack my body.

What causes stress? In general, stress results from unmet expectations. Stress is the *gap* between what we expect ourselves and others to do and what actually happens. The bigger the gap, the greater the stress. The result is hurt feelings, frustration, irritation, hostility, guilt, and unforgiveness. Unrelieved stress often keeps one awake at night, worrying and overly concerned about the future.

I have lain awake a lot at night over the past two years.

During that period, I retired and then unretired. I signed the biggest publishing contract of my career. I dealt with major ministry reorganization. I spoke at many large conferences. I managed some sticky neighborhood and family problems—and on and on it went. I had too much on my plate and failed to effectively manage my stressed-out emotions. One of Dr. Colbert's statements really grabbed my attention: "If we don't control our stress level and reduce the flow of these damaging hormones, there are many other diseases we can develop."[26]

I already have two diseases; I don't want any more.

Dr. Colbert's book gave me a wake-up call. I realized that I had more to learn about healthy self-care. I prayed, "Lord, teach me from this day what I need to do to start managing my stress." The insights I'm sharing with you in this book have completely changed my life. Today I feel much more relaxed, at peace, resting. In fact, my blood pressure has returned to what it was in high school!

These days I'm adding the following four actions to my self-care program. These steps work together to drop my stress to manageable levels. I make these four steps part of my prayer every morning before I get out of bed.

1. I start off my day by reducing all my earthly expectations to as close to zero as I can get. I no longer expect life to unfold according to my will, my timeline, and my desires. Whether it be traffic, income, ministry plans, the behavior of others, or anything else, I want all of my expectations to be in line with God's expectations and his timetable.[27] I want to wait on God for everything.[28] I've started making a list of my expectations and giving them over to God. I still have strong passions, dreams, and goals about loving people and ministering, but I am willing to wait for God's timing. It was the timing issue that nearly killed me. From now on, the Lord is my shepherd and I will never want again. I will graze in green pastures, by quiet waters, expecting only that God will continually restore my soul and guide me every day to righteousness.[29]

2. I receive everything that happens to me as filtered by God. If God chooses, he can block any bad experience from reaching me. So if he allows it to hit me, I will receive it as something he allowed to pass through his filter. And what's okay with God is okay with me! If a single sparrow can't drop from the sky without his knowledge and consent, how much less could something hit me without first passing through his filter?[30]

God tested me on this conviction a few days after my transplant.

My doctors and nurses had instructed me to keep away from animal waste, especially bird droppings—highly toxic to a kidney-transplant patient. One day, since I was allowed to walk around a bit, I left the hotel where I was recuperating. I didn't walk more than twenty feet before I felt something plop on my head. I reached up to feel what it was and saw a dark, black substance all over my fingers . . . bird droppings! I had never had this happen to me—*why now?* Two weeks earlier, I might have gotten angry. I might have felt frustrated. But instead I relaxed and said, "God, somehow you let that happen. So if it's okay with you, it's okay with me. In fact, God, that was a good one!" And I actually saw the humor in it. By the time I showered twice, I was over it.

3. Every upsetting experience is an opportunity to worship God. When I face a frustrating experience, I ask, How is this thing good for me, and how is it bringing me closer to Christ, making me more loving and more like him? And I remind myself of three truths:

- God causes all things to work together for good to those who love him. If I let them, all trials can result in more love for him and others. I become complete in him through trials.[31]

- Emotional disturbances remind me that God is all I need. I can use difficulties to recall my love for him and my utter dependence on him. He will go ahead of me and protect me from behind. He is my very sustenance. He will guide and comfort me. He is everything I will ever need.[32]

- I get a chance to hunt for "treasure," to recognize all of the benefits of my stressful experiences. God turns ashes to beauty, sorrow to joy. Through my pain, he transforms me into something strong.[33]

4. I rest in God, listen quietly, and ask him what he's telling me to do. I ask God to reveal his will for me, and then I ask others if they can confirm for me what I thought I heard. I want to be more like my wife, Norma—careful and thoughtful. I don't want to be in a hurry anymore. I want to wait for God to renew my strength.[34] My biggest change is listening to my wife more.

You want to know something embarrassing? Twenty years ago I not only knew these principles, I lived by them. Twenty years ago, every morning before I jogged, I would say, "Lord, thank you that you are my life. Thank you that all I need is you. Thank you that all my needs are met in Christ Jesus."

But that was twenty years ago. Somewhere along the way, I let those lessons slip away from me—and I wound up with a body full of stress, resulting in one heart attack and one pair of failed kidneys. But God is gracious! And he's given me yet another chance. I now have the rest of my life to get up each morning and practice healthy self-care.

Even though you may not be on the brink of a heart attack or kidney failure, you may be danger in other ways if you are not taking good care of yourself. Remember the advice in this chapter: listen to your emotions, let them inform you about danger signs. Then tend to yourself spiritually, emotionally, intellectually, and physically. Keep your battery charged. And when you do, you will be prepared for deeply satisfying relationships.

I believe the next chapter offers the greatest communication method on earth. By using it, you can eliminate the main causes of strained or broken relationships.

LIFE IS RELATIONSHIPS;
THE REST IS JUST DETAILS.

ONE-MINUTE REVIEW
SELF-CARE: KEEP YOUR BATTERY CHARGED

1. **Self-care is essential to all relationships.** If you don't take care of yourself, you will have nothing to give to a relationship.

2. **We must love God above all and love others as we love ourselves.** This great commandment indicates that we can love others only as we love ourselves. When we take care of our whole selves—spiritually, emotionally, intellectually, and physically—we set ourselves up for healthy relationships.

3. **Your emotions are your information system.** Your emotions inform you about what you are feeling.

4. **Listen to your emotions.** Identify your emotions, and evaluate whether or not they are true.

5. **Self-care is not selfish.** Taking good care of yourself is one of the best things you can do for your family, friends, and coworkers.

6. **Good self-care involves receiving, attending, and giving.** You need to receive from others, attend to your legitimate needs, and give to others out of your fullness.

7. **You can release your stress and find peace:**

   - *Reduce expectations.*
   - *Receive everything that happens as filtered by God.*
   - *Use every stressful experience as an opportunity to worship God.*
   - *Rest in God, listen quietly, and ask him what he's telling you to do.*

7

EMOTIONAL COMMUNICATION: LISTEN WITH THE HEART

During a rocky period in Bob Paul's marriage, his wife, Jenni, let him know that she did not feel loved. Her revelation practically killed Bob because he loved Jenni very much. The situation frustrated him beyond words. He just couldn't figure out what she meant.

Bob considered himself pretty skilled at opening his heart to receive God's love and to feel lots of love for Jenni and others. The fact that she could still feel unloved baffled him. No matter what he did, his love didn't seem to get through. Bob wondered why he seemed almost completely inept at getting love from his heart to hers.

One day Jenni walked by and, in a playful gesture, Bob pinched her bottom. She stopped abruptly and glared at him, as if steam poured from her reddening ears. And Bob thought, *Come on. Lighten up! I'm just trying to flirt with you.*

Another day while on his way home from work, Bob thought he'd surprise his wife and sweep her off her feet. He had it all planned.

He'd walk in the door, put down all his stuff, and find her in the kitchen, where she'd be preparing dinner. He would quietly sidle up to her, pick her up, swing her around, and give her a big, passionate kiss. He figured it would make her day.

So that's what he did.

What was Jenni's response? She glowered at him, making no effort to hide her red-hot anger. Once again Bob was baffled. He thought, *What is your problem? Here I am, acting out every woman's dream. I'm being Joe Romance—and you are angry at me! What's the deal?*

The two encounters caused Bob to reevaluate how he interacted and communicated with his wife. He realized that although his goal had been to show Jenni his love, he wasn't getting the job done. Obviously Jenni still did not feel loved. So whatever he was doing, it was not working.

"As a guy," Bob told me, "it got to the point where I thought, *This is dumb. I'm tired of being a total failure. No matter what I do, it never works.* So finally I said to myself, 'Maybe I should find out why this isn't working for her and see if there's something else I could do. I'm sick of being a relational goat. I want to be a hero.'"

None of us wants to be a relational goat. We all want to be relational heroes. Right? If so, I advise you to pay close attention to this chapter. What I'm about to tell you has the potential to radically improve all your most precious relationships. In fact, the research of Howard J. Markman, Scott M. Stanley, and Susan L. Blumberg indicates that learning and practicing the method of communication shared here will eliminate the four main causes of divorce.[1] You enter into the two deepest levels of communication, where the most relational satisfaction is found in all relationships. I call it the greatest communication method on earth. I have watched it revolutionize my own marriage and family, and I've witnessed thousands of couples and singles using it to enrich their relationships. It's not necessarily easy to learn, but it's very powerful when you do.

Beyond Words to Feelings

Do you want to know one particularly nasty myth that keeps many people—including my friend Bob—from experiencing the tremendous benefits of effective communication? Somewhere along the way, they have come to believe that real communication occurs when they understand the other person's *words*. They equate effective communication with accurately noting the words and phrases they hear.

But in fact, good communication is more than that. True communication usually does not occur until each person understands the *feelings* that underlie the spoken words. People generally feel more understood, cared for, and connected when the communication focuses on their emotions and feelings rather than merely on their words or thoughts.

Consider this the magic of effective communication. Our goal must go beyond understanding the spoken words to grasping the emotional nugget underlying the words. It's far more important to discover and address the emotions beneath the situation than to parrot the words we hear. Ask yourself, "What is the emotional impact of these words?" not merely, "What exact words did I just hear?"

Suppose a wife says, "I really don't think our kids should go to public schools. I think we should homeschool them."

What did she mean? Consider carefully her two sentences. The woman used no "feeling" words but all "thinking" words. So if her husband replies, "So what you're saying is that you don't think our kids should go to public schools," he's completely missed the point. He has accurately reflected to her the words she just spoke, but he remains completely in the dark about her real concern.

But what if he listens for the emotions beneath the words? What if he listens with his heart? What if he said, "Are you saying that you feel really concerned about our kids"? Presto! This time, he's "got it." He listened beyond his wife's words to her heart, to her real concern. He's tapped into her emotional message—her fear for their kids.

A lot of people get stuck in the Fear Dance at precisely this point. They use "thought" words about their actions instead of talking about their feelings or deepest concerns. They remain stuck until they finally learn to look for the emotional nugget. They free themselves only when they discover how to go beyond the expressed thoughts and opinions and to get to the underlying feelings—the place of real concern and deep emotional experience.

I Care about You

When we work to uncover the emotional nugget, we say to our family member, friend, or partner, "I care how you feel. Your feelings matter to me." And when our loved ones get *this* message, they feel deeply cared for. That's when they feel loved.

But if we don't relay this message—even if we understand the words the person has spoken—he or she still will not feel loved, and real communication will grind to a halt.

A lot of us (especially men) struggle with this skill. Men tend to think in a linear way: cut to the chase, get to the bottom line. We want to solve a problem and complete a task, not deal with emotions. We want only to figure out how to "fix it."

Without listening for and responding to the emotions, however, all of the problem solving in the world won't get us to the real problem. We have found that only when we understand the feelings involved can we effectively start the task of problem solving. Once my friend Bob understood this and then started acting on it, his rocky marriage got not only a lot smoother but also more enjoyable.

"I chose to become a 'student' of Jenni, to learn about what she thinks and feels," Bob said. "Later that night after dinner was done, I asked her, 'Hey, how come you got so upset when I came in and swung you around and kissed you?'"

Jenni's quick reply struck a chord of fear in Bob, all the way down to the tips of his toes. She looked at him and said, "Do you *really* want to know?"

Bob thought, *Oh, man—do I really want to know?* He wasn't sure, but by that point he felt committed to hanging up the goat's hat in favor of the one that said Hero. So he said, "Yes, I really want to know."

"When you did that," Jenni explained, "at that moment, I had about ten things on my mind. I was rushing around, just trying to get dinner together—and it felt as if you wanted me to drop everything I was doing and just focus on you, as if nothing else in my life mattered to you. You didn't care about me or about anything going on in my life."

Bob swallowed hard, then replied, "Okay, that's really not what I wanted to do. That's not what I was trying to accomplish. I was trying to bless you, to do something that would make you feel loved. What could I have done instead?"

"Hmmm," Jenni replied. "You really want to know?"

Bob gulped again and said, "Yes, I really want to know."

"Well, if you had paused for a moment when you got to the doorway of the kitchen and just noticed what was going on with me, and then either rolled up your sleeves and started doing the dishes, or even asked how you could help, I would have felt so loved."

Immediately Bob thought, *You know, this is not that complicated.*

Next he asked her, "When I flirted with you and pinched you a few days ago, you also got very upset. What was the deal with that?"

"You really want to know?"

"Yes, I really want to know."

Jenni explained that some types of affection felt very private to her—including that playful pinch. "The kids were doing their homework in the next room. I'm not comfortable when you do something like that when they are nearby. That's a private gesture to me, not something to be done in the kitchen."

Bob told me later, "That's not the way I feel about it. I'm doing my Tarzan routine, wanting to show the whole world how much I love my woman—but it just angers her."

When Bob asked Jenni what she would have liked him to do differently, she had no ideas. But at that moment, he remembered a situation with their eldest daughter. When Jessica was young, she would occasionally come up to Bob and plant the most inappropriate kisses on his mouth, and it would bother him. He would ask Jenni, "Can you help me here? I don't know what to do about Jessica's kisses."

Jenni came up with a great idea. "The next time Jessica comes to give you a kiss," she suggested, "turn your head and let her kiss you on the cheek. Then you give her a kiss." He did that, and it worked great. And that gave Bob an idea.

"How would you like it," he asked Jenni, "if, instead of pinching you, I gave you a really affectionate kiss on the cheek? I really just want to get the affection from my heart to yours."

Jenni just melted. "I would *love* that!" she exclaimed.

And Bob thought again, *This is just not that hard.*

THE REAL MESSAGE IS OFTEN THE EMOTION BENEATH THE WORDS. ←

Effective communication comes down to listening and speaking with your heart. When people feel understood emotionally, they feel cared for. This is very different from listening to someone from the head—that is, looking merely for the content of the person's words, without paying attention to the emotion. The goal of effective communication is to understand the *emotional* message of the speaker. You have to ask yourself, *What is this person feeling?*

Allow Others' Emotions to Touch You

It is one thing to hear these emotions and say, "Boy, I can really tell you are upset." But it is another thing to allow these emotions to penetrate your heart, to allow yourself to feel the pain or the sadness. The key is not merely to understand these feelings but also to allow the feelings to touch you. This is one of the primary ways that people feel cared for and loved.

When I take the time to find out what is going on inside of my loved ones—when they know that I care how they feel and that their feelings deeply affect me—they feel loved and cared for. If Norma is hurting and I really care about her, I allow her hurt to touch me. I hurt because she is hurting. Why? Because I love her.

Just a few nights ago, I was lying in bed and thought of a conversation I had with my son Greg. He said that he didn't feel as if I understand the pain he went through recently in a very hurtful situation at work. "Do you really care?" he asked me. At the time I didn't know the depth of his feelings. So before I went to sleep, I chose to walk in his shoes during the past year and experience it with my heart. So many feelings came to me; it was quite overwhelming. I felt his pain and suddenly understood how he could have felt. I almost started crying. I met with him two days later and shared what I had done and explained how I started to understand his pain. He looked at me and said, "That's all I needed from you. Just knowing you understand settles it for me." What I did was so helpful for me to feel the pain of others, I did the same thing the next night for my wife, my other children, and grandkids. Now I do it often, and it allows me to feel with people after I have met with them and need to really understand them.

In his new book *Scandalous Freedom*, author and radio host Steve Brown talks about the necessity of allowing the hurt of others to affect us:

> I have a dear friend who, in the last two or three years, has come close to tears whenever we talked about certain important matters. I'm a fixer, and fixers, when they see tears, see a problem in need of fixing. I offered all kinds of sugges-

tions to my friend to stop the tears and to make her feel better. Finally, after a number of failed attempts, she said to me, "Stop it! Just stop it. My tears are good."

When I asked my friend to please explain herself, she told me that for many years she felt separate from her own pain and the pain of others. "I was, I suppose," she said, "compassionate in a way. I cared about what people were going through—but there was this thing about not being able to really feel the things that hurt them. There was even a way I separated myself from my own pain." Then my friend said something profound. "Steve," she said, "my tears are good in that they, for the first time in my life, let me know that I'm real."[2]

In just this way, effective communication benefits not only the ones with whom we want to connect but also ourselves. It lets us know we're "real." Still, the primary beneficiary is the one who sees how his or her pain genuinely affects us.

Does this sound like a lot of work? Do you think it makes more sense just to make a decision, without really understanding what the other person is feeling? Be careful! Just making a quick decision will not solve your problem. When people don't feel understood and cared for, they may "agree" to some decision, but they won't get on board with it. Relationally, it doesn't feel to them like a satisfying or effective solution. And in the end, you'll have to talk about these things all over again.

Listening Does Not Equal Agreement

Some people—again, men in particular—hesitate to use this method of effective communication because they confuse it with the idea that they'll have to do what the other person wants them to do. Some also hesitate because by talking this way, they feel they are agreeing with the other person or they might be exposed to guilt if too many feelings come out during the conversation.

But I can really care about how a person is feeling, even if I do not agree with what that person is saying. When I see that Norma is hurting, I can make it clear that it matters to me that she hurts. True, she might falsely believe that something I said or did caused her hurt, even if I didn't really do or say it. But her misperception does not keep me from caring about her pain. When I allow her pain to affect me, it's not the same thing as saying, "I hurt because I see what I did to you." She hurts, and I want to understand and give comfort.

When I say, "Norma, I really understand that you are hurting, that this has wounded you," I am not necessarily saying, "Norma, I agree with you, and I was wrong." Rather, I am saying, "I could tell that this really hurt you, and your feelings mean the world to me. I care how you feel!"

At other times some of us shy away from effective communication because we feel very vulnerable in the presence of deep emotion. We feel out of control. We don't know where or how deep it is going to take us—and we fear being out of control.

But when we refuse to go to that place, it makes us seem uncaring. Remember Steve Brown's friend? When we refuse to allow the feelings of the other to affect us emotionally, we seem uncaring. And no relationship will grow when the other person thinks we don't care.

Let's take this a little further. When we say things like, "You shouldn't feel this way," we are really saying, "I don't care how you are feeling. Your feelings are wrong; they should be different." And who feels cared for by someone who says, "I don't care how you feel"?

Perhaps the communication method I'm proposing sounds risky to you. Maybe it makes you feel far too vulnerable. I feel that way sometimes. But even though it's a risk, I know I can do it. Why? Because I have already chosen to take responsibility for myself. I already have attended to my own self-care. And you know what? I find that I multiply my ability to care for others a hundredfold when I know that I have taken good care of myself. Had I let that slip, it *would* seem too risky. It *would* throw me into a tailspin. That's why we talked about the Power of One and Self-Care before we got here. It really does make all the difference.

Effective communication makes room for people to actually feel what the other is feeling. This communication method allows people to understand their heart and to be okay with dipping into their emotions.

A Dynamic Process of Discovery

My colleague Bob Paul likes to say, "Effective communication is a dynamic process of discovery that maintains energy in the relationship." And what does that mean? Let's look at each part of his sentence.

First, effective communication is *dynamic*. It changes. It shifts and wiggles and squirms and jumps and turns. It never stands still; that's why you can't plug somebody's words into an electronic translator and come out with a perfect understanding of the intended message. That's also why you have to pay careful attention during the conversation. If you take a break, the conversation may move on and you may miss something. It's *dynamic*.

The other day my friend Jim was asking me about using my John Deere tractor, and he told me about his son, who is moving to Oklahoma City for his doctoral residency. My friend was feeling good that his son would be so close to our hometown. Then Jim mentioned how happy he was about seeing his grandson more often. He started tearing up while sharing a deep feeling about his grandkids. All of Jim's grandparents died before he could remember them. He has always felt cheated by that experience. As he was telling this story, I wondered if it was related to our recent conversation about his increased travel at our company. So I asked him, "Jim, you seemed to react to me the other day when we talked about increasing your travel time." Then the tears started flowing. He admitted that his need to be with his grandkids more often was so strong that he didn't want to travel more often. Finally I understood where the reaction came from, and we started working on how to free his schedule instead of increasing his travel. That is what we mean by dynamic.

"EFFECTIVE COMMUNICATION ← IS A DYNAMIC PROCESS OF DISCOVERY THAT MAINTAINS ENERGY IN THE RELATIONSHIP."

Second, effective communication is a *process*. If you see communication as a destination rather than a process, you will miss things. Important things get communicated along the way, things that would never come out if you approached the conversation as a set-in-stone collection of words and sentences that tell you everything you need to know. As a process, effective communication takes time—just like the process of making homemade ice cream. Do you simply throw eggs and sugar and cream and flavorings in a chilled bowl and drink the concoction? You could if you wanted to, but you wouldn't be getting ice cream. Real ice cream—the delicious kind—gets made only when you follow a certain process. And if you cut short the process, you spoil the dessert. The same is true with effective communication. It's a *process*.

Third, effective communication leads to *discovery*. Through it, you learn things you didn't know before and couldn't have guessed. Real communication does not occur when you "skip ahead" and try to predict what the other person is going to say next. It shuts down when you pretend to listen but really are deciding how best to respond. People discover things when they open their ears and eyes and allow what's happening around them to clue them in to something they didn't know before.

You might say to the other person, "I really want to learn about you, about how you are feeling. I want to learn about what God is doing in this." Be genuinely interested in learning about what is going on and about the other person's emotions.

Interestingly, when you see communication primarily as a dynamic process of discovery rather than one of solving problems, you often solve the problems almost by default. Sometimes you find that the solutions are much less important to the other person than feeling understood and cared for. Often, this understanding alone ends the conflict, even without finding a "solution." We make exciting finds in communication when we treat it as a process of *discovery*.

Last, effective communication *maintains energy in the relationship*. That's psychologist-speak to say that it keeps things between the two of you fun, exciting, satisfying, and healthy. When you learn to communicate with each other at a heart level, you experience more of what God made you to be. You feel more vibrant. Life seems more intriguing. You wake up eager to charge into the world and share your experiences with the ones you love. You find energy you never had before and thank God that he gave you breath.

A friend of mine, Dr. Bob Burbee, illustrates for me the "discovery factor" of this powerful model of effective communication. Several years ago Bob and his wife, Mary Jo, were trying to decide whether they should have more children. At the time they had a five-year-old daughter, Erin, and a three-year-old son, Tyler.

One day Mary Jo asked, "What about having another baby?" From Bob's perspective, they already had the perfect family. It made no sense to him to threaten family harmony with more children.

Mary Jo, on the other hand, really wanted another child and wouldn't let the issue drop. Consequently, they got locked into a conflict and made no progress for months.

Finally, on a holiday road trip, they experienced a breakthrough. When the subject of more children came up, Bob started thinking, *Here we go again*—but something prompted him to think, *What if I listen to Mary Jo as if I were listening to her for the very first time?*

As Bob chose to set aside his own agenda, he began to hear some things Mary Jo had probably tried to tell him before. She described what it meant to her to be a mom. She spoke of the fulfillment and sense of personal worth and self-esteem she derived from loving and caring for their children. She said she thought of motherhood as a divine calling and expressed her desire to mother more than two children.

"It began to dawn on me," Bob said, "that being a mother to her was very different from what being a father was to me. Being a good husband and father are important to me, and I have always felt committed to the role and responsibility of being a loving father. Still, if I were truly honest, my sense of self-esteem and accomplishment are not so tightly attached to my role as father as they are to Mary Jo's role as a mother."

This insight helped Bob understand why Mary Jo couldn't let go of the issue. As his perspective grew, the issue took on new complexity. And something else—something very interesting—happened as they continued to talk.

"Maybe my efforts to really understand Mary Jo inspired her to try to understand my feelings as well," Bob said. "I described my anxiety about not having enough of me to go around with more children in the family. I described the additional strain on our finances and the changes to our lifestyle. We had just gotten out of the 'diaper stage,' and the thought of starting that again did not appeal to me."

By the end of Bob and Mary Jo's drive, they had not made a decision, but their relationship had moved to a new and better place. Think about that! On the surface, this issue looked as if it required a final decision: they either would have more children or they wouldn't. But remember, the problem is rarely the problem. Bob and Mary Jo discovered that trying to make a decision had resulted only in more conflict and a stalemate. When they stopped trying to "solve" the problem and simply worked at understanding each other's emotional state, their relationship took several steps forward.

"The resolution came," Bob said, "not in making a decision but in allowing ourselves to truly understand each other's emotions, and then letting that understanding shape us so the issue took on a new, more complete definition."

Eventually, Bob and Mary Jo did resolve their difference—but you'll have to wait until the next chapter to find out what happened!

Complex, Not Simple

"I don't think this relationship is going to work out," Cyndi tells Chuck. "I wanted to go to Hereford's Steak House yesterday, and you took me to Shrimp's Seafood instead."

"Wait a minute," Chuck replies, dumbfounded. "You want to break up with me because we went to the wrong *restaurant?*"

"Of course not," Cyndi answers. "But see there? You did it again."

"I did *what* again?"

"Oh, honestly! You just don't understand me! How could we be right for each other if you don't 'get' me?"

"But I asked you yesterday where you wanted to eat. You said you didn't care!"

"*Please!* You shouldn't have to ask. You should just know. I can't be with someone who seems unable to catch perfectly obvious hints. Good-bye, Chuck."

Have you ever overheard a conversation anything like this? Maybe you've been involved in one, either on the giving or receiving end. It reflects a very common reason why many people fail at healthy, positive relationships. They fail because they believe that effective communication between people in a relationship should be simple. Easy. Effortless.

It's not! Actually, it is quite complex. And it takes a lot of hard work. But, trust me, it is worth every second of effort!

Many of us get really frustrated with each other when a misunderstanding arises. We even get angry, as if the other person intentionally did something stupid or purposefully failed to "get it."

I remember a situation at the site where I was to give a talk some years ago. When I arrived at the auditorium, I found a very messy stage. I rushed around, trying to get everything straightened out and prepared. Soon I noticed a woman sitting in the auditorium, all alone. I tried, very politely, to recruit her help. I told her I was in a rush and asked for her assistance. She smiled and nodded her head. I thanked her, turned around, and started cleaning again.

But in a couple of minutes when I looked out from the stage, I saw the woman still sitting there. *What is this woman's problem?* I wondered. Irritated, I stopped and got her attention. Once more I appealed to her again to help me, and once more she smiled, nodded . . . and continued to sit where she was.

Finally I quietly lost patience with her and started to walk off when I heard her say something in Spanish. It had never occurred to me that we might be using completely different languages!

In real life, sadly, misunderstandings come even when we speak the same language. If we forget that effective communication is a complex process that takes a great deal of work, we can easily find ourselves getting angry with the other person and wondering how he or she can be so dense.

It helps to remember that we are the only creatures on earth who, as far as we know, communicate with the kind of sophistication that characterizes human interaction. Every time we hear a word or sentence, we have to go through an amazing process of interpretation. Human language can be imprecise; words have so many meanings. Body language and other nonverbal signals convey huge meaning, but we miss much of it. The chance of misunderstanding is enormous.

EFFECTIVE COMMUNICATION ← TAKES WORK.

Perhaps we really ought to start with the expectation that, at least on some level, we are bound to misunderstand and misinterpret one another. We might even admit it out loud: "More than likely, I am going to say some things that you could take wrong, misunderstand, or misinterpret." If we did this, I think we would tend to be more cautious, more deliberate. We would be more careful to make sure that understanding really takes place.

But let's make this a little more personal. If you hear something that hits you wrong, instead of just reacting—"How could you say

143

such a thing?"—you might instead try saying, "This is what I just heard, and this is what I think you meant. Before I get upset, I need to find out if I'm right." Check it out before you jump to a wrong conclusion.

I have been humbled countless times by thinking that I understood the malicious intent of a person and so reacted harshly—only to discover that what I thought he said was not what he meant. I totally blasted or misjudged the person and so damaged our relationship.

It helps to remember what the Bible says: "The purposes of a man's heart are deep waters, but a man of understanding draws them out."[3] What lies within often lies *deep* within, requiring careful and sustained effort to draw it out.

Think of effective communication as something of a deep-sea dive. If you want to visit the rusting hulk of the HMS *Titanic*, silently resting two and a half miles down on the bottom of the Atlantic Ocean, you don't just jump into the water and start swimming. You have to prepare. You have to know what you're doing. You have to know what kind of submersible you will need. You have to allow sufficient time for both the long descent and the even slower ascent. Without sufficient preparation, you won't be seeing anything but a lot of cold water (and maybe an occasional hungry shark).

Effective communication is a complex business. If you go into it expecting things to flow easily and without a lot of effort, you're just kidding yourself. I recommend that you adjust your expectations from "simple" to "complex," especially in three key areas:

1. Expect problems and misunderstandings. Even the best communicators sometimes fail to understand others, or they fall short of making themselves understood. We're all human. We don't always follow through on what we know to be best. We don't always use the proven techniques that we know work. Often we don't even know for sure why we act or feel a certain way. Effective communicators expect problems and misunderstandings. Because they do not look for seas as calm as glass, they don't feel surprised when a nor'easter hits. They prepare themselves to work through the storms to reach the sunny skies waiting on the other side of the rain clouds.

2. Expect that you'll need a lot of patience. Effective communication takes time. You and the other person may not connect or get on the same wavelength on the first or second (or third or even fourth) attempt. Impatience can doom the goal of genuine understanding. Being in a hurry works against the commitment to care that is essential to all effective communication. How can you genuinely care for someone while you're tapping your feet and reaching for the door?

Instead, relax. Be careful. Recognize that effective communication deserves patience and a deliberate attempt to understand not only the words being said but also the emotions behind the words. Slow down until you get that. It will make the communication much easier and much more effective.

3. *Expect a lot of trial and error.* People have different ways of communicating. While all of us can master and use a powerful set of tools for effective communication, the way we use those tools varies from person to person.[4] We get the best use out of them by adapting them for our own style and personal bent—and that requires trial and error.

You didn't give up on driving a car just because you felt a little intimidated the first time you sat behind the wheel, did you? You didn't abandon your pursuit of reading when you choked on a few words from *The Cat in the Hat*, did you? You didn't swear off all future attempts at tying your shoes when you bungled your first attempts, did you? Of course not. It takes trial and error to get good at any skill—and that includes the skill of communicating effectively.

Effective communication is a complex business. But you grease the skids for its success when you start out from the right position.

You Can Start on Your Own

A lot of people mistakenly think that they can't practice the elements of effective communication unless they get the full cooperation of the other person, but that is not true. In fact, you can do a lot of effective communication even without the conscious cooperation or understanding of the other person. In fact, you have a tremendous impact, all by yourself.

You can choose to listen for the heart and clearly communicate what you're sensing, regardless of whether the other person knows the process you're using. You can choose to speak more articulately, in a way that the other person can more easily understand. You can also choose to listen carefully and grasp the other person's feelings.

You can exercise the Power of One. You can have a positive influence on your relationship even if the other person does not fully cooperate. You can do a significant amount to make a huge difference, even without a lot of cooperation from the other person.

So don't stay stuck. Don't stay in neutral. Put to work the strategies I've just outlined for you—and start building a stronger relationship *today*.

Effective Communication Saves Time

Does it seem as if identifying the emotional nugget will take far more time than other methods of communication? A lot of guys think so! But, in fact, it actually *saves* tremendous amounts of time.

Think about it. If you don't have to repeatedly go back over the same old ground, then you can spend your time on other things. Many husbands who come in for counseling initially balk at the idea of trying to identify and focus on their wife's core emotion. Yet they soon come to embrace it, once they see that by getting to the emotional nugget, conversation on the topic can get wrapped up pretty quickly.

Guys, take note: *Effective communication is ultimately more efficient and takes less time than any other method.* A lot of men feel frustrated when their wives seem to go on and on. They don't understand that the reason they go on and on is that they don't feel *emotionally* understood. If these husbands took the time to actually uncover their wives' emotional concern, the conversation would move on and they wouldn't have to hear the same thing a dozen times, from six different angles. When guys finally "get" this, the lightbulb goes on for them. They get excited about their ability to condense the conversation.

"That's all I have to do—help her see that I truly understand her feelings?" they ask, amazed and delighted.

Yep. That's it. Sounds great, doesn't it? This may sound selfish on a man's part, but when you think about it for a second, why wouldn't you want to save time and reduce frustration?

Guys, hear me: If the woman in your life—whether she is your wife, your dating partner, your daughter, your friend, or your colleague—repeats the same thing over and over, I can almost guarantee that she does not believe you understand her heart. You could say at that point, "I noticed that you are repeating yourself, and that causes me to question whether you believe I am understanding you. Am I missing something?"

It is amazing what happens when a woman feels deeply understood emotionally. She will be much more inclined to stop talking about the issue, for she no longer has any reason to keep going.

The last thing I want to do is spend any more time than necessary on unpleasant topics. Sure, if you shut down the communication, you might not have to deal (at least immediately) with more words—but you probably *will* have to deal with the cold shoulder, the distance, or all the other things that come from not taking the time to attend to a person's feelings.

Is this method easy? Not in one sense—it's probably very different from what you've done to this point in your life. But practice makes perfect! And over time it gets much more efficient. At first, I admit, it feels awkward. It feels very unnatural, and you may be clumsy at it. But as you get more practice, it gets easier. It streamlines. In fact, this is the most streamlined form of communication that I know.

So learn to listen with your heart. Put your problem-solving urges on hold for a while, and listen with your heart. Problem-solving skills remain extremely valuable, of course, but they are much more effective after you understand the emotions involved. So save time! Get efficient! And look for the emotional nugget.

Safety First . . . and Second

What would happen if you discharged a loaded cannon in your bedroom? Not a pretty sight. But what if you made sure that you used only the best artillery shells and the latest guidance systems? How about if you first read the most up-to-date manual, talked to a retired gunnery sergeant, and made sure the weapon was clean and thoroughly inspected before you fired a live round into your ceiling?

"Who's stupid enough to do something like that?" you ask. "Everybody knows that you don't fire a cannon in your own bedroom!"

Why not? That's easy—it's a question of environment. No matter how good your equipment and supplies might be, if you use a cannon in the wrong environment, you'll get disastrous results.

It's exactly the same story when it comes to effective communication. You can have the best tools, the latest insights, the greatest determination, and the most powerful strategies and *still fail* if the environment is wrong.

So what is the "right" environment for effective communication? We talked about safety a couple of chapters ago, but it's worth a review here. In a safe environment, no one has to worry about being shamed or rejected or punished or attacked for stating personal beliefs and feelings. In a place like that, heartfelt communication can bloom and grow.

When I believe someone is allowing me to feel the way I feel, without judging my feelings, I feel cared for. On the other hand, I never feel cared for when someone tells me that I "shouldn't feel that way," that my feelings are "stupid" or "wrong" or "excessive." If they tell me that my feelings are anything other than what they are, I do not feel cared for. And I don't feel safe.

Effective communication ought to begin with a simple and firm commitment to the goal of safety. Of course, agreeing on basic ground rules and an effective strategy for communication can help to create a safe environment.[5] But the commitment to safety must come first. Make safety your goal, and watch intimacy blossom. Otherwise, you may find the ceiling raining down in chunks.

But it doesn't end there! In fact, the way you communicate also *creates* a greater measure of safety. If you listen with your heart, to the point that the other person feels deeply understood and cared for, you increase the person's sense of safety. The more safety that exists in your relationships, the more openness, real intimacy, and connection will occur. When a person feels safe, he or she is more inclined to become a willing participant in the relationship.

In other words, a safe environment makes effective communication easier, and effective communication creates more safety. They work off of each other to improve your relationships.

Whose Fault Is It?

One last issue needs to get unpacked before we can move on to the next chapter. Many of us spend a whole lifetime consistently "missing" each other because we remain in the iron grip of a deadly myth.

Let's take a little quiz. Here is the question: *When you find yourself in a conflict with someone, how much of your conversation includes questions like the following?*

- Who is right? Who is wrong?
- Whose fault is this mess? Who's to blame?

- What really happened here?
- How will we solve the problem?

Probably 90 percent of the people who come to us for relationship help begin their sessions by asking exactly these questions. They really believe that if they can establish "who's right" and "what happened," they will set the stage for effective communication. They think that by doing so, they'll improve their relationships.

But you know what? They rarely do.

When we focus—at least, as a place to start—on trying to determine who is right and who is wrong, we embark on a totally useless pursuit. Starting anywhere other than attending to the emotions will get you derailed most of the time. When we begin by attempting to figure out who is to blame or what really happened, we succeed only in fueling power struggles and hurtful disagreements.

When people feel emotionally heard and understood, on the other hand, they tend to relax and to trust that you really care. Eventually they will be able to move toward determining right and wrong. What really happened might be useful to know in finding a solution. But it is very hard to get on the same page and to feel relaxed if you do not first feel that your emotions are being heard, cared for, and understood.

Effective communication makes thorough understanding its goal. The Bible counsels, "Wisdom is supreme; therefore get wisdom. Though it cost all you have, get understanding."[6]

COMMUNICATION IS ← UNDERSTANDING, NOT DETERMINING WHO'S RIGHT.

The apostle Paul had healthy relationships in mind when he said, "Let us stop passing judgment on one another. Instead, make up your mind not to put any stumbling block or obstacle in your brother's way."[7] Rather than trying to fix blame or nail someone to the wall, Paul tells us, "Let us therefore make every effort to do what leads to peace and to mutual edification."[8]

And what best leads to peace? What builds us up, as almost nothing else can? The sense that we have been genuinely heard and deeply understood! That's the goal we're after. That's the treasure we seek.

It Gets Even Better

Remember my friend Bob, the one who flirted with his wife but didn't get the reaction he wanted? He desperately wanted that treasure. He longed for the gold of true understanding. So do you know what he did?

Bob chose to create a list of things that would be surefire winners—things that would make Jenni feel really loved. He said. "I created that list either from things I witnessed or asked her about. And I created another list, equally long, of things she didn't like, things not to do. I knew that if I stopped doing the things on the second list, she would begin to feel loved. I started doing the things on my first list, and sure enough, over time, she started to feel very much loved."

But it gets even better for this man who chose to practice effective communication. "In fact," Bob continued, "these days, Jenni feels deeply loved. We hardly ever fight anymore. We have learned to manage our differences wonderfully, and we trust each other. Things are in a very, very different place at this stage. I wouldn't trade this relationship for anything. The last thing in the world I would ever want is to start over. I can't think of anything more unappealing. I've spent more than two decades getting to this point, and I want to ride this out for as long as I can and enjoy it for the rest of my life."

Would you like to enjoy your relationships for the rest of your life? Would you like to ride them out for the long haul? You can! When you choose to master the art of effective communication, you, like Bob, can help all of your loved ones to *feel* truly loved. And a loving relationship is a growing relationship!

How would you like to win most of your disagreements with others? Read on!

LIFE IS RELATIONSHIPS;
THE REST IS JUST DETAILS.

:01

ONE-MINUTE REVIEW
EMOTIONAL COMMUNICATION: LISTEN WITH THE HEART

1. **Listen beyond the words to the feelings.** People generally feel more understood, cared for, and connected when the communication focuses on their emotions and feelings rather than merely on their words or thoughts.

2. **The real message is often the emotion behind the words.** When you listen with your heart and listen for the heart of the other person, you show that you care.

3. **Allow others' emotions to touch you.** People feel loved when they know you truly understand their feelings.

4. **Effective communication is a dynamic process of discovery that maintains energy in the relationship.** When you see communication as a dynamic process of discovery rather than one of solving problems, you often solve the problems by default.

5. **Effective Communication starts with safety.** When you listen rather than judge or correct, you create a safe environment for understanding to blossom.

6. **Communication is understanding, not determining who's right.** Your relationships will thrive if your priority is understanding the other person.

8

TEAMWORK: ADOPT A NO-LOSERS POLICY

A number of years ago Bob Paul found himself in a heated disagreement with his son Chris, who was a young boy at the time. Because Bob felt passionate about his position, he pressed pretty hard with his son. Bob felt Chris was not agreeing with him and had "tuned him out." More discussion was basically a waste of their time, but Bob continued the conversation. "Chris," he said, "if you don't get this, you could get into real trouble."

No matter how Bob explained his deep concern, however, Chris kept missing the point. "I didn't know if he was purposefully dodging me or what," Bob says. "I was using the best persuasive skills that I could muster. I'd come at it from one angle, and he'd dodge it. So I'd rethink my strategy and try it from another perspective. This went on for an hour and a half, and I couldn't understand why we weren't getting anywhere."

Eventually Bob broke through his son's resistance, and Chris finally understood. Bob felt so relieved that he fell back on his bed, stared at the ceiling, and breathed a prayer of thanks. Even from his prone position he noticed his crestfallen son walking out of the room with his head hanging low, but he thought, *He'll get over it. At least he understands my point.*

For fifteen or twenty minutes Bob sat on the bed, gathering himself after his grueling encounter. When he got up, walked out of the bedroom and down the hallway, he noticed Chris sitting in the dining room at the head of the table, all by himself. He looked totally dejected.

"At that moment," Bob says, "I felt such a sense of conviction. And then God dropped an idea in my head that had never occurred to me before. It really made sense."

Bob walked over to his son and sat next to him at the table. "Hey, Chris," he said, "if you look back at that conversation, who do you think 'won'?"

His son thought for a moment, then replied, "You know, Dad, in some ways neither of us. But for the most part, you did."

Bob shook his head and said, "Son, if that's the case, then I lost."

Chris gave his dad a look that said, "What do you mean *you* lost? You are *so* weird."

Back in those years, Chris played on a Little League baseball team with a friend named Chuckie. "Look at it this way," Bob explained. "Is there ever a time when you and Chuckie are playing ball, when you win and Chuckie loses?"

"No."

"How about when Chuckie wins and you lose?"

"No."

"How come?"

"Dad," Chris said in exasperation, "we're on the *same team.*"

"Exactly, Son," Bob replied. "And you and I are on the same team. I'm not your enemy; I'm on your team. And if our conversation made you feel as if you lost, then I lost too. If you lose, I lose. We both need to win."

The Greatest Ploy

Does the power struggle between Bob and Chris sound at all familiar to you? Are you at odds with family members or friends? Do you often feel as if you win—or lose—in those relationships?

Power struggles can be very destructive. Why? In every power struggle, people become instant adversaries; they take up opposing positions and try to crush their opponent. And do you know what? Every time that happens, Satan is very pleased. He can just fold his arms and walk away. Why? Because he knows that friends-turned-adversaries will hurt and perhaps even destroy one another. If he can get partners to see themselves as adversaries, he's already accomplished his dirty work. He doesn't have to do anything more.

Never forget that your true enemy is not the other person. The enemy of our souls and relationships wants with all his evil heart to destroy your healthy relationships. If he can get you to perceive the other person as the enemy, as an adversary, he's already won.

So if squaring off with our friends and partners causes so much damage, why do we so quickly make them into adversaries? Why do we so easily jump into power struggles? Once more, I think the reaction is rooted in fear. It is a very natural thing to feel threatened by someone who disagrees with us. Conflicts feel inherently threatening. We very naturally consider that our opinion or way of seeing things is the "right" or "better" way. If we didn't, we'd change our opinion or way of seeing things. So when people suggest that our way *isn't* right or better, we fear that they will take us someplace we don't want to go—and that creates fear. We tend to dig in our heels and try to prove our point, to get them to see things our way, and to admit how wrong they are.

Once we square off as adversaries, however, the outcome is already assured. We don't even have to play the game. We've already lost. Because when you're on a team, win-lose is a total illusion. There is no such thing. You have only two options: You either both win, or you both lose.

A No-Losers Policy

After his encounter with his son, Bob started thinking about the way he handled most of the relationships in his life. When he applied the dynamics of his encounter with Chris to his own marriage, it dawned on him that he set up almost every interaction with his wife in an adversarial way.

"I always felt frustrated about whether or not I won my point," he said. "I couldn't understand why it always felt like a loss. Everybody knows that feeling—where you win something but still feel as if you lost. It's a hollow victory, at best. I decided at that moment that I wouldn't fall for this anymore. I was sick to death of being a relational failure. I was sick to death of being ineffective. I had a choice, and I chose to stop the madness."

So Bob determined to abandon the old, failed model and make a commitment to a new way of doing things. He and his wife, Jenni, established what they called a no-losers policy. They agreed that from that point on it would never be acceptable for either of them to walk away from any interaction feeling as if they had lost. Each spouse had to feel good about what happened. That was their new goal. Both had to "buy into" whatever decision they made as a couple.

Such a commitment radically improves any relationship. No wonder author and speaker Zig Ziglar once said, "Many marriages would be better if the husband and the wife clearly understood that they are on the same side."

Remember the conflict between Bob and Mary Jo Burbee from the last chapter? They couldn't agree on whether to have more children. Mary Jo wanted to add to their family, but Bob worried that he couldn't provide for a larger family. Their conflict went on for some time. Eventually they managed to help the other understand their very different gut-level feelings, and each made a commitment to make sure that the other didn't feel like a loser. So what happened?

"Interestingly," Bob said, "the decision about more children was made for us. We discovered not long after this trip that in spite of using contraception, Mary Jo was pregnant."

So did Mary Jo win and Bob lose? People often ask Bob this very question. "My answer," he said, "has everything to do with those hours we spent on that road trip, listening and trying to understand one another in a fresh way. Without a new, expanded perspective on the issue gained from understanding what motherhood meant to Mary Jo, I have no doubt the news of our pregnancy would have been very difficult for me to take. The broader perspective didn't eliminate my anxiety, but it did allow me to embrace the pregnancy and join Mary Jo in her excitement about another baby. In fact, I so enjoyed having the third child, I like to take credit for suggesting that we have a fourth. Eighteen months after Allison was born, our fourth child, Travis, joined our family—and I can't imagine my life without them."

And what does this have to do with a no-losers policy? "We kept talking because we chose to work on the issue until we both felt some satisfaction that kept us talking about the issue of more children," Bob explained. "Mary Jo wasn't going to trick me, and I wasn't content to let her feel as if she were losing. It took us awhile, but the principle of no-losers kept us working at the issue until we finally hit on the mutual understanding that we so desperately needed." And then God took care of the rest.

Once you establish a no-losers policy, things start changing pretty quickly, often dramatically. This is true even if only one person in the relationship commits himself or herself to the no-losers policy. Remember the Power of One. Once the other person discovers that you *will* consider his or her feelings and needs, those same feelings and needs cease to be something to worry about. Consider a no-losers policy a potent vaccination against the worry of getting the shaft.

Laura and her sister Sally are often at loggerheads. But if Laura makes it clear that she will not feel satisfied about a decision or issue until Sally also does, then all of Sally's worry about losing goes away. She starts to relax and becomes far more cooperative. She knows that Laura will never force her to accept a solution that she doesn't feel good about.

Shortly after a no-losers policy gets established in a relationship, it starts to become almost automatic. Neither person has to say, "Okay, let's implement the no-losers policy here." It becomes a constant, almost like the law of gravity. You both see it as a nonnegotiable: Either you both win, or you both lose. Period.

So does a no-losers policy end all conflicts in a relationship? Does it do away with all relational losses? That would be nice, but Bob Paul admits it hasn't turned out quite that way.

"I'm not going to say that I never set up adversaries in relationships anymore," he says. "It happens. It's happened plenty of times—it's just not okay. It's not acceptable."

Such a commitment goes a long way toward creating the kind of relationships that yield joy and satisfaction rather than grief and frustration. It's worked for Bob and Jenni, it's worked for Bob and Mary Jo, and it can work equally well for you, regardless of the type of relationship in which you apply it.

A Different Definition of Winning

To make this new dance step work for you, you have to come up with a different definition of winning. If you make winning about getting your own way—in any way, shape, or form—you're still locked into the old pattern and still headed for the relationship rocks.

Many of us resist at this point because we really do think we know what's best in any given conflict. We usually have a fairly high opinion of our own perception of a sticky situation. God knows this ugly fact about us; that's why he calls us to humility. He asks us to admit that we really don't have a corner on the wisdom market. He reminds us, "There is a path before each person that seems right, but it ends in death."[1] Sometimes, by insisting on our own way, we kill our most cherished relationships.

So be open to the possibility that even though a particular course of action seems right to you, it really may not be the best alternative. And it certainly isn't the only one. Therefore, don't lock yourself into a single view (yours). Don't insist on your path and no other. Sure, you want to win. I do too. But maybe winning isn't about getting your own way.

Remember, you're part of a team. Therefore you have to redefine winning as *finding and implementing a solution that both people can feel good about.* A winning solution goes beyond a plan of attack that seems merely acceptable or tolerable to you both. That's compromise, and compromises rarely make anyone feel good.

→ WINNING IS FINDING A SOLUTION BOTH PEOPLE FEEL GOOD ABOUT.

"A compromise is a deal in which two people get what neither of them wanted," says one anonymous definition. "A compromise is the art of dividing a cake in a way that everyone believes he has gotten the biggest piece," declares another version.[2] Compromise usually leaves a bad taste in someone's mouth, and therefore it seldom, if ever, is the answer. Collaboration works. Compromise and capitulation don't.

A win-win solution that makes both parties feel good gives positive movement to the relationship and leaves it in a better place than it was before. You take a trip and end up someplace other than where you started, a beautiful and delightful place. And how do you get there? It varies.

"Sometimes we have ended up doing exactly what Jenni wanted to do from the beginning," Bob Paul says, "but by the time we got there, I felt great about it. It didn't feel like a loss for me. At other times the opposite has happened; we've done exactly what I wanted to do, but by the time we got there, Jenni felt fine about it. So it wasn't a loss for her."

The ideas generated through such a commitment to win-win solutions often come as a total surprise to both parties. At the beginning, neither partner may foresee or predict the eventual solution.

Bob and Jenni often feel this way. "Sometimes we come up with creative solutions that neither one of us would have thought about before," he says. "At other times we negotiate and piece something together—a little of hers, a little of mine. But our goal—both of us feeling good about our decision—remains the same, no matter how we get there."

Has this new way of defining "winning" changed anything in the Paul household? "It's made a huge difference," Bob says. "It's positively affected our relationship in many ways. For one thing, our home feels safer. Neither of us has to worry about getting railroaded into something we don't want."

You tend to relax when winning becomes finding and implementing a solution that both people can feel good about. Why? Because you don't have to worry that the other person will accept a solution that makes him or her feel bad.

"At times I've gotten so focused on what I wanted that, after a while, I beat Jenni down," Bob admits. "Eventually she wore out and gave up. But it always catches me when she says, 'Okay, just go ahead and do it.'

"I'll respond, 'Do you feel as if you're losing here?'

"'Well, yes,' she'll say, 'but I'm just too tired to keep tussling.'

"'Jenni, I'm sorry. That's not okay. I'm sorry I let it go that way. Rather than just drop it, I'd like us to keep at this thing until we come up with something that both of us feel good about.'"

Is Bob being merely kind or altruistic when he walks down this road? Hardly. He realizes it's the only way he can win. He's part of a team, and everyone on a team either wins or loses together.

Working Together

Even though the Bible doesn't talk about what our culture calls team sports, it does have a lot to say about working together for a common goal. Rather than using the image of a team, it draws on the picture of a body to convey the same idea. The apostle Paul wrote, "There should be no division in the body, but . . . its parts should have equal concern for each other. If one part suffers, every part suffers with it; if one part is honored, every part rejoices with it."[3]

Imagine what would happen if your body tried to function according to the rules of a win-lose system. Suppose your heart and your kidneys got into a heated debate about which one most needed a steady blood supply, winner take all.

"Hey, I pump blood through the whole body," declares the heart. "Without me, every organ dies—including you!"

"That may be," retorts the kidneys, "but if the blood doesn't go through me, all you accomplish with your incessant pumping is to poison the entire system. And then guess who dies?"

Silly? Of course it is. Does it really matter who "wins" the debate? Because both the heart and the kidneys live as part of a single body, what affects one affects them both. The heart cannot "win" at the expense of the kidneys any more than the kidneys can "win" at the expense of the heart. They *have* to find a win-win solution because a win-lose solution is nothing but a loss. Could the heart "win" its debate by arguing that the body would die almost immediately without its services? Maybe. But if the kidneys lost and shut down, both organs will die anyway—and in a great deal of pain.

In a relationship there is no such thing as a win-lose solution. There is either win-win or lose-lose. No other options exist.

→ IN HEALTHY RELATIONSHIPS EVERYONE WINS.

The apostle Paul labored to get his young churches to understand this basic principle. In passage after passage he pled with them to cooperate, to work together, to find solutions that benefited everyone. He told one church, "Don't be selfish; don't live to make a good impression on others. Be humble, thinking of others as better than yourself. Don't think only about your own affairs, but be interested in others, too, and what they are doing."[4]

His advice is a no-losers policy. When we commit ourselves to implementing such a cooperative strategy in all our significant relationships, we set ourselves up for success. In other words, we all win!

Different Dynamics for Different Relationships

Even though the no-losers policy applies to every successful relationship, it does not apply in exactly the same way. Why not? Because different kinds of relationships—husband-wife, parent-child, employer-employee, teacher-student, supervisor-volunteer, friend-friend—have different starting points and different ground rules.

Consider marriage, for example, the closest kind of relationship that two humans can enjoy. In marriage a man and a woman come together before God and pledge themselves to one another in a binding commitment of love, what the Bible calls a "covenant." As we noted earlier, God considers a husband and a wife "united into one."[5] Jesus explicitly said, "They are no longer two but one."[6] In the case of marriage, then, we can apply the no-losers policy quite literally. If either husband or wife loses in a given situation, the relationship always loses. Since they are no longer two but one, they *have* to find win-win solutions. They have no other option if they want to enjoy relationship success.

The scene shifts a little, however, for other kinds of relationships. Other types of relationships do not involve the kind of "two becoming one" that marriage does. Therefore, while the no-losers policy cannot always be applied literally, it should always be applied in spirit. In *every* relationship you can make it your explicit goal that both people in the relationship feel good about a decision or course of action—even though you might occasionally fall short of your goal. The very existence of the goal, however, improves the relationship.

Think of the relationship between a parent and a child. The parent has legitimate, God-given power and authority that the child does not, and therefore that parent may have to make some decisions that the child may dislike. But what happens when a son knows that his dad considers both of them on the same team and that he wants both of them to win? What happens when a daughter knows that her mom wants, as much as possible, to find solutions that they both can support? What happens when the kids hear, "I want you to know that I am going to try hard to come up with a solution that you can feel good about, and I won't feel satisfied with something that you don't feel good about"?

I know a dad who occasionally says to his kids, "I know you really like this idea, but I have to tell you that, as a caring father, this does not feel good to me. This concerns me, and in good conscience I can't let it happen. Let's see if we can come up with something else, and we'll just keep at it until we find a solution that works for all of us." Sometimes they can't come up with a plan that suits all of them, and my friend has to say, "I'm sorry, but right now it doesn't seem as if we can come up with anything. So therefore I am going to have to make a decision, even though you may not like it." You wouldn't believe what a positive effect it has on these kids to know that their dad is trying hard to work according to the spirit of the no-losers policy!

The spirit of the no-losers policy also applies in the workplace. If I know that my boss feels very concerned about making decisions that work for me, I can relax and give my best to my job. I feel good about being his or her employee. Of course, at times an employer has to make difficult and unpopular decisions for the health of the company. But even then, the spirit of the no-losers policy can come into play. People committed to win-win will find a way to walk through even a layoff or termination so that people feel valued, honored, and convinced that the employer did everything possible to make the situation work.

Even in relationships that do not have the authority structure that a parent-child relationship or a boss-employee relationship has, you can still have the same win-win spirit. You can work toward a no-losers policy in friendships or between neighbors or among volunteers at church or anywhere else. When the other person in a relationship knows that you are always looking for a solution that both of you can feel good about, the clouds part and the sun shines through—even if the eventual decision disappoints one or both of you.

The bottom line is this: The no-losers policy conveys a deep sense of caring. Whether you apply it literally or in spirit, your spouse or children or family members or friends will know that you care about their feelings and that you will do whatever you can to treat them as valuable human beings.

Seven Steps to Win-Win Solutions

Once we choose to establish a no-losers policy, we never again have to worry about losing or about protecting our own agenda. We find little to fuss about and quickly learn how to reach efficient and quick decisions over matters that used to cause ugly problems. Let me offer a seven-step process to reaching win-win solutions.

STEP 1: ESTABLISH A NO-LOSERS POLICY

When you consciously establish a no-losers policy, you create a positive tone that tends to radically improve how you treat one another. You could say, "I need you to know that I will not feel okay with any solution that you do not also feel good about." All either one of you has to say is, "I don't feel good about this decision," or, "I feel as if I'm losing here," and that's it. You back up and start over. It simply is unacceptable for either of you to feel as if you're losing.

A no-losers policy is like a fire extinguisher that puts out a dangerous flare-up. It says to each person, "You don't need to feel threatened because we won't go forward until both of us feel good about it."

If you did nothing more than this, you would see an enormous improvement in your relationships. The worry simply dissipates.

STEP 2: LISTEN TO HOW THE OTHER FEELS

Talk to each other. Listen for the heart. Try to understand the emotions the other is feeling and why he or she prefers a particular solution. Why does it seem like the right way to go? Why is it important? Try to understand the "big deal" for the other. Work at it until both of you feel completely understood.

Once you finish this, take your separate ideas and set them aside. Put them on the shelf. You don't throw them away or pursue them; you simply set them aside. Keep them handy in case you want to go back to them at a later time.

STEP 3: ASK GOD FOR HIS OPINION

Some conflicts get resolved very quickly once you ask God whether he has an opinion on what you ought to do. Pray about the issue you are trying to resolve. Share your perspectives about what you think the Bible says about the issue, remembering that the Bible will not speak to every issue, of course.

But do you want to know something really awesome? It virtually does not matter in the end whether God has an opinion on the matter. For in the very act of coming together to discover God's perspective, you're working toward unity.

I have a friend who had a pretty good squabble with his wife over what color to paint their bedroom. Now, I doubt very much that God cares a fig about what color their bedroom should be, but the act of coming together and prayerfully asking him whether he had an opinion—coupled with the commitment to yield to him if he did—immediately reestablished unity in this couple. By seeking God's will together, they got on the same page.

If you discover that you really don't feel like praying together over some issue, it's probably a good indication that you shouldn't be trying to resolve the conflict quite yet. If you go ahead anyway, you're more likely to speak like adversaries than partners. So hold off until you can both find God's grace to help you.[7]

STEP 4: BRAINSTORM ABOUT A WIN-WIN SOLUTION
Look for creative solutions. Hear each other out. Give each person an opportunity to lay on the table any suggestion he or she thinks might work. Make sure that this is a "green light" session, a time when both of you feel safe to share ideas. Don't judge the ideas at this point. Just get them out where you can both consider them. It's fair to ask clarifying questions about some of the ideas, but don't judge them until you've exhausted your creativity. Then, revisit them all, highlighting the ones that might help you to solve your dilemma. If you feel you need more input, do some research at the library or on the Internet. You might consult with an expert. The goal is to explore lots of options.

STEP 5: SELECT A WIN-WIN SOLUTION
Now it's time to find a win-win solution, something that you both can feel good about. It doesn't matter who suggests the proposed solution; the only important thing is that both of you can endorse it.

When I think back on how Norma and I have worked through this process, I can point to many times when I have ended up doing exactly what Norma wanted to do from the beginning. But by the time we got there, I had endorsed her perspective. It ceased being a win-lose and became a win-win. We also have ended up doing exactly what I wanted to do from the beginning. But by the time we got there, Norma decided that my suggestion was the one we should pursue. As long as we both feel great about the decision, we find a win-win solution. And that's what we're after.

STEP 6: IMPLEMENT YOUR SOLUTION
After you hammer out something that looks as if it might work for both of you, try it out. But go into it with the same spirit that helped

you to identify this option—making sure that both of you still consider it a win-win.

I think of the way Norma and I used to do vacations. Norma liked to have everything scheduled and planned, long before we took off. We knew where we were staying, what we would be doing, the whole works. And as a person who likes spontaneity, I hated it. So on other vacations, I forced Norma to camp for three weeks in one spot, next to a stream—which drove her almost insane. While I love to fish, she loves to shop and visit antique stores and malls.

Finally, we listened to each other's heart and chose to work toward a win-win solution. We decided to combine our tastes. On our favorite vacations, we don't know where we're going to stay the first night. We rent a car, ask for the best direction to drive, and head that way. We have found the most incredible places to stay! The best thing is, I'll drive until I find a great river or stream, where I'll stop and fish for an hour. Meanwhile, Norma reads in the shade, something she loves. Then we'll enter a town, find a great place to stay, and I'll help her look for an antique shop. By the end of the day, we both feel so fulfilled. We both feel like winners!

STEP 7: EVALUATE AND REWORK
YOUR SOLUTION IF NECESSARY

A real win-win has to stay a win-win. At times in the past Norma and I ended up doing what I wanted to do, and I had the attitude, "Okay, you agreed to it, so now you are going to live with it, whether you continue to like it or not." Not good! If at any point the solution stops working for either of you, then someone feels like a loser, and that hurts the team. For the solution to be a win-win, it has to stay a win-win.

Many times we think we have dreamed up a really great idea, only to find out that it doesn't work as well as we'd hoped. "I didn't think about that," we say, or, "That's not nearly as good as I thought it would be." If you make such a discovery, don't sweat it. Just rework your solution. Remember, you want to start and end with a win-win. You want to make sure that your team stays on the successful side of things.

Forty-Five Minutes to a Win-Win

Bruce and Samantha, just three weeks away from their wedding day, kept having the same argument. Samantha wanted the wedding videographer to tape what happened in Bruce's dressing room as he got himself ready for the ceremony. Bruce resisted the idea and wouldn't agree to the taping.

The couple came to our counseling center for a premarital intensive training day, and we helped them work through the seven steps to win-win solutions.

Step 1: Establish a no-losers policy. We reminded them that they were on the same team and both needed to feel good about whatever solution they picked. We helped them commit to a win-win solution, no matter what it took.

Step 2: Listen to how the other feels. We helped them talk about and listen to their emotional messages. Samantha thought it would be very meaningful if she could later see what Bruce was doing and saying before they said their vows. She felt hurt and misunderstood by his resistance to the idea. Bruce said that he did not want these very private moments to be the subject of a video, seen by all their friends and family members. Eventually they both really heard the other's point of view and saw its validity and importance.

Step 3: Ask God for his opinion. The two of them prayed together and later told us that neither of them felt God had an opinion about the video. However, they did see the need to be respectful and gentle with one another as they negotiated the issue.

Step 4: Brainstorm about a win-win solution. As the brainstorming began, the options flowed:

- No video in dressing rooms.
- Video in dressing rooms.
- Take still photos of this time.
- Audiotape this part.
- Create a separate, "private" tape for themselves that would include this preparation time. They could show an alternate version to others, not including this footage.
- Have a groomsman take a private, amateur video of this part of getting ready so Samantha could watch it later; but it wouldn't be included on the professionally produced video.
- Call each other by cell phone from their separate dressing rooms and check in with one another.

Step 5: Select a win-win solution. They both liked the sound of option 6.

Step 6: Implement your solution. They agreed to try out option 6.

Step 7: Evaluate and rework your solution if necessary. They agreed to revisit their plan three days before the wedding and make sure they both still felt good about it. This would also give them time to work on an alternative, if necessary.

Bruce and Samantha told us that they both felt great about the process—and it took them only about forty-five minutes to pull off a win-win!

Who's to say that you couldn't pull off something similar in even less time than that? You're probably not even having last-minute jitters!

Two Objections Answered

Some people who have never seen a no-losers policy at work hesitate to implement it in their relationships. They have two objections:

1. It will take too much time. "I don't have the time to go through all of these steps," some say. "With all the disagreements we have, it would take *forever!*"

But do you know what I have discovered? A no-losers policy actually saves huge chunks of time, especially once it becomes a habit. Here's why.

When you feel as if you have to defend your territory, you tend to dig in your heels for a protracted and tiring tug-of-war. The battle continues until one or the other person just wears out—and that can take a long, long time.

When you implement a no-losers policy, however, you stop having to worry about protecting your agenda. You no longer feel anxious that your feelings won't be considered. And when those issues go away, the substance of your disagreements usually turns out to be pretty small. Since you now have very little to fuss about, you move through the process quickly. It's very efficient and doesn't take much time at all. Much of it, in fact, becomes almost unconscious, like breathing.

2. What if we cannot come to an agreement and somebody has to make a decision? You know what? It hardly ever happens. Remember, the problem is rarely the problem. If you follow through on the new

167

dance steps I'm teaching you, you'll hardly ever arrive at the difficult situation described above.

But what if you do? Let me tell you something else I've discovered. Most "urgent" decisions—things that drive me to hurry up, that tell me that I'm almost out of time, that insist I'm about to miss the opportunity of a lifetime—almost always end up being less than urgent. The opportunity either was not as good as it looked (something I couldn't know from my vantage point), or another, even better, opportunity had not yet presented itself. I often realize that if I had moved on the first decision, I would have missed out on the second.

In general, I prefer to hold off on such decisions until the other person and I can arrive at a place of unity. But if the decision really does need to be made, I try to determine who appears to be the most qualified to make it—based on experience or training or something else—and let that person decide. Too often guys say things like, "Listen, I'm the man, so therefore I need to say what goes!" It almost becomes a Tarzan chest-thumping exercise, and it can kill you.

These days, if I feel compelled to make a decision that Norma opposes, I'll do it with great caution. I'll tell her, "I feel led to make this decision, but I have to tell you that because you and I are not together on this, I'm open to the possibility that I might be wrong. Therefore, I will make the decision, but I want you to know that I will also take the heat if I'm wrong. And I will be the one to answer to God. You are off the hook." This is very different from saying, "I'm the man, so back off because I make the decisions around here!"

You Can Choose

Picture yourself in a rowboat, gliding down the river with your friend or coworker or spouse. Suddenly an argument erupts. You see a shotgun resting in the bottom of the boat, and to make your point, you seize the gun and start blowing holes in the bottom of your little vessel.

You might get your point across—but what happens to the boat? It sinks. And who's in the boat? Your partner . . . and you. What a fine time you'll have, celebrating your "victory" all the way to the bottom of the river!

Remember this: In any kind of significant relationship, you can't win unless the other person also wins. So in your own best interest, you have to make sure that he or she wins. For exactly the same reason, the other person has to make sure that you win. The only alternative is that you both lose.

When you choose to enter into a significant relationship with another person, you're also choosing to become a member of a team. All relationships involve choice. You can choose whether that team is going to succeed or fail. You decide whether it brings you pain or delight. It's your choice.

In the 1988 Olympics, the powerful U.S. men's volleyball team made it to the semifinals. One of its players, Paul Samuelson, cursed at a referee during a game. Judges assessed the U.S. team one penalty point, ultimately costing the Americans the game and a chance at a gold medal.

The next day the U.S. team returned to the arena to play for the bronze medal. As the team took the court, observers noticed that many of its members had shaved their heads. The spectators wondered why. Was it for improved aerodynamics? Was it to somehow spite the judges? Was it to make a fashion statement? No. The players did it for one simple reason: They had a bald teammate named Paul Samuelson. Through their unusual hairstyle choice they were telling the world, "Paul may have been wrong, but he is still our friend. He blew it, but he is still part of our team."

Members of a team win together, or they lose together. Partners in a relationship experience exactly the same thing—except that in relationships you choose every day whether you will win or lose.

What will you choose?

LIFE IS RELATIONSHIPS;
THE REST IS JUST DETAILS.

ONE-MINUTE REVIEW
TEAMWORK: ADOPT A NO-LOSERS POLICY

1. **Adopt a no-losers policy.** When one person in a relationship loses, everyone loses. A no-losers policy works toward mutual understanding and a win-win.

2. **Winning is finding a solution both people feel good about.** Winning is not compromise but a true sense of win-win.

3. **In healthy relationships, everyone wins.** If we see relationships as teamwork, we can commit ourselves to working on cooperative strategies.

4. **Seven steps to win-win solutions:**

   - Step 1: Establish a no-losers policy.
   - Step 2: Listen to how the other feels.
   - Step 3: Ask God for his opinion.
   - Step 4: Brainstorm about a win-win solution.
   - Step 5: Select a win-win solution.
   - Step 6: Implement your solution.
   - Step 7: Evaluate and rework your solution if necessary.

PART THREE
THE NEXT STEP

9

WHAT WE CAN CHANGE

"I did everything you told me to," an agitated client says, "and it doesn't work. I identified my core fear, took personal responsibility, tried to create a safe environment, did good self-care, improved my communication skills, worked hard on teamwork—and still my spouse drives me crazy. I'm telling you, it doesn't work."

We don't hear complaints like this very often, but we do hear them. We usually reply with something like this: "If you carefully follow the plan of action we've laid out, we firmly believe that you'll be well on your way toward building a strong, healthy, growing relationship. But we have to say that it's possible to do all the 'right' things and still not get the relationship that you most desire. We would be less than honest if we said that by learning and practicing the effective relationship principles we've just taught you, you're 100 percent assured of getting everything you want out of a relationship. You're not."

I know, that's a bitter pill to swallow. It disillusions some people almost to a crippling extent. But it really doesn't need to.

A Caveat

Relationship experts have to make sure that we don't nurture the hurtful fallacy that "if you do this, this and this, then you're *guaranteed* to have great relationships." Such an unrealistic promise can set us up to feel very discouraged and disillusioned.

Once again, here's the cold, hard reality: You can do everything I've outlined in this book and *still* not get the relationships that you want. Somehow this unsettling reality seems missing from most books about relationships. It's not hard to see why. Who wants to admit the possibility of less than perfect success? Authors and seminar leaders want everyone to believe that when they finish this book or complete that conference, they will have all the power they need to "make it happen."

While in some ways such a claim speaks genuine truth, in another very fundamental way it does not. It *is* true that by applying these powerful concepts and techniques to your relationships, you will set yourself up for your best chance at success. It *is* true that by living in the way God has outlined, you create a fertile environment in which healthy relationships can grow and flourish. We can tell you what we have found are the easiest paths to great relationships. That's all true—but it's a far cry from a guarantee of success. And such a realization frustrates us.

And yet that emphatically does *not* mean that the concepts and techniques in this book "don't work." Far from it!

The Change God Most Wants

In my experience, "It doesn't work" most often means, "My partner's habits and behavior continue to make my life miserable." "It doesn't work" usually translates into some form of, "I can't get my partner to change."

But what if that isn't what God most wants? What if God most wants to change *you*?

My colleagues ran headlong into this dilemma a couple of years ago during a difficult marriage intensive. The husband had habitually and seriously mismanaged his family's finances. He spent a lot of money to cover debts on crazy investments that lost his family thousands of dollars, and then he tried to hide everything from his wife. Whenever she found evidence of his reckless use of the household funds, he'd fabricate a chain of lies. To make things worse, the man served as an elder in his local church. The wife felt beside herself with frustration.

This woman desperately wanted her husband to change and to

become a person of integrity—not at all a bad desire! The trouble was, she thought she could somehow *force* her husband into becoming the kind of person she wanted. She kept telling us, "I've gone to the conferences. I've read all the books. We've been to counseling three different times. And none of it works."

Do you see her problem? Her idea of "what works" came down to "whatever will force my husband to change." In our view, she had been doggedly pursuing the wrong goal. She wanted to know, What can I do to get my husband to act like I want him to act? What system, what technique, will manipulate him into acting in a more responsible way? As long as this woman defined "what works" as "what forces my husband to change," she felt angry. She didn't reach a turning point until she started thinking about her problem in a new way.

"What happens," we asked her, "if you ask a different question? Instead of asking, 'What will work to get him to change,' what if you asked, 'What kind of person should *I* be?'"

The question caught her up short. Eventually it put her on a new path. She started to realize that the crazy woman whom she heard yelling at her husband was not the person she wanted to be. She finally admitted to herself that all the energy she expended acting as her own private detective—trying to find out whether he lied or told the truth—amounted to wasted time and a totally ineffective use of her limited resources. So she stopped asking, "What will work to get my husband to change?" and instead began to ask, "How can I choose to become the person God wants me to be?"

Remember a relationship truth we mentioned in an earlier chapter: Choice equals change. When we choose a path, it will always involve change. Even though change may feel threatening, in this case it is the right path.

I think you'll find it most helpful to follow her excellent example. Think of it this way: To the extent that you define the problem or the goal in terms of the other person, you remain paralyzed. You will have no power to change anything. You'll remain as helpless to *make* that person change as a quadriplegic remains helpless to leap up from a wheelchair and set a world record in the 100-meter dash.

YOU CAN'T FORCE THE ←
OTHER PERSON TO CHANGE.

I suggest that you'll find the key in rethinking your answer to the question "What am I trying to accomplish?" Could it perhaps be more helpful to develop some objectives that hold out a high probability of success? And please believe me, a goal of changing the other person does *not* rank high on any such list.

Personal Change and Serendipity

It's a shame that the word *serendipity* doesn't get used much anymore. It's a great word. It means an aptitude for unexpectedly making desirable discoveries.

Serendipity often happens when you ask God how he might want to change *you* rather than focusing on what you can do to change the other person. When we make it our goal to change our own behavior rather than the other person's, that person often notices the positive transformation taking place in us and begins his or her own journey of personal change.

That's not a promise. But serendipity happens.

Remember the man who badly mishandled his family's finances and then lied about his despicable behavior? When his wife exercised the Power of One and started focusing on the kind of person God wanted *her* to be, she started to enjoy life. She stopped screaming at her husband and gave up trying to catch him in his lies. She didn't do this to try to force her husband into becoming a man of integrity. She did it for herself and for her own peace of mind. She wanted her husband to change, of course—who wouldn't?—but regardless of how he responded, she intended to pursue God's pathway for her.

Eventually, this woman walked into a wonderful serendipity. As she began to move in the direction of spiritual and emotional maturity, her husband's own irresponsibility became increasingly evident to him. Since he no longer spent so much time resisting her, he had much more time to focus on his own shortcomings. In time, the illogic and dysfunction of his own behavior became painfully clear to him. Eventually he felt convicted enough to change, *but not because his wife nagged him to do so.*

→ THE ONLY PERSON YOU CAN CHANGE IS YOURSELF.

This woman enjoyed a happy ending to her story only because she consciously changed her focus. She shifted her attention from changing her husband to changing herself. At no point along the way did she *cause* or *force* her husband to change; she understood that she had no control over his behavior. But as her husband saw the positive difference in her, God's presence within him prompted him to make his own necessary changes.

Thank God serendipity happens!

What If Your Desires for Change Go Unfulfilled?

Most of us like the word *guarantee* better than the word *serendipity*–but if we insist on the former, we may get only a broken heart. What if the steps you take to change yourself don't result in any change in the other person? What if *nothing* prompts him or her to change?

In such a case, serendipity can still happen–just not, perhaps, the one you longed for. If you choose to travel the road of personal transformation, the worst that can happen is that you will end up with a life that's far more enjoyable, satisfying, fulfilling, and helpful to others than the one you had while you continued to insist on changing the other person. Even so, I have to admit, you may never get your heart's desire.

A woman reported an amazing serendipity in one of my small support groups recently. The seventy-year-old shared her story of being married to a very self-centered man. She tried to change him the first few years and finally gave up. She asked God to change *her* instead. She says that the best thing she learned was to give up any expectation that her husband would ever change and to work only on herself. She prayed for her husband, but gave up other expectations. The only thing she tried to stop him from doing was buying her expensive jewelry. But he refused and continued to buy the jewelry.

Even though the woman could not get her husband to change, she could change herself. And she did. She became a happy person by loving and receiving love from family and friends and by letting God fill her with the fullness of himself.[1] After her husband retired, he lost all of their savings in various foolish investments and left the couple completely broke. How do you think they survived the next few years? You guessed it. By living on the sale of the very expensive jewelry she had resented. In a serendipitous provision, God used the jewelry to provide for the woman and her husband.

We at the Smalley Relationship Center and the National Institute of Marriage have no magic cures for relationships, no guaranteed secrets for making all your dreams come true, no fail-safe promises of relational paradise. While we have helped more than 90 percent of the troubled couples that visit us to find new satisfaction and fulfillment in their relationships, there remains that just-under 10 percent that still winds up in divorce court. Despite our best efforts and the expressed desire of at least one person in each couple to remain together, the relationship breaks up.

How can this be? If the desire is there—a desire that God himself endorses—then shouldn't there always be a happy ending? Shouldn't things always turn out the way we want? Shouldn't there be some guarantee that if we do things a certain way, we'll always get what we most hope for?

Well, maybe there should be. But it doesn't look as if there is. Serendipity, perhaps. Guarantees, no.

David, the biblical king of ancient Israel, made this disconcerting discovery thousands of years ago. He wanted to build a temple for the God he loved so deeply. One day he asked the prophet Nathan about his idea, and Nathan told him to go for it. David then eagerly set about gathering the necessary craftsmen and supplies and resources to build a magnificent temple for the God of Israel. Everything seemed to be going great.

But the next day Nathan reappeared with some startling news, decisively derailing the king's hopes and plans. "Are you the one to build me a temple to live in?" God asked David.[2] God informed him, "Since you have shed so much blood before me, you will not be the one to build a temple to honor my name."[3] Yet don't miss a critical part of the story. At the same time, God also expressly told David that it was "right" to have this desire to build the Temple!

Please don't miss the point. Was it a good thing that David desired to build a temple for his God? Emphatically, yes! God himself endorsed David's desire, telling the king, "It is right for you to want to build the Temple to honor my name."[4] Yet did God allow David to actually build the Temple? No, he did not. The happy job of Temple construction fell to David's son and successor, Solomon. While God approved of David's desire, he also refused to fulfill his desire.

I think this ancient episode has much to teach us today. It tells us that, at least sometimes, it is possible to have a good desire in our hearts—a desire that God himself endorses—and yet never see that desire completely fulfilled.

A hard truth to take? You bet. But never forget about serendipity! God certainly doesn't.

David had to feel enormous disappointment when it became clear that he would never be able to fulfill his good desire. The divine decision came as a complete surprise to him; he had already started to put things in motion. Yet God had not exhausted his surprises! God knows a thing or two about serendipity. He subsequently told David that, although he would not permit him to act on his good desire to build a house of worship, God would instead build a "house" for David—a family tree that would eventually produce the Messiah, Jesus Christ, the Savior and Lord of the world.[5] Amazing! While David did not see his heart's desire fulfilled, God had something different (and even greater) in mind for him.

That's serendipity. And that's also a stunning picture of what God can do for you. You may lose a spouse, fall into disharmony with grown children, or lose a close friend through a disagreement, but it doesn't mean those relationships are lost forever. You and I know of situations in which people have reunited later in life, much to their joy.

What Power Do You Have?

If you find yourself saying, "It's not working," then it may be time to ask, "What am I trying to accomplish? What is my goal or objective?"

If your goal is to change the other person, then you have set yourself up for frustration. Instead, try asking yourself, "What power do I actually have?"

It seems to me that the best answer to that question—the greatest goal with the highest likelihood of success—is to become the man or woman that God has created you to be. You have a lot of say and a lot of power over your own personal transformation. Your choice to focus on yourself certainly has the potential to affect the other person, but only as a secondary consequence—a serendipity—rather than as a goal.

Does this feel like a difficult challenge? I don't deny it. If the other person has checked out of the relationship, you naturally want to do something to bring him or her back. But if you make that your major objective, understand that you're setting yourself up for frustration.

I've even seen people insist that their main goal was to become the man or woman God wanted them to be—even as they continued to pursue the other goal. All of us are fully capable of playing mind games with ourselves. But what happens when we do this? The other person usually senses the manipulation, and so all our efforts fail.

Panicked, Tim called me one morning, expressing his fear that his wife was leaving him that very day. Tim didn't know that his wife, Sarah, had already told me. Two days before she left, she said, "I tried on numerous occasions to get Tim's attention. But he never seems to hear me." When she finally took off, Tim just came apart. He felt crushed, broken. At that point, our conversations took a completely different turn. Finally I could say things that Tim had refused to hear many times before.

One of the chief topics we discussed involved Tim's need to focus on the things he had the power to change rather than on the things out of his control. "You can stay where you are if you want," I said, "but the problem is, if you stay there, you instantly put yourself in a powerless position. As long as you think of everything that's going on as outside of you, you remain a victim. You have no control over anything, no power in your situation at all. You can stay there if you want—but I know I would prefer to focus on the things I do have power over, so at least I can have some say or some hand in making things better for me."

Even with the Best of Intentions

Let me clear up one more possible misconception before we move on to the final chapter. Some people get discouraged, not because they fail to get the relationship they always desired, but because they don't enjoy such a relationship all of the time. They wrongly think that once they understand and put into practice the principles in this book, they can kiss all relationship conflicts good-bye.

The truth is, it's possible to know all about the Fear Dance and what pushes your own button. It's possible to become skilled at all the new dance steps that allow you to do a new dance. But any of us can fall back into the hurtful steps of the Fear Dance, even when we have the best of intentions.

Michael and his wife, Amy, are very aware of the Fear Dance and of their personal core fears. Yet sometimes, they—like Norma and me, and anyone else—still fall into the old patterns.

Sundays are usually pretty hard for Michael and Amy. Every Sunday night about fifty high-school students from their church meet at their house. Michael and Amy have to get ready for the group at the same time that they take care of their own young family.

One day Michael and Amy got home from church and immediately had to start cleaning. They both felt very tired, but since Amy had been up much of the previous night with their baby, Michael said, "Why don't you get some sleep? I'll start cleaning now, and when you wake up, everything will be fine."

"That would be great," Amy replied. So she slept for two hours. Meanwhile, Michael cleaned. He cleaned the whole time. But because he takes after his dad (I'm ADHD), he doesn't clean the way Amy does. He goes from one thing to another; he never completes anything in one sweep.

Finally Amy woke up. She came upstairs, saw that Michael had made the bed and picked up Cole's shoes, but he hadn't yet cleaned up the mess on the floor. She was frustrated that the job had not been done well, and she reacted by accusing Michael of loafing.

"Wait a minute!" Michael said. "Let's be fair. You've been sleeping for *two hours* while I've been cleaning the whole time. Why are you so upset?"

His question didn't make her mood any better, and she started belittling him and his efforts at cleaning. He soon felt hurt and bruised emotionally. Finally he decided to gather the kids and leave the house, which by this time felt totally unsafe to him. When he announced his plan, Amy protested, so he and the kids ended up staying.

Later that day, after things had calmed down, Michael thought he would be Mr. Helpful. He approached Amy in the bedroom and said, very softly, "Hey, can we talk about today? I'm really hurt and confused over what happened."

"Sure," she replied.

"Look," he said, "here's the deal. The way you treated me today made me feel bloodied and bruised. I felt like a corpse lying in its own pool of blood. When you treat me like this, it makes me want to die to you or to desensitize myself to where I just don't want to care." He figured he spoke the truth, and that this was a good thing.

Amy didn't.

She reacted with strong words, and her negative reaction totally baffled Michael. When he saw this conversation going nowhere, he dropped it.

The next day they didn't talk about the incident. Then came Tuesday, the day they help lead a small group from church. Michael asked Amy, "I think we're stuck on our conflict. What if we ask the group to help us?"

Not only did Amy not want to discuss their conflict with the group, she didn't even want to go to the group meeting. "But Amy," Michael pleaded, "this is what the group is all about. We can't avoid it."

They ended up going to the group and telling their story. Their pastor, who is very aware of the Fear Dance, said to Michael, "Don't you see how you tapped into her fear when you acted as you did?"

"No," Michael replied, completely unaware. "What are you talking about?"

"Well," his pastor reminded him, "her fear is fear of abandonment or rejection."

Suddenly everything made total sense. When Michael threatened to leave the house, he pushed Amy's fear button, big time. It took a third person to bring clarity. Their pastor's comments opened up both Michael and Amy and produced a very powerful moment for the two of them.

"Here I thought I had been so perfect and nice and healthy," Michael said, "when I hadn't been at all." And Amy also saw how she had gone on the attack.

Even with the best of intentions, even when we know this material backward and forward, we can still slip into the old patterns and make a mess of things. But, thank God, when we realize our mistake, we have the ability to stop the madness and get back to sanity—and back to building a healthy, safe, satisfying relationship.

One More Time

I could not feel more strongly that the five new dance steps to healthy relationships I just told you about in this book give us all the best chance for relationship success. We greatly increase our odds for achieving great relationships if we put into practice the new dance steps—even though I can't guarantee that either you or I will always get everything we want.

So let me say it one more time. I have no magic pills. No secrets of guaranteed relationship success. Even so, I do have some solid and strong reassurance for those who may feel uneasy at the thought of a world without guarantees. I feel so confident because the reassurance comes straight from God's Word. And it drips with sweet serendipity:

> Even though the fig trees have no blossoms, and there are no grapes on the vine; even though the olive crop fails, and the fields lie empty and barren; even though the flocks die in the fields, and the cattle barns are empty, yet I will rejoice in the Lord! I will be joyful in the God of my salvation. The Sovereign Lord is my strength! He will make me as sure-footed as a deer and bring me safely over the mountains.[6]

You and I can literally start a relationship revolution together—as long as we go with God. And so to the heights we set our gaze. May I tell you about the most important opportunity and exciting challenge I've been called to do for the next decade or more?

LIFE IS RELATIONSHIPS;
THE REST IS JUST DETAILS.

ONE-MINUTE REVIEW
WHAT WE CAN CHANGE

1. **You can't force the other person to change.** It is futile to try to make the other person change.

2. **The only person you can change is yourself.** The only responsibility you have is to change yourself. Allow God to change you, then leave the rest up to him.

3. **Leave room for serendipity.** Allow change to happen in unexpected places.

10

YOU CAN MAKE A DIFFERENCE

LIFE IS RELATIONSHIPS;
THE REST IS JUST DETAILS.

If you still don't believe me, just ask someone on death's door about what is most important. I will never forget that moment—the time my life almost came to an end.

As a fresh morning breeze brushed my face, the music of birds and of water splashing over stones in the nearby creek produced a soundtrack of sheer delight. I took a deep breath. The sweet scent of flowers and plants filled my senses, and I thought, *It's so very good to be alive*. Except for the sounds of nature, all was quiet. As I stood there that morning and gazed out across the landscape, I took another deep breath as a new day dawned. A sense of completeness and satisfaction flooded my spirit.

A twig snapped beneath my feet, and as I stopped, my hunting partner, Junior, and I spotted a wild turkey off in the brush. Although in my boyhood years I used to be an avid hunter, I fumbled with my gun—*has to be the excitement of my first turkey hunt,* I thought. But as I took aim, an unfamiliar unease gripped me; I could hardly breathe. Junior anxiously motioned with his finger pressed against his lip. "*Shhh,* stop breathing so loud!"

As the trophy-sized turkey inched closer, I lowered my gun. *What's wrong with me? Why don't I have any strength?* Junior's raspy whisper urged me on: "Shoot! Shoot!"

Pressed into action, I again lifted my gun and aimed. I pulled the trigger. At the same moment the turkey fell over, I also crumpled. As I lay moaning on the ground, Junior assumed that a rush of adrenaline had overwhelmed me, and he reached down to help me to my feet. Yet I could feel that something far worse had happened. Later I learned that a major artery near my heart had torn.

I was having a heart attack.

My father died of a heart attack at age fifty-eight; my older brother died of the same thing at age fifty-one. Another brother has endured triple-bypass surgery three times. Years ago I radically altered my eating and exercise habits to fend off this moment. But at age sixty-one, I found myself unwillingly conforming to my genetic heritage—yet another Smalley victim of heart disease.

As Junior ran for the truck, I lay motionless on the ground, paralyzed by the pain. And yet, I'll never forget the peace that overcame me. I felt ready to die. "Lord," I whispered, "I'm ready to come home."

At that moment I had but one desire: to see my wife and kids one last time. None of the books I'd written, videos I'd made, conferences I'd addressed, couples I'd counseled, awards I'd won, or any other accomplishment mattered. I longed for only one thing: to be with my family, the people who mattered most to me.

As Junior carried me out of the woods, I didn't know if I would live or die. Truthfully, I didn't understand why I hadn't already died.

Back at our vehicle, precious moments ticked by as we discovered that our remote location put us out of cell phone range. Halfway down the mountain, we connected with the paramedics on a two-way radio. Emergency vehicles rushed to meet us. I hung on to every breath; I just had to see my family once more.

I finally reached Norma by phone, but before I could tell my wife what had happened, she said, "I have someone in my office; I'm putting you on hold." As I listened to the "on hold" music, I thought,

Perfect! I'm going to die while my wife has me on hold. When she finally picked up the line and I explained my situation, she yelled, "Why didn't you tell me?" Then she hung up and raced toward the hospital.

Paramedics flew me to a hospital about fifty miles from my home. Greg, my older son, lived there, so he arrived first at the hospital. As they wheeled me into the emergency room, my eyes locked onto Greg. *I made it!*

I don't remember much of what happened next. No, my life didn't flash before my eyes. But I recall frantically trying to tell Greg what to say to each family member. It felt like trying to cram sixty-one years of relationships into several sentences. *What should I say?*

I'm sure my instructions sounded like the ranting and ravings of a lunatic. The more I tried to articulate my good-byes, the more frustrated I became. Finally, Greg leaned over me and said something that instantly calmed me down. "Dad," he whispered ever so gently, "we know."

At that very moment—when I thought I was about to die—I realized that my family already knew everything I wanted to tell them. They knew how proud I felt of each of them. They knew how valuable they were to me. But most important, they knew that they were loved.

As I held my son's hand, everything seemed to slow down. I thought about how much happiness and laughter had filled my life as a husband, father, and grandfather. Even as I wondered whether my life had come to its end, I felt fresh appreciation for the love I had been able to receive and to give. And over the next forty-eight hours in the hospital, I paused frequently to ask myself what I had lived for and what had given me such a sense of completeness and satisfaction.

I realized anew that the most important thing in my life is relationships—not only with my family and friends and the people I meet all over the world, but with the God who walks with me even "through the dark valley of death."[1] The rest is just details.

The Need of the Hour

My brush with death convinced me more than ever that we cannot simply go on doing business as usual. *Something* has to change.

We face relationship crises everywhere we look. Perhaps we see it most clearly in marriage. Nearly all of us have been touched somehow by divorce, either in our own families or in the lives of close friends.

And Christians are not immune from the crises. Did you know that "Baptists have the highest divorce rate of any Christian denomination and are more likely to get a divorce than atheists and agnostics, according to a national survey"? George Barna, president of Barna Research Group, said about this report, "While it may be alarming to discover that born-again Christians are more likely than others to experience a divorce, that pattern has been in place for quite some time."[2]

Barna's report stirred up many people in the Christian community and earned him a few angry retorts. In response he wrote a letter to his supporters, declaring that he stood by his data, even though it upset many. "We rarely find substantial differences" between the moral behavior of Christians and non-Christians, he said. Barna Project Director Meg Flammang added, "We would love to be able to report that Christians are living very distinct lives and impacting the community, but . . . in the area of divorce rates, they continue to be the same."[3]

But serious relationship struggles are not limited to marriages. Most of us also have experienced strained parent-child relationships, broken friendships, unresolved conflict in our workplaces and our churches. The front pages of our newspapers remind us every day that relationships are in crisis.

What will we do about it? How should we combat these relationship disasters? What can we do to make sure our fractured relationships don't stand in the way of God's bringing a mighty and much-needed revival to our churches and to our land?

In response to the crisis in marriage, Mike Huckabee, governor of Arkansas and an evangelical Christian himself, has declared a "marital emergency." He has set a goal to reduce the divorce rate by half in his state by 2010, from 6.1 per thousand to about 3. Frank Keating, former governor of Oklahoma, has initiated a similar campaign in his own state. By 2009 he wants to reduce the divorce rate by a third, from 6 per thousand to about 4 per thousand.

Similarly, Kerby Anderson of Probe Ministries has said, "I think it is time for the church to get back to basics. Pastors must preach about marriage from the pulpit, and churches should encourage their members to attend marriage conferences that provide God's blueprint for marriage. Christian marriages should set the example for the world."[4]

But addressing the marriage problem is only the beginning. We must do more to strengthen families, friendships, work relationships, and others.

I want to extend a challenge. I want to encourage you to get "life-on-life" with others, to help those outside of your closest circle to enjoy the benefits of strong, healthy relationships. The need of the hour cries out for you to do what you can to help multiply healthy, satisfied, revitalized relationships among the people all around you. Together we can lock arms and work toward change. We've done it before in our country's history.

A Revolution in the Making

"We have it in our power to begin the world anew," wrote Thomas Paine in his 1776 instant best seller, *Common Sense*, a potent little book that rallied fellow patriots and fired them with resolve to change their world. His inspiring words moved the people of the American colonies to organize, band together, and fight for their freedom.

Today we need another revolution—a relationship revolution. We need a revolution to free us from the chains of relationship discord, misery, and collapse.

I believe the American Revolutionary War provides several strategies that will help us in the relationship revolution. Several historians believe the Revolutionary War succeeded for at least three reasons:

- The average person understood what was happening and where events appeared to be leading.
- The people learned how to get their leaders to address their growing problems with England and to nurture a grassroots response.
- The people took decisive action.

If we are to respond effectively at this historical crossroads to the relationship crisis we face—if we are to succeed in bringing about a relationship revolution—then we must do as America's first patriots did.

1. We must open our eyes to the relationship crisis. If we are to succeed in bringing about a relationship revolution, we must also recognize what is happening to relationships all around us and realize where we will end up if we do not take steps to prevent the disaster. Throughout this book we have noted the alarming relationship collapse that continues to grow more frightening with each passing year. Do you see what is happening all around you? Can you envision where these appalling trends will take us if we do nothing?

2. We must connect with leaders and nurture a grassroots response. In an age when women had no role in combat, Deborah Samson disguised herself as a young man and presented herself as a willing volunteer for the American Revolutionary army. She enlisted as Robert Shirtliffe and went where the action was, serving for the whole term of the Revolutionary War. She offered her services, giving whatever she could to the cause. Why did she do it? She was afraid of what would happen if she did nothing. She allied herself with a grassroots effort, knowing that if people worked together, they would succeed.

If we are to successfully pull off a relationship revolution, we must connect with our leaders, the opinion makers, as well as the movers and shakers to craft a plan of action, understanding that lasting change must happen from the bottom up. And that means you and me.

3. We must take action. The American Revolution lasted more than six bloody years and cost the lives of thousands of people on both sides of the conflict. It wasn't quick, and it wasn't easy—but history reveals what an enormous and vital role it played (and plays still) on the world's stage. The patriots who dreamed of freedom did more than talk; they took action. They did what they needed to do to make their dream into a reality.

So must we.

It is time to take action. We must not merely talk about a relationship revolution; we must act in decisive ways to bring one about.

We can hold meetings. We can write letters. We can hold small home groups in which neighbors and friends can come together to begin the change. We can talk with our pastors and other church leaders about igniting a relationship revolution in our community. We can teach a class focusing on relationships, or we can recruit participants for such a class.

It's time to get busy. Will you answer the call?

What Will You Do?

We have reached a watershed moment in this country when what we decide to do now about the national relationship crisis will determine for generations to come the plight of America. Will we stand by and do nothing? Or will we take the necessary steps not only to strengthen and energize our own relationships but also to help others find the satisfaction and fulfillment they also crave from their relationships?

Consider these three important ways you can begin immediately:

1. *Pray regularly for troubled relationships in your neighborhood, school, church, and community. Start a prayer journal, and have others pray for these relationships as well.*
2. *Go to www.thednaofrelationships.com and sign up to receive a free*
   - Study guide for *The DNA of Relationships*
   - Relationship evaluation test, which we have found to be 90 percent accurate with married couples
   - DNA e-letter with weekly insights for strengthening *all* your relationships
3. *If you are a pastor, chaplain, or church leader, go to www.thednaofrelationships.com and*
   - Download free sermons based on the principles in *The DNA of Relationships*
   - Download Gary Smalley's video message for leaders on "How to lead a Relationship Revolution"
   - Receive information on TV simulcasts and monthly conferences in the USA and Canada
   - Find information about launching a DNA of Relationships small group.

Change can begin in this country when we start to understand God's blueprint for interpersonal connections, the DNA of relationships. When we consistently apply these principles, our relationships will begin to heal, grow strong, and become truly satisfying. Friendships will be restored, marriages will thrive, and families will discover the joy of harmony.

Let's together spark a generational shift right now. Let's help our kids and grandkids to succeed at relationships. Join us in spreading the great news about what can happen when people really start loving each other the way God designed us to love.

Let's start today!

HOW TO HAVE A
RELATIONSHIP WITH GOD

You have a relationship with God, whether or not you acknowledge it. That relationship is an important factor in your relationship with others and with yourself.

How would you describe your relationship with God? Is it distant? Is it intimate? Do you ignore him? Is he the center of your life? Do you know God personally?

Maybe you are consumed with a "try harder" religion. You believe that if you work hard, take care of your duties, and watch after your family or others, God will look over your whole life and conclude that in the end you are okay. Perhaps you believe that giving up your bad habits will place you in God's good graces.

A relationship with God is not based on what you do—or abstain from doing. It is not about your best efforts. It is about a God who loves you and wants a relationship with you. In fact, the Bible says that "he is a God who is passionate about his relationship with you" (Exodus 34:14). Think about that. How many people are passionate about a relationship with you? Well, the God of the universe is. He loves you right where you are. He loves you despite your past. He wants a relationship with you no matter who you are or what you have done.

How can you have a relationship with God? Through his Son, Jesus Christ. As the Bible says, "There is only one God and one Mediator who can reconcile God and people. He is the man Christ Jesus" (1 Timothy 2:5).

We have a natural desire to be independent, to be the master of our own lives, to live by our own standards. It's the old "look out for number 1" attitude. The biblical word for that attitude is *sin*. Our sin cuts us off from God. Every single one of us struggles with this problem. "All have sinned; all fall short of God's glorious standard" (Romans 3:23). Therefore, in and of ourselves, we can never measure up. Yet, the story doesn't end there.

Jesus Christ, and his death on the cross, has made it possible for you to be in a relationship with God. The first step is to admit that God has not been first place in your life. Believe that Jesus died to pay for your sin, and ask him to forgive you. With that admission you are given this promise: "If we confess our sins to him, he is faithful and just to forgive us and to cleanse us from every wrong" (1 John 1:9).

You may be asking, "So what's the catch?" There is no catch! God's forgiveness is free. We don't deserve it, but God wants to give it to us anyway. If there were a way you could earn it, then Christ's death on the cross would be meaningless. His death paved the way for us to give God all of the credit. "God saved you by his special favor when you believed. And you can't take credit for this; it is a gift from God. Salvation is not a reward for the good things we have done, so none of us can boast about it" (Ephesians 2:8-9).

If you would like to begin a personal relationship with God today, pray something like this simple prayer as an expression of your decision.

Dear Father, thank you for loving me, even when I've been unlovable. You have not been first place in my life until today. I submit my life to you. Thank you for sending your Son, Jesus, to die on that cross. He took care of my sins. Please forgive me. I want to follow you. Make me a new person. I accept your free gift of salvation. Please empower me to grow now as a follower of Jesus.

To begin your new relationship with God, start with the basics. Here are some excellent books to understand more about knowing God:

* *The God You're Looking For* by Bill Hybels (Thomas Nelson)
* *Reaching for the Invisible God* by Philip Yancey (Zondervan)
* *Discover God* by Bill Bright (NewLife Publication)
* *Knowing God* by J. I. Packer (InterVarsity Press)

- *The Grace Awakening* by Charles Swindoll (W Publishing Group)
- *Secrets of the Vine* by Bruce Wilkinson (Multnomah)
- *Discover the Real Jesus* by Bill Bright (Tyndale)
- *The Jesus I Never Knew* by Philip Yancey (Zondervan)

IDENTIFY YOUR CORE FEAR

1. IDENTIFY THE CONFLICT: Identify a recent conflict, argument, or negative situation with your spouse, friend, child, neighbor, coworker, or whomever—something that really "pushed your buttons" or upset you. Think about how you were feeling and how you wished the person would not say or do the things that upset you. You might have thought something like, *If only you would stop saying or doing ___, I would not be so upset.*

2. IDENTIFY YOUR FEELINGS. How did this conflict or negative situation make you feel? Check all that apply—but "star" the most important feelings:

___ Unsure	___ Uncomfortable	___ Frightened
___ Apathetic	___ Confused	___ Anxious
___ Puzzled	___ Worried	___ Horrified
___ Upset	___ Disgusted	___ Disturbed
___ Sullen	___ Resentful	___ Furious
___ Sad	___ Bitter	___ Other:
___ Hurt	___ Fed up	
___ Disappointed	___ Frustrated	___ Other:
___ Wearied	___ Miserable	
___ Torn up	___ Guilty	___ Other:
___ Shamed	___ Embarrassed	

3. IDENTIFY YOUR FEAR: How did this conflict make you feel about *yourself*? What did the conflict "say" about *you and your feelings*? Check all that apply, but "star" the most important feeling.

✓ Or *	"As a result of the conflict, I felt . . ."	What That Feeling Sounds Like
	Rejected	The other person doesn't want me or need me; I am not necessary in this relationship; I feel unwanted.
	Abandoned	The other person will ultimately leave me; I will be left alone to care for myself; the other person won't be committed to me for life.
	Disconnected	We will become emotionally detached or separated; I will feel cut off from the other person.
	Like a failure	I am not successful at being a husband/wife, friend, parent, coworker; I will not perform correctly; I will not live up to expectations; I am not good enough.
	Helpless	I cannot do anything to change the other person or my situation; I do not possess the power, resources, capacity, or ability to get what I want; I will feel controlled by the other person.
	Defective	Something is wrong with me; I'm the problem.
	Inadequate	I am not capable; I am incompetent.
	Inferior	Everyone else is better than I am; I am less valuable or important than others.
	Invalidated	Who I am, what I think, what I do, or how I feel is not valued.
	Unloved	The other person doesn't care about me; my relationship lacks warm attachment, admiration, enthusiasm, or devotion.

✓ Or *	"As a result of the conflict, I felt . . ."	What That Feeling Sounds Like
	Dissatisfied	I will not experience satisfaction in the relationship; I will not feel joy or excitement about the relationship.
	Cheated	The other person will take advantage of me or will withhold something I need; I won't get what I want.
	Worthless	I am useless; I have no value to the other person.
	Unaccepted	I am never able to meet the other person's expectations; I am not good enough.
	Judged	I am always being unfairly judged; the other person forms faulty or negative opinions about me; I am always being evaluated; the other person does not approve of me.
	Humiliated	The relationship is extremely destructive to my self-respect or dignity.
	Ignored	The other person will not pay attention to me; I feel neglected.
	Insignificant	I am irrelevant in the relationship; the other person does not see me as an important part of our relationship.
	Other	_____ _____

4. IDENTIFY YOUR REACTIONS: What do you do when you feel [insert the most important feeling from question #3]? How do you *react* when you feel that way? Identify your common verbal or physical reactions to deal with that feeling. Check all that apply— but "star" the most important reactions:

✓ Or *	Reaction	Explanation
	Withdrawal	You avoid others or alienate yourself without resolution; you sulk or use the silent treatment.
	Escalation	Your emotions spiral out of control; you argue, raise your voice, fly into a rage.
	Try harder	You try to do more to earn others' love and care.
	Negative beliefs	You believe the other person is far worse than is really the case; you see the other person in a negative light or attribute negative motives to him or her.
	Blaming	You place responsibility on others, not accepting fault; you're convinced the problem is the other person's fault.
	Exaggeration	You make overstatements or enlarge your words beyond bounds or the truth.
	Tantrums	You have fits of bad temper.
	Denial	You refuse to admit the truth or reality.
	Invalidation	You devalue the other person; you do not appreciate what he or she feels or thinks or does.
	Defensiveness	Instead of listening, you defend yourself by providing an explanation.
	Clinginess	You develop a strong emotional attachment or dependence on the other person.
	Passive– aggressive	You display negative emotions, resentment, and aggression in passive ways, such as procrastination and stubbornness.

✓ Or *	Reaction	Explanation
	Caretaking	You become responsible for the other person by giving physical or emotional care and support to the point you are doing everything for the other person, who does nothing to care for himself or herself.
	Acting out	You engage in negative behaviors, such as drug or alcohol abuse, extramarital affairs, excessive shopping or spending, or overeating.
	Fix-it mode	You focus almost exclusively on what is needed to solve the problem.
	Complaining	You express unhappiness or make accusations; you criticize, creating a list of the other person's faults.
	Aggression or abuse	You become verbally or physically aggressive, possibly abusive.
	Manipulation	You control the other person for your own advantage; you try to get him or her to do what you want.
	Anger and rage	You display strong feeling of displeasure or violent and uncontrolled emotions.
	Catastrophize	You use dramatic, exaggerated expressions to depict that the relationship is in danger or that it has failed.
	Numbing out	You become devoid of emotion, or you have no regard for others' needs or troubles.
	Humor	You use humor as a way of not dealing with the issue at hand.

✓ Or *	Reaction	Explanation
	Sarcasm	You use negative humor, hurtful words, belittling comments, cutting remarks, or demeaning statements.
	Minimization	You assert that the other person is overreacting to an issue; you intentionally underestimate, downplay, or softpedal the issue.
	Rationalization	You attempt to make your actions seem reasonable; you try to attribute your behavior to credible motives; you try to provide believable but untrue reasons for your conduct.
	Indifference	You are cold and show no concern.
	Abdication	You give away responsibilities.
	Self-Abandonment	You run yourself down; you neglect yourself.
	Other:	_____ _____

5. Look at the items you starred in response to question 3. List the three or four main feelings. These are your core fears:

Core fear #1 _____

Core fear #2 _____

Core fear #3 _____

Remember that most core fears are related to two main primary fears:

1. The fear of being controlled (losing influence or power over others)

2. The fear of being disconnected (separation from people and being alone)

More men fear losing power or being controlled, and more women fear being disconnected from relationships with others.

6. Look at the items you starred in response to question 4. List your three or four main reactions when someone pushes your core fear button.
    Reaction #1 _____
    Reaction #2 _____
    Reaction #3 _____

Your responses to these exercises should help you understand your part of the Fear Dance: your core fear button and your reaction. Remember that it's very common for your reactions to push the core fear button of the other person in the conflict. If the other person can figure out his or her core fears and reactions, you will see clearly the unique Fear Dance the two of you are doing. But even if the other person isn't able to be involved in the process of discovering his or her part of the Fear Dance, you can take steps to stop the dance. (See chapters 4–8.)

THE DNA OF RELATIONSHIPS
STUDY GUIDE

"Life is relationships; the rest is just details." How you feel about life often boils down to how you feel about your relationships. As human beings, we are designed for relationships with others, with ourselves, and with God. It's part of our relational DNA. When those relationships are balanced and healthy, life is good. But too often we live with broken, strained relationships, accommodating ourselves to the pain without taking constructive action to address the underlying issues. Too often we unknowingly damage the most important relationships in our lives with destructive habits. Too often we don't take care of ourselves. Too often we ignore the most important relationship—our spiritual connection with God.

It would be easy to read a book like this and never quite get around to applying its principles. The purpose of this study guide is to help you start taking constructive action to improve the quality of all your relationships. You'll find elements useful for individual study, for couples to work through together, and for group study. You'll even find some questions designed to point you to Bible passages that speak to the issue of healthy relationships. The questions in the study guide will challenge you to think through the issues surrounding your most important relationships, help you begin to take responsibility for your role in your relationships, and give you positive, practical steps toward building healthy relationships in every area of your life.

Whether you've already read through the book or plan to read it and work through the study guide simultaneously, you will find that the questions often take you back to the text to help you grapple with the important principles of building healthy, thriving relationships. Although the book at times focuses on marriage relationships, the questions in this study guide are applicable to all relationships. Therefore, if you are studying *The DNA of Relationships* with a group, you can encourage people at any stage of life to join you. In fact, a variety of members—married or single, young or old—will likely enhance discussions by bringing to the table several different perspectives that might not be considered in a less diverse setting. Whether you're working through the lessons on your own or with your spouse or a close friend, you'll find much to apply to your own life.

If you are using this study guide in a group context, keep several things in mind. First, relationship conflict is not always easy to discuss, and emotions can often run high. If you share details about a relationship that is in conflict, be respectful about how you talk about the other person(s) in the relationship. A group discussion is not a place to put down other people. If the other person, a spouse for instance, is also in the group, do not use the discussion time as a means of gathering support for your "side" of the conflict. Remember to keep the focus on yourself, not on the other person. Second, we all have different levels of comfort in revealing details about our personal lives. Respect each other's limits. Never force someone to talk about something if he or she is not comfortable. Third, listen empathetically and look for every opportunity to encourage one another. Help others to be honest with their part in the conflict. Remember, the only person we can change is ourself. Fourth, confidentiality is essential in any group discussion, but that is especially true when discussing interpersonal conflict. People who share in a group setting must have the confidence that what they say will not be discussed outside the group. Fifth, pray for one another, allowing God to direct and bring healing in circumstances that seem impossible to resolve.

Before beginning the study questions, spend some time reflecting on your important relationships. What do you want to accomplish in your relationships? Growth requires reflection, so allow time for that. What you learn in this book could change your life. And when you join the growing network of people committed to healthy relationships, you could very well change your world—one relationship at a time. *The DNA of Relationships* is our invitation for you to become a part of a relationship revolution. It's time to make your relationships the best they can be.

PART ONE:
THE FIRST STEP

*"Everything in life that truly matters can be
boiled down to relationships."*

Getting Started

1. "Life is relationships; the rest is just details." List the key relationships in your life. You might include family and friends, as well as relationships from your workplace, church, neighborhood, and organizations to which you belong. What does your time investment in each area tell you about where your relationships fit into your priorities? (It might be difficult, but answer based on what is actually true rather than on what you may think your response should be.) What often gets in the way of your investing in relationships? Consider external factors, such as job responsibilities, and internal factors, such as personal weaknesses.

2. What expectations or hopes do you have for this study? Do you have a particular relationship that needs help?

Recapping the Chapter

1. This book will help you grow in your relationships, especially those in which you face some conflict. If you are married, do you and your spouse ever do a destructive dance? Do you ever get stuck? What about your other relationships? Where might you be stuck in destructive patterns with a sibling or a coworker? Write your responses, and share them with others if you are comfortable doing so.

2. If you could hope for a "greatest discovery" in your important relationships, what would it be?

3. Review the five teaching principles (five new dance steps) summarized on pages 11–12. Which one is the most challenging for you? Why?
4. "I long for you to experience and enjoy the same newfound life and vitality in relationships that I've come to experience in the past few years as a result of applying the concepts in this book" (page 11). Describe what an *alive* or *vital* relationship looks like compared to a dead or stagnant one.
5. Review the list of "headlines" on page 13. In all likelihood, you've personally been touched by at least one of these issues, and you probably could name people in your life—relatives, friends, or acquaintances—who've experienced nearly all of them. Go a bit deeper now and consider the human bond. How has every person alive been affected at some level by all the examples on that list?

Applying Principles from the Bible
1. Let's take another look at the first human relationship God created. Read Genesis 2:18-23: "The Lord God said, 'It is not good for the man to be alone. I will make a companion who will help him.' So the Lord God formed from the soil every kind of animal and bird. He brought them to Adam to see what he would call them, and Adam chose a name for each one. He gave names to all the livestock, birds, and wild animals. But still there was no companion suitable for him. So the Lord God caused Adam to fall into a deep sleep. He took one of Adam's ribs and closed up the place from which he had taken it. Then the Lord God made a woman from the rib and brought her to Adam. 'At last!' Adam exclaimed. 'She is part of my own flesh and bone! She will be called "woman," because she was taken out of a man.'" Adam enjoyed the greatest relationship possible—a close intimacy with God, whom he had all to himself. However, God knew that Adam needed other people. List the ways that your life is blessed because of relationships.
2. The term *friend* can apply to any relationship. You can be friends with your spouse, children, other relatives, coworkers, and . . . well . . . your friends. Which principles of friendship do the following verses embody: Proverbs 17:17; 18:24; 27:9; Ecclesiastes 4:10?

Making It Real
What effect do you want to have on the people in your life? Spend some time developing your answer to this question, because you're es-

sentially defining what you want your life to be about. The purpose of this exercise is to focus your mind and heart on your personal responsibilities and goals for your relationships.

The Final Word

Dear friend, I am praying that all is well with you and that your body is as healthy as I know your soul is. 3 JOHN 1:2

CHAPTER 2 —
THE DNA OF RELATIONSHIPS

"Even when they are hard, difficult, or just plain frustrating, you need relationships. It's the way you are wired. You have a longing to belong to someone, to be wanted and cherished for the valued person you are."

Getting Started

1. Comment on the idea that relationships are not an option. Describe a time when you have pulled away from a relationship due to miscommunication or conflict. What was the situation, and did you ever seek reconciliation? Why is it a blessing that we cannot escape relationships?

2. Reflect on the "blame game" humans have been playing since Adam and Eve's time. Oh, how we love an excuse to blame someone else! Think about the times when you have excused your own actions by pointing the finger at someone else. What does "passing the buck" really reveal about you? Don't hurry through this question; it's an important one to consider thoughtfully.

Recapping the Chapter

1. Name the three strands that make up the relationship DNA code (see page 20). Which of these strands are already integrated into your thinking about relationships? Which strands are new to you?

2. Name the three kinds of relationships and summarize each one (see pages 22–37). Discuss the importance of keeping all three relationships in balance and how each one affects the others.

3. "It's never just about the other person." Think of a current relationship

in which you are experiencing conflict. What is your part in the conflict? Consider the true root of the problem. If you're working through this study guide with others, share with the group (if you feel comfortable) your feelings about the situation and how you're processing it now. This will require some vulnerability, but growth happens through being honest.

4. Spend time thinking through your relationship with yourself. How much are you affected at a deep level by others' perceptions of you (close friends and family, as well as acquaintances and even strangers)? How are you affected by their words? Is your overall self-image an asset or a liability in your relationships? What improvements do you need to make in the way you see yourself?

5. Okay, now focus on your relationship with God. Follow the same thought processes as above but apply the questions to how you relate to God. Do you think he is pleased with you? Do you think he is pleased with the depth of your relationship? Why or why not?

6. It is important to understand that you are made with the capacity to choose. When a relationship turns sour or hits a rough spot, it's easy to conclude that there's nothing you can do about it. Think about a relationship problem that left you feeling helpless, feeling as if you couldn't do anything about it. Based on what you've read in chapter 2, what new insights do you have regarding that situation? How is avoidance a choice in itself? What are some effects of avoidance you have seen?

7. Look at the One-Minute Review for chapter 2. In what areas do you need to take responsibility for yourself? In what areas do you need the most growth?

Applying Principles from the Bible

1. Throughout history, people have gone to great lengths to avoid taking the blame for their own actions, often compounding their mistakes in an effort to cover up for themselves. Think of a time when, like Adam and Eve, you shifted the blame onto someone else for your own decision. What were the consequences of your refusal to take personal responsibility?

2. In order to have healthy relationships with ourselves and others, we must first see ourselves through God's eyes and have a growing relationship with him, our Creator. After all, who could understand us better than the One who wired us? However, it's easy to become con-

fused about God's view of us. For clarification, read Deuteronomy 30:10; Psalm 147:11; Isaiah 43:1-4; Micah 7:18-20; Romans 8:38-39; and James 1:18. Which verse(s) mean(s) the most to you today?

Making It Real

Personalize the three kinds of relationships in your life (with others, with yourself, and with God). Which one takes the highest priority? Which one is healthiest, and which one needs the most improvement? Spend a few minutes writing a note—it could be one paragraph or several pages—to the person with whom you are struggling most (yes, this person might be yourself, another person, or God). Share your feelings about that person and the relationship as a whole, including your hopes, regrets, fears, and hurts. Consider the lengths to which you are willing to go to help that relationship be as healthy and vital as possible. What, if anything, is keeping you from working on it? Depending on your situation, you may want to send the note or read it to the person, or save it to share at another time. The point is to get your feelings on paper. Writing something down can open up new thought processes and validate circumstances in your own mind and heart. It may even clarify new direction for you.

The Final Word

Love each other with genuine affection, and take delight in honoring each other. ROMANS 12:10

CHAPTER 3 —
THE DANCE THAT DESTROYS RELATIONSHIPS

"Without identifying your own core fear and understanding how you tend to react when your fear button gets pushed, your relationships will suffer. Every time! . . . One of the worst things about the Fear Dance is that, eventually, it makes us dependent on other people for our happiness and fulfillment."

Getting Started

1. Throughout the book, we use the analogy of dance to describe our patterns of relating to one another. Dancing is often a learned skill–think

of the skyrocketing interest in ballroom and swing dance classes of recent years. What happens when one partner doesn't dance well? Feet get stepped on, right? When that happens, one partner feels pain and the other feels somewhat embarrassed or ashamed. Share your ideas about how these feelings correlate to people learning the skills of relating to one another.

2. Discuss the times when you have observed the truth of the following statement: "When people exclude God and try to navigate their own way through the relationship maze, we see much more fear prevalent in their lives." What are your particular fears in your relationships? How has fear hindered the development of your relationships?

Recapping the Chapter

1. In relationships, "the external problem is rarely the real problem." Think about a recent or current relationship conflict. What was/is the apparent problem? Now, explore deeper. What might be some of the real issues underlying the surface problem? How does understanding the underlying issues change your perspective of the conflict and your role in it?

2. What are the two core fears that most men and women have (see page 42)? Do you recognize them in yourself? Explain your observations of those fears in the people in your life (remember to be cautious of privacy issues). How do those fears play significantly into the relationships that you struggle with? How does understanding your own fear and the other person's fear affect how you interact with each other?

3. Explain the steps of the Fear Dance (see page 45). Think back on a conflict from one of your relationships. Identify the steps of the dance as they played out in the conflict. With the information from this chapter, what could you have done differently to halt those steps and refocus the resolution?

4. "When you expect people, places, and things to fulfill your wants, you will be disappointed." How do *misplaced expectations* confuse us about our role in finding solutions to conflicts? Think about your relationship struggles. Are you looking to the other person to fulfill your wants? If you are, how does that expectation play into the conflict? What can you do about it?

5. Discuss the twenty-five wants and fears listed on pages 48–49. Which ones are most personal for you? Share your thoughts about the list of reactions and explanations on pages 51–52. How do you tend to react

when your fear buttons are pushed? when you fear that your wants won't be met?

6. What does it mean to be "functionally dysfunctional" (see pages 55–57)?

7. Look at the One-Minute Review for chapter 3. Which of the six main points from the chapter were the most interesting or enlightening? Explain. With your new understanding of these concepts, which one do you think will have the greatest affect on your relationships? Explain.

Applying Principles from the Bible

1. Read Psalm 27. Throughout his life, David was chased and threatened by enemies, some of whom were his own relatives, people he would have expected to love him the most. His reputation was constantly at stake, and as king he undoubtedly could not please everyone all the time. What do you see in this psalm that shows where (or in whom) David placed his confidence and security? How did that assuredness help him through the roughest circumstances, including relationship problems with his closest relatives (see verse 10)? How does David's security in God encourage you to see yourself through God's eyes in regard to your human relationships?

2. Read 1 Corinthians 13:4-7 and discuss the qualities of love. Now take a look at 1 John 4:17-19. What role does love play in demolishing fear?

Making It Real

If you haven't identified your core fear(s) by working through appendix B, do so now. What realizations did you come to? What, if anything, surprised you? What insights did you gain about how your fear(s) and responses affect your relationships? How will you apply this information in your relationships?

The Final Word

God has not given us a spirit of fear and timidity, but of power, love, and self-discipline. 2 TIMOTHY 1:7

PART TWO:
NEW DANCE STEPS

CHAPTER 4 — THE POWER OF ONE: TAKE PERSONAL RESPONIBILITY

"If you decide to take control of how you react to the challenges, insults, difficulties, and conflicts that inevitably come your way, then a whole new world opens up—a world marked by peace."

Getting Started

1. How is our power to choose both a freedom and a responsibility? Take into consideration all kinds of choices, from the mundane to the life altering, from the most personal to those that affect vast numbers of people.

2. The overarching message of this chapter is that we have the power to change our relationships, even in those instances where we are certain that the problem is the other person's behavior. If this is true, what implications does it have for your troubled relationships?

Recapping the Chapter

1. When you have conflict in your relationships, where do you tend to place the blame? On the other person? On external circumstances? Or on yourself (taking responsibility for your own responses)? What can you do to take personal responsibility for your thoughts, feelings, and actions?

2. "You can choose your reaction, and your reaction is based on your thoughts." Discuss the power of your thought life over your actions and emotions. How important is it to gain control over your emotions? Give specific reasons for your answers.

3. Name the six steps for gaining control of your emotions and reactions to life (see the discussion starting on page 67). Regarding the first step, discuss your thoughts about the following statements: "Whenever you focus your attention on what the other person is doing, you take away your own power. You make yourself weak." What does that mean? Do you agree or disagree? Why?

4. Truth time: As far as your comfort level goes, share about a time when you caught yourself (or were caught by someone else) attempting to change someone's opinions or actions through unhealthy, manipulative ways. (We've all been there!) What was the situation, and what was the outcome? Did you end up pushing the other person's buttons? If you could redo your actions, would you have responded differently? If so, how?

5. Look more closely at the fourth step for gaining control of your emotions: "Don't look to others to make you happy." Reflect for a few moments on your current level of happiness. On a scale of one to ten (ten being the highest), what rank would you give to your happiness? What would it take to make you happier? How can you change your thoughts about your circumstances to help raise your own degree of fulfillment?

6. "Everything negative that happens to us can be reframed into something positive." Do you agree or disagree? Do you generally apply this philosophy to your problems? Think back on how you've grown from tough times. Brainstorm about ways to remind yourself to view troubles and conflicts as opportunities to practice a more positive outlook.

7. Summarize the two actions involved in forgiveness (see page 83). Take time to discuss the second action, in particular, as it is often overlooked in most explanations of forgiveness. If you're willing, honestly share about a time when you struggled to extend forgiveness. As always, keep in mind issues of privacy and propriety.

8. Look at the One-Minute Review for chapter 4. Of the six main points from the chapter, which one do you most need to put into practice in your relationships?

Applying Principles from the Bible

1. Take a look at the following Bible verses: Proverbs 16:23; Isaiah 26:3; Philippians 4:8-9; James 1:19, 23-25. Discuss how each one speaks to the power of our thoughts in relation to our feelings and reactions. What hope do you find in the following verses for taking responsibility for and gaining control of your thoughts: Psalm 94:19; Romans 8:6; 12:2; Philippians 4:6-7; James 1:5-7?

2. Much of this chapter focuses on the fact that no one else can *make* us happy. Where do joy and strength come from? Read the following verses for assistance: Psalms 19:8; 28:7; 40:16-17; Jeremiah 15:16; Ephesians 3:19; Philippians 3:1. Where does *your* joy come from?

3. Forgiveness is essential to resolving conflict. What insights about forgiveness do you gain from the following passages: Matthew 6:14-15; Colossians 3:13; Hebrews 12:14-15? What can make forgiveness difficult?

Making It Real

The sixth step in taking personal control of our thoughts, feelings, and reactions is to recruit assistants to help us take care of and be responsible to ourselves. Do you have people who fit that role in your life? If not, make a list of family members and friends who may be willing to partner with you for that accountability. Perhaps you can do the same for them. Prayerfully consider each one, then take the first step and ask one or more to assist you in identifying your fear buttons and practicing healthy ways to respond when those buttons are pushed.

The Final Word

We are each responsible for our own conduct.   Galatians 6:5

CHAPTER 5 —
SAFETY: CREATE A SAFE ENVIRONMENT

"This second new dance step will help you create a safe climate in which you can build open relationships that will grow and flourish. It will help you build relationships in which you and the other person will feel cherished, honored, and alive. It's almost as if this step changes the background music to your dance, setting a soothing tone that will allow you to feel relaxed in your relationships."

Getting Started

1. Have you ever felt unsafe in a relationship—emotionally, physically, or in some other way? What were your fears based on? How did you deal with those feelings?

2. Discuss what a truly safe relationship looks like. Consider all forms of safety: emotional, physical, spiritual, mental, and environmental.

Recapping the Chapter

1. In general, do you feel safe in your relationships to open up and reveal your deepest thoughts and dreams, as well as your weaknesses and mistakes? How deep do most of your relationships go? Are they satisfying—do you feel that others know you for who you truly are—or do most of your relationships leave you feeling somewhat empty? If you're studying the book with a group, share your responses as far as your comfort level allows.

2. "Too often you and I are hopelessly stuck, afraid to open up with others because we're not quite sure what they will say or do or how they'll use what they learn about us." Has someone ever used your mistakes or weaknesses against you, either by holding the mistakes over your head as a reminder or by making you feel ashamed about the mistakes privately or publicly? How did you respond? How did the experience affect your willingness to let down your guard around that person or in other relationships?

3. Now turn the tables: Have *you* ever used others' mistakes or weaknesses against them, either by holding them over their head as a reminder or by making them feel ashamed about them privately or publicly? How did they respond? How did the experience affect the relationship?

4. Review the steps to safety on page 91. Which one is the most difficult for you to put into practice? Why? Regarding the first step, what two things can you do to encourage another person to take down a wall of safety he or she has put up (see page 93)? What are possible negative effects of trying to bulldoze through someone else's wall?

5. The second step to safety is "honor others." The word *honor* might evoke numerous images for you. One could argue that the concept of honor has been somewhat diluted in today's society; it might seem that many people's main goal in life is to get ahead, regardless of what ethics they have to compromise or how many "casualties" lay in their wake. Share your thoughts on what honor is and what it means to honor someone.

6. "If a relationship is to feel like a safe place, it must make room for *all* of both people." Because no two people are the same, differences inevitably will create conflict somewhere along the way in any relationship. Name a difference between you and one important person in your life.

Are there any qualities you find irritating in that person that reveal your own imperfections? How can (or do) you make your differences work *for* your relationship?

7. Review the principle of trustworthiness discussed on pages 102–106. What does it mean to be trustworthy with yourself? What are two possible responses to choose when people treat you badly? Explain your understanding of the following statement: "When I remain trustworthy to myself, I can afford to give others a whole lot of freedom in relationships."

8. Look at the One-Minute Review for chapter 5. Of the six main points from the chapter, which one do you most need to put into practice in your relationships?

Applying Principles from the Bible

1. Let's imagine what the Garden of Eden was like in terms of safety. Read Genesis 1:1–2:25. In what ways was Eden an ideal environment for Adam and Eve, physically, emotionally, and spiritually (before they sinned)? Consider what it might have been like to walk so closely with God and with each other. What negative characteristics were absent before they sinned (think about bitterness, jealousy, etc.)?

2. Review the story of Armon, the six-year-old trapped after an earthquake in Turkey (see page 96). He never doubted his father's loving tenacity to search for him through the pile of rubble. Throughout the pages of the Bible, we observe God's constant pursuit to save us and give us more than we could ever hope for. Much of this pursuit is shown through Jesus' life. We can learn much about how to lovingly and faithfully care for others in the hopes of eventually working our way to their hearts through any walls they've put up. Read John 10:2-4, 10-11, 14-15. What does Jesus call himself? What does he do for his sheep? Now read Matthew 18:12-13. How does Jesus' gentle approach as a shepherd caring for his flock differ from the idea of a bulldozer tearing down a wall? From Jesus' example of dealing with people, what can we learn about creating a safe environment for those we care about?

Making It Real

Create your own Honor Journal, as described on page 96. Designate one or more pages for each significant person in your life—family members, friends, coworkers, neighbors, ministry partners, civic leaders, etc. Give yourself five minutes for each one, and write down as many positive qualities as you can think of that are true of that person. Then spend a minute or two praying for each name on the list; ask God to bring grateful thoughts to mind to help you grow in honoring each person. Then open the communication lines with the people closest to you; talk about how you can enhance one another's feelings of safety in your relationship.

The Final Word

Be to me a protecting rock of safety, where I am always welcome.   PSALM 71:3

CHAPTER 6 —
SELF-CARE: KEEP YOUR BATTERY CHARGED

"If you take responsibility for yourself and attend to your own self-care, you can act from a position of wholeness, not neediness. And that sets you up for relationship success."

Getting Started

1. In your opinion, what emphasis does our society as a whole put on self-care? Give examples to support your view. Which examples are positive and which are negative?
2. What recharges you? What drains you? What importance do you typically place on taking care of yourself? Think about ways you could improve your self-care as well as some healthy habits you've established to cope with life's stresses. What insights do you hope to gain from this chapter's study?

Recapping the Chapter

1. Are you taking good care of yourself physically, mentally, emotionally, and spiritually? Do you value yourself as God does? Write down and/or discuss three ways in which you can choose to honor God by taking better care of yourself.
2. Think of someone you know who appears to have a healthy balance between caring for others and making time for himself or herself. What

habits or disciplines does that person practice to make sure he or she stays energized?

3. Consider your important relationships. Which ones drain you, and which ones fill you up? What survival techniques have you developed to keep yourself going in the draining ones? Are those techniques proactive and positive, or merely reactive—just to get by with the bare minimum of getting your needs met? Now think about your own qualities that might drain others. (This is not easy to admit!) If you're willing to be vulnerable, share your thoughts in the group discussion.

4. "You make the best decisions when you use your feelings to inform your brain." Do you agree or disagree? Explain your opinion.

5. Discuss what it means to evaluate the truth of your emotions (see pages 115–18). What is the purpose of emotions? (You may come up with several responses.) Which is generally more difficult for you: identifying your emotions or evaluating the truth of them? Explain your response.

6. Summarize the three components of good self-care, as described on pages 124–25. Why is the act of giving such an important component of self-care?

7. Review the four self-care actions discussed on pages 127–29. Which one(s) could be most helpful to you? How are you doing on each one?

8. Look at the One-Minute Review for chapter 6. Which of the seven main points from the chapter were the most interesting or enlightening? Explain. Were any of these concepts new to you? If so, how will your new understanding affect your approach to self-care?

Applying Principles from the Bible

1. To varying degrees, we all battle negative feelings about ourselves, emotions that chip away at our health and effectiveness in relationships. In order to place the right amount of emphasis on taking care of ourselves, we first must understand how God sees us. Read 2 Samuel 22:19-20; Psalms 18:19; 37:23; 72:13-14; Luke 12:6-7. What do these verses tell us about ourselves from God's point of view?

2. The Bible is filled with verses about finding our wholeness and strength in God. Here are several to study: Exodus 15:2; Psalm 59:9, 16-17; Ephesians 3:16-19; Philippians 4:13; 2 Thessalonians 2:16-17. What freedom does finding your true satisfaction in God give you? How can putting your relationship with God first enrich your level of self-care?

Making It Real

Invest a couple of hours paying attention to your needs. It may take some preparation to clear your schedule, but the results can be worth it. In order to make the most of this refreshment time, brainstorm in advance for ideas that would reap the most benefits. You may want to spend the time in a quiet room with the Bible or another good book; or perhaps lunch with a friend or your spouse would do you good. Schedule this getaway time once a month for starters, and then work toward twice a month.

The Final Word

Don't let anyone condemn you by insisting on self-denial. . . . We grow only as we get our nourishment and strength from God.   COLOSSIANS 2:18-19

CHAPTER 7 —
EMOTIONAL COMMUNICATION:
LISTEN WITH THE HEART

"Effective communication comes down to listening and speaking with your heart. . . . [It] deserves patience and a deliberate attempt to understand not only the words being said but also the emotions behind the words."

Getting Started

1. In your opinion, what is involved in meaningful communication? Discuss how the depth of communication and the depth of a relationship are related. Is one the result of the other—does a relationship grow as communication grows, or does communication grow as a relationship grows?

2. What are your communication strengths and weaknesses? What effect do these have on your relationships? Talk about various successes and failures you've experienced in your (lifelong) communication learning process. What are things other people sometimes do or say that shut down your feelings of freedom to communicate honestly? What can you do to accentuate your strengths and avoid your weaknesses?

Recapping the Chapter

1. Have you ever experienced a situation like Bob and Jenni's (the situation described at the beginning of chapter 7), a time when nothing you

said or did seemed to invite a positive response from someone else? If you are doing this study with others, share your experience with them. How did the situation eventually turn out? What could you have done differently to avoid the miscommunication glitch(es)?

2. Review the section "Beyond Words to Feelings" on pages 132–33. What are your thoughts on the following statement: "True communication usually does not occur until each person understands the *feelings* that underlie the spoken words"? Describe some ways in which people have helped you open up in the past. What makes you feel understood?

3. What are the differences between "thinking" words and "feeling" words? Give an example. What is the value of using feeling words? How is a relationship enhanced when two people simply feel understood, even in the midst of significant unresolved issues?

4. Bob Paul experienced a significant breakthrough in his marriage when he decided to become a "student" of his wife, Jenni, in order to learn about what she thinks and feels. Expand on this idea of being a student in every relationship. What attitudes are necessary to embrace when taking on a learning role? How can you take steps to become a student of the people in your important relationships?

5. "Some of us shy away from effective communication because we feel very vulnerable in the presence of deep emotion. We feel out of control. We don't know where or how deep it is going to take us—and we fear being out of control." Explore these statements (on your own or with your group). What past experiences have caused you to become fearful of deep emotions?

6. Review the section subtitled "A Dynamic Process of Discovery" beginning on page 138. What are four qualities of effective communication? Explain your understanding of each of the four qualities. Which one is most meaningful to you? Give reasons for your response.

7. What are the hazards of focusing too much attention on deciding who is at fault in a conflict? Why is it often difficult to steer clear of the tendency to assign blame? What can be gained by *not* focusing on blame?

8. Look at the One-Minute Review for chapter 7. Of the six main points from the chapter, which one do you most need to put into practice in your relationships?

Applying Principles from the Bible

1. This chapter focuses on listening to understand the emotions behind the words people speak. Because we're not mind readers, we need to

learn the skill of truly reading between someone's words. Read Proverbs 2:2-3; 3:13-14; 14:33; 18:2; 19:8. What do these verses reveal about the importance of understanding?

2. No one sets a better example of paying attention to people's emotions than Jesus did. He also showed great understanding. What can we learn from his words in Matthew 13:12 and Mark 4:23-25? Discuss why listening does not necessarily equal understanding.

Making It Real

Make a commitment to become a *student* in your relationships. In one or more of your most important relationships, talk with the other person about how you can listen for understanding. Ask if there are any frustrations that he or she would like to work through. Sometimes, walls can be melted just by asking questions in a caring way. Practice listening and asking questions to show you care and to grow in understanding the people who are God's gifts in your life. You may want to collect your thoughts and information you've gathered and write them in your Honor Journal.

The Final Word

I pray that your love for each other will overflow more and more, and that you will keep on growing in your knowledge and understanding. For I want you to understand what really matters. Philippians 1:9-10

CHAPTER 8 —
TEAMWORK: ADOPT A
NO-LOSERS POLICY

"In a relationship there is no such thing as a win-lose solution. There is either win-win or lose-lose. No other options exist. . . . When we commit ourselves to implementing such a cooperative strategy in all our significant relationships, we set ourselves up for success. In other words, we all win!"

Getting Started

1. When you are in a conflict, are you generally more concerned about being right—winning—than you are about what is happening in the re-

lationship? What do you consider to be a good outcome of a conflict: having people agree with you or arriving at a solution that respects the needs of all the people involved?

2. Do you tend to remain firm in a conflict until you feel you've won, or are you typically the person who concedes to keep the peace? Spend time thinking about your attitudes toward conflict—whether you avoid it or see it as an opportunity for growth.

Recapping the Chapter

1. We've all been involved in a power struggle at some point. As humans, our nature is to want a measure of control over the circumstances of life. No one wants to feel powerless or always susceptible to someone else's dominance. Describe the last power struggle you found yourself in. What was the issue, and what was the outcome? Did you "win" or "lose"? Based on the discussion in this chapter, was the true outcome a win-win or a lose-lose?

2. Consider the idea of compromise. Many people consider compromise to be a positive solution to relationship conflicts. Summarize the reasons given in the chapter for viewing compromise as a negative solution—or only a tolerable one at best. Instead of compromise, what should our goal be for resolving conflicts in relationships? (You may want to refer to page 158.) Explain the basics of a no-losers policy. How does "finding and implementing a solution that both people can feel good about" differ from compromise? What steps may be necessary to implement a no-losers policy in your relationships?

3. Based on what you know about marriage (whether you're married or not), how is that relationship unique in its no-losers policy? (Refer to page 161, if necessary.) How is a no-losers policy really in one's own best interests (in any relationship)?

4. Now focus on your workplace. Think about your work environment (if you work at home, you can answer in general or based on past outside work experience). How well do coworkers support one another? What is the level of conflict or tension in an average week? Share your thoughts about possible ways you can encourage a no-losers policy in your company.

5. Summarize and discuss the seven steps to win-win solutions (as outlined on pages 162–65). Have you ever implemented a majority of these steps, either consciously or subconsciously? Which one or ones

do you think are needed most in some of your significant relationships? Explain your thought processes regarding your answer.

6. Describe the two common objections that many people give against applying a no-losers policy (see pages 167–68). Tell about an experience when you discovered that a decision that seemed urgent really wasn't in the end.

7. Look at the One-Minute Review for chapter 8. Discuss how the four points naturally support the goal of teamwork.

Applying Principles from the Bible

1. A no-losers policy is all about unity and teamwork, key concepts discussed throughout the New Testament. Identify an important principle from each of the following passages that shows the importance of working together for a common good: Matthew 12:25; 1 Corinthians 1:10-13; Philippians 1:27; 4:5; 2 Timothy 2:14-15; James 3:16-18.

2. When our relationship with God is on track and thriving, the Holy Spirit grows various qualities in us known as the fruit of the Spirit. Read Galatians 5:16-26 for powerful revelations about how this fruit helps us work toward unity in our relationships. Discuss how living by our sinful natures differs from living filled by the Holy Spirit. How do these two ways of life affect conflict resolution in our relationships? How does 1 John 1:7 support the idea of unity through the Holy Spirit's power?

Making It Real

The Bible challenges us: "Don't worry about anything; instead, pray about everything. Tell God what you need, and thank him for all he has done. If you do this, you will experience God's peace, which is far more wonderful than the human mind can understand" (Philippians 4:6-7). Whether you are accustomed to praying or rarely pray, this challenge can inspire you to take every confusing, problematic relationship issue to God. He promises to answer when those who love him pray to him. He cares deeply for you, as well as for every person in your life. Spend a few minutes today, and each day this month, taking your relationship concerns to God. Ask for direction, clarity, peace, forgiveness, hope—whatever is on your heart. Ask him to show you his answers and to give you his wisdom for handling conflicts. Then watch for him to work.

The Final Word

Work hard at living in peace with others.　1 PETER 3:11

PART THREE:
THE NEXT STEP

CHAPTERS 9 AND 10—WHAT WE CAN CHANGE AND YOU CAN MAKE A DIFFERENCE

"Instead of asking, 'What will work to get him to change,' what if you asked, 'What kind of person should I be?' . . . If you choose to travel the road of personal transformation, the worst that can happen is that you will end up with a life that's far more enjoyable, satisfying, fulfilling, and helpful to others than the one you had while you continued to insist on changing the other person."

Getting Started
1. Ask yourself these questions: What kind of person should I be? What would the "ideal you" look like in terms of your relationships? How can you choose to become the person that God wants you to be? What needs to change? What strengths can you build on?
2. In your closest relationships, what are you trying to accomplish? If your close relationships were exactly as you would like them, what would they look like? (Remember to keep your focus on your own role and responsibility in each relationship.)

Recapping the Chapters
1. Most times our complaints in a relationship focus on what we'd like the other person to do differently. Think about your relationships, whether they're going strong or struggling. Chances are, you can think of one or two ways you'd like to adjust the other person's habits—even in your best relationships. In all honesty, how much do you focus on what your loved ones are doing right versus what they could improve?
2. "What if God most wants to change *you?*" Have you ever asked your-

self how God might want to change you? What feelings are evoked in you at the thought of God's desire to work in your life? Fear? Excitement? Anxiety? Wonder?

3. Expand on the following statement: "To the extent that you define the problem or the goal in terms of the other person, you remain paralyzed." How can pointing the finger back at yourself actually be freeing and empowering?

4. With your answer to the previous question in mind, discuss the following statement: "As long as you think of everything that's going on as outside of you, you remain a victim." Do you ever catch yourself acting like a victim, always ready with an excuse involving someone else's behavior to explain your own life problems? How do others respond to you when you do that? How has acting like a victim affected your relationships? What can you do to begin taking responsibility for your life?

5. Discuss your understanding of *serendipity* when it comes to trusting God to provide what you need (see pages 176–79). Describe your current level of hope in God to give you something he knows is better than something you may be asking of him. How are you encouraged or challenged by the idea of serendipity?

6. Look at the One-Minute Review for chapter 9. Of the three main points from the chapter, which one do you most need to put into practice in your relationships? How will you start?

Applying Principles from the Bible

1. God doesn't expect us to truly change without his help. Read Job 12:16; Psalms 44:3; 68:28; 69:29; Isaiah 40:29; Habakkuk 3:2; Matthew 21:21-22; 2 Corinthians 3:17-18; and Ephesians 4:1-3, 15-16, and discuss what each example from biblical history tells you about God's work in people, his expectations, and the strength he offers. Talk about how each verse explains God's power and how it can help you change in a relationship, whether or not the other person changes.

2. Do you believe that God has your best interests at heart? Do you trust that he has all the issues of your life in his control and that he's working right now on your behalf? Read Exodus 34:9-11; Isaiah 43:1-7; 46:3-4; Romans 8:28; 1 Peter 5:6-7. What do these verses say about God's miracles and timing? How can you apply the hope of each promise to your own circumstances?

Making It Real

Create an action plan. Start by taking inventory of your life. What do your actions and time commitments reveal about where your priorities truly are (not necessarily where you *think* they should be)? What circumstances would cause you to redirect some priorities that may need refocusing? Set aside fifteen minutes or so to write a letter to God asking him to reveal to you where he wants you to spend your time and energy. Will you take an additional challenge and commit to being an active part in a relationship revolution? Share those thoughts with God, including any hesitations you may feel. Once you have your action plan on paper, seal it in an envelope and place the envelope in a spot where you'll see it frequently over the next couple of months: posted on your refrigerator, tucked in your vehicle's visor, or taped on the inside of your medicine cabinet door. Every time you see the envelope, pray for your relationships and how God may want to see you grow through them (and for them).

The Final Word

I have not kept this good news hidden in my heart; I have talked about your faithfulness and saving power. I have told everyone.   PSALM 40:10

NOTES

CHAPTER 1–A RELATIONSHIP REVOLUTION
1. This phrase was coined by Dr. Scott Sticksel.

CHAPTER 2–THE DNA OF RELATIONSHIPS
1. Genesis 2:18.
2. See Genesis 2:15-17; 3:1-6.
3. Sharon Begley, "Your Brain on Religion," *Newsweek* (May 7, 2001).
4. Exodus 34:14.
5. See John 10:10.
6. Rick Warren, *The Purpose-Driven Life* (Grand Rapids: Zondervan, 2002), 22–24.
7. See Isaiah 43:3-4.
8. If you need a reminder, read John 3:16 to see what lengths he went to in order to pay the price for every one of your bad choices.
9. Matthew 22:37-39.

CHAPTER 3–THE DANCE THAT DESTROYS RELATIONSHIPS
1. These and other names in this book have been changed to protect the privacy of the people whose stories we share.

CHAPTER 4–THE POWER OF ONE: TAKE PERSONAL RESPONSIBILITY
1. Archibald D. Hart, *Habits of the Mind: Ten Exercises to Renew Your Thinking* (Dallas: Word, 1996), 11.
2. Ibid., 8–10.
3. Ibid., 5.
4. Philippians 4:8.
5. 2 Corinthians 10:5, NIV.
6. See Philippians 4:19.
7. Romans 12:18, NIV, emphasis added.
8. James 1:2.
9. Luke 17:3-4, NIV.
10. Luke 17:5-6, NIV.
11. Matthew 6:12.
12. That truth is even more clear in a statement Jesus made right after he

taught his disciples the prayer. He said, "If you forgive those who sin against you, your heavenly Father will forgive you" (Matthew 6:14).
13. Ephesians 4:32.

CHAPTER 5—SAFETY: CREATE A SAFE ENVIRONMENT
1. Genesis 2:24.
2. Romans 13:7 tells us to "give respect and honor to all to whom it is due." And Romans 12:10 reminds us, "Love each other with genuine affection, and take delight in honoring each other."

CHAPTER 6—SELF-CARE: KEEP YOUR BATTERY CHARGED
1. Mark 12:30-31.
2. I am not suggesting that you ignore it if you believe God is nudging you to do something because a loved one *is* in danger. You don't want to doubt that. But you do want to discern when you are getting yourself worked up and when God is nudging you.
3. See Matthew 14:23; John 6:15.
4. See Mark 15:41.
5. See Matthew 21:18; John 4:7.
6. See John 2:24; 11:6.
7. See Matthew 26:36-38.
8. See Luke 4:28-30.
9. See Luke 12:30.
10. See Matthew 11:28.
11. Ephesians 5:29.
12. 1 Timothy 5:23, NIV.
13. Ephesians 5:18, NIV.
14. Psalm 149:4.
15. John 10:10.
16. Psalm 103:1, KJV.
17. See Matthew 6:21.
18. See Isaiah 43:4.
19. See 1 John 2:14; 1 Corinthians 4:10.
20. See Philippians 2:15, NIV; 2 Corinthians 3:3; Ephesians 2:19.
21. 1 Corinthians 6:19-20.
22. Ephesians 2:21-22.
23. Luke 2:52.
24. Don Colbert, *Deadly Emotions: Understand the Mind-Body-Spirit Connection That Can Heal or Destroy You* (Nashville: Nelson, 2003), 16.
25. Ibid., 17.
26. Ibid., 25.
27. See Colossians 3:1.
28. See Ephesians 3:1-17.
29. See Psalm 23.
30. See Matthew 10:29-31.

31. See Romans 8:28; James 1:1-4.
32. See Isaiah 52:12; Psalm 23.
33. See Isaiah 61:3.
34. See Isaiah 40, especially verse 31.

CHAPTER 7—EMOTIONAL COMMUNICATION: LISTEN WITH THE HEART

1. Howard J. Markman, Scott M. Stanley, and Susan L. Blumberg, *Fighting for Your Marriage* (San Francisco: Jossey-Bass, 2001).
2. Steve Brown, *Scandalous Freedom* (West Monroe, La.: Howard Publishing, 2004), from chapter 3, "The Perfection We Desire . . . and the Forgiveness That Sets Us Free."
3. Proverbs 20:5, NIV.
4. For some very effective communication tools, see Gary Smalley, Greg Smalley, and Michael Smalley, *Men's Relational Toolbox* (Wheaton, Ill.: Tyndale, 2003).
5. To learn more about what we call LUV talk (Listen, Understand, Value), see Greg Smalley, *The Marriage You've Always Dreamed Of* (Wheaton, Ill.: Tyndale, 2005).
6. Proverbs 4:7, NIV.
7. Romans 14:13, NIV.
8. Romans 14:19, NIV.

CHAPTER 8—TEAMWORK: ADOPT A NO-LOSERS POLICY

1. Proverbs 14:12; 16:25.
2. Variously attributed to both Paul Gauguin and former West German Chancellor Ludwig Erhard.
3. 1 Corinthians 12:25-26, NIV.
4. Philippians 2:3-4.
5. Genesis 2:24.
6. Matthew 19:6.
7. Hebrews 4:16 reminds us that we can "come boldly to the throne of our gracious God. There we will receive his mercy, and we will find grace to help us when we need it."

CHAPTER 9—WHAT WE CAN CHANGE

1. See Ephesians 3:19.
2. 2 Samuel 7:5.
3. 1 Chronicles 22:8.
4. 1 Kings 8:18.
5. See 2 Samuel 7:8-16.
6. Habakkuk 3:17-19.

CHAPTER 10—YOU CAN MAKE A DIFFERENCE

1. Psalm 23:4.

2. The Associated Press, December 30, 1999; from the Smart Marriages Archive, www.divorcereform.org/mel/rbaptisthigh.html.

3. John Rossomando, "Born-Again Christians No More Immune to Divorce Than Others, Says Author," CNSNews.com (January 21, 2002); see www.cnsnews.com/viewculture.asp?Page=/culture/archive/200201/CUL20020121b.html.

4. Kerby Anderson, "Divorce Statistics," Kerby Anderson Commentaries, January 12, 2000; see www.probe.org/docs/c-divorce.html.

THE CENTER FOR RELATIONSHIP ENRICHMENT JOHN BROWN UNIVERSITY

Enriching relationships for a lifetime.

The Center for Relationship Enrichment (CRE), under the leadership of Dr. Gary Oliver, equips people for healthy relationships through biblically based consulting, education, enrichment, resources, research, and assessment. Several initiatives or programs that the CRE uses to accomplish its mission and vision include the following:

1. CHURCH RELATIONSHIP INITIATIVE

An important part of the mission of the CRE is to partner with church leaders to increase their effectiveness in ministering to the wide range of personal and interpersonal needs represented by those in their congregation. As a part of this mission, CRE has designed the Church Relationships Survey.

2. CONSULTING AND TRAINING SERVICES

The CRE offers consulting and training services to Christian leaders and organizations in order to contribute to the effectiveness and health of personal and interpersonal ministries. As part of our Church Initiate, we administer the CRE Church Relationships Survey. The survey gives us detailed and specific information on the health and effectiveness of the relational ministries that are being offered to the church congregation. This information is then given to the staff, pastors, elders, deacons, and lay leaders.

For more information about the Church Relationships Survey or consulting and training services, please contact Judy Shoop at (479) 524-7105 or jshoop@jbu.edu.

3. SPECIAL SPEAKING

The CRE speaking team, including Dr. Gary and Carrie Oliver and Dr. Greg and Erin Smalley, is well equipped to provide you with the necessary tools for enriching marriage and family relationships. We would love the opportunity to discuss your specific needs and customize a speaking event that will have maximum impact for you. To schedule our speakers, please contact us at (479) 524-7105 or cmfs@jbu.edu.

NATIONAL INSTITUTE OF MARRIAGE

The National Institute of Marriage was originally founded as the Smalley Marriage Institute under the leadership of Dr. Greg Smalley. Because of the growth of this ministry and the ever growing national presence, we renamed the organization the National Institute of Marriage (NIM), which more accurately represents the ministry being accomplished. Led by co-presidents Dr. Robert S. Paul and Mark Pyatt, the NIM team members have a wide variety of training and expertise, but one single passion: making an eternal difference in the lives of couples.

Through our nationally recognized Intensive programs, the team members accomplish two very important goals: to remain dependent on God's transforming power as marriages are restored, and to continually learn, apply, and teach the life-changing concepts that result in successful marriages.

Exponentially expanding the impact of ministry, NIM is focusing on presenting the principles, concepts, and tools from the Intensive Program to professional counselors, chaplains, pastoral leadership, marriage mentors, and small group leaders. We believe that as we enrich and equip these leaders who are influencing a multitude of other couples, a marriage revival will take place that could change the world.

For more information on these programs, to inquire about speaking engagements, or to become a ministry partner, visit www.nationalmarriage.com or call (417) 335-5882.

the **DNA** *of*
RELATIONSHIPS

CAMPAIGN

Relationships are in crisis.

Daily newspaper headlines give snapshots of people in deep relational crises:

- A mother abandons her family and children.
- A teenager starts a shooting spree over a deeply held grudge.
- Random terrorist attacks reveal ethnic and religious hatred.
- Divorce rates continue to skyrocket.

This is the tip of the iceberg.
Millions upon millions of men and women struggle with relationships with family, friends, coworkers, and neighbors.

→ YOU CAN MAKE A DIFFERENCE!
Join **The DNA of Relationships campaign,** and start to strengthen your own relationships—as well as relationships around you.

Log on to *dnaofrelationships.com* and receive

- Relationship resources that help you with difficult relationships
- Self-tests that help you discover the source of relationship conflict
- Study guides for small groups that want to have an impact on relationships
- Sermon ideas to highlight the importance of relationships to God
- *More information about upcoming DNA of Relationships books, videos, and seminars*

Go to the Web site, become a member, and start making a difference—today.

BOOKS IN
THE DNA OF RELATIONSHIPS
CAMPAIGN

HAVE YOU EVER FELT AS IF YOU'RE . . .

Repeating the Same Mistakes in Your Relationships?

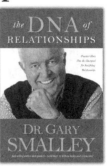

Dr. Smalley, president of Smalley Relationship Center and host of the nationally syndicated radio show *Smalley LIVE!,* tells you the whys and hows of relationships.

His insights are based on his own experience with disappointing and fractured relationships, as well as a five-year study that has demonstrated amazing results:

- 90 percent success rate in resolving conflict
- 72 percent increase in relationship satisfaction

Turn to Dr. Gary Smalley for help with

- relational conflict with bosses or coworkers
- difficult people in your neighborhood or at church
- destructive behavior patterns with relatives and in-laws
- problems with your kids or teens
- sibling rivalry

*"The DNA of Relationships is sure to be a defining work—
a catalyst for a relationship revolution that will touch millions."*
DRS. LES & LESLIE PARROTT

Have you ever wondered if your marriage could be better?

Dr. Greg Smalley directs Church Relationship Ministries for the Center for Relationship Enrichment at John Brown University. He also maintains a counseling practice for couples in crisis through the National Marriage Institute's marriage intensives. Couples come to the marriage intensives with broken and failed marriages, often ready to divorce the next week. Greg and his colleague, Dr. Robert S. Paul, help couples understand the destructive relationship cycle that threatens their marriages—and how to heal the damage. Dr. Smalley bases his insights on five years of research conducted in his marriage intensives.

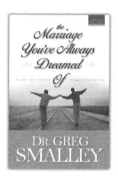

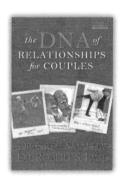

In this book Dr. Robert S. Paul and Dr. Greg Smalley use the journeys of four couples through their highly successful Marriage Intensive program to illustrate how to change your marriage for the better. The key to experiencing healthy relationships is seeing healthy relationships at work. Whether you want to learn techniques and behaviors that will keep your own marriage healthy and growing or you desire to heal a damaged relationship with your spouse, this book is for you.

What about dating relationships?

Check out Michael and Amy Smalley's *Don't Date Naked* book for straight talk about relationships for singles who are dating. In this book you'll find advice for both guys and girls, from Michael and Amy Smalley's differing perspectives. We don't have to let MTV or FOX television shape our views of sex, dating, and relationships anymore. Read Michael and Amy's book to get a fresh perspective on what healthy dating is.

ABOUT THE AUTHORS

 DR. GARY SMALLEY, the cofounder and chairman of the board of the Smalley Relationship Center, is America's relationship doctor. He is the author and coauthor of more than forty books, including the best-selling, award-winning books *Marriage for a Lifetime, Secrets to Lasting Love, The Blessing, The Two Sides of Love*, and *The Language of Love*. Recent releases include *Men's Relational Toolbox, Food and Love, Food and Love Cookbook, One Flame, Bound by Honor*, and the Redemption fiction series (with Karen Kingsbury). In addition to earning a master's degree from Bethel Theological Seminary, Gary has received two honorary doctorates, one from Biola University and one from Southwest Baptist University, for his work with couples. He is the host of the nationally syndicated radio show *Smalley LIVE!* In his thirty years of ministry, Gary has appeared on national television programs such as *Oprah, Larry King Live, Today, Sally Jessy Raphael*, as well as numerous national radio programs. Gary has been featured on hundreds of regional and local television and radio programs and has also produced films and videos that have sold millions of copies. Gary and his wife, Norma, have been married for nearly forty years and live in Branson, Missouri. They have three adult children and eight grandchildren.

 DR. GREG SMALLEY is the director of Church Relationship Ministries for the Center for Relationship Enrichment at John Brown University. He also maintains a counseling practice for couples in crisis. Greg earned his doctoral degree in clinical psychology from Rosemead School of Psychology at Biola University. He is the author and coauthor of several books including *The Marriage You've Always Dreamed Of, The DNA of Relationships, The DNA of Parent and Teen Relationships, Men's Relational Toolbox, Life Lines: Communicating with Your Teen, Winning Your Wife Back*, and *Winning Your Husband Back*. Greg has appeared on television and radio programs, including *Focus on the Family* and *Hour of Power*. Greg and his wife, Erin, have three children and live in Siloam Springs, Arkansas.

 MICHAEL SMALLEY earned a master's degree in clinical psychology from Wheaton College and was an international speaker on relationships for ten years. Currently, Michael is director of marriage and family for The Woodlands United Methodist church in Texas. Michael has authored or coauthored relationship advice books such as *Communicating with Your Teen*, *Men's Relational Toolbox*, and *Don't Date Naked*. He and his wife, Amy, live in Texas with their three children.

 DR. ROBERT S. PAUL is co-president and CEO of the National Institute of Marriage and is the director, primary innovator, and creator of their highly acclaimed Intensive programs. Bob received a master's degree from Georgia State University and a diploma in Christian counseling and honorary doctorate from Psychological Studies Institute. He is a licensed professional counselor and a national certified counselor. Bob is a former professor at Evangel University, where he taught in both the Biblical Studies and Psychology departments, specializing in marriage and family counseling, human sexuality, and the integration of faith into all areas of life. Bob and his wife, Jenni, have four children and live in Branson, Missouri.